W9-AEJ-869

STANDARDS
for Educational and Psychological Testing

American Educational Research Association
American Psychological Association
National Council on Measurement in Education

Published by the
American Educational Research Association
1430 K St., NW, Suite 1200
Washington, DC 20005

Printed in the United States of America

Prepared by the
Joint Committee on the *Standards for Educational and Psychological Testing* of the American Educational Research Association, the American Psychological Association, and the National Council on Measurement in Education

Library of Congress Cataloging-in-Publication Data

American Educational Research Association.
    Standards for educational and psychological testing / American Educational Research Association, American Psychological Association, National Council on Measurement in Education.
        pages cm
    "Prepared by the Joint Committee on Standards for Educational and Psychological Testing of the American Educational Research Association, American Psychological Association and National Council on Measurement in Education"—T.p. verso.
    Include index.
    ISBN 978-0-935302-35-6 (alk. paper)
    1. Educational tests and measurements—Standards—United States. 2. Psychological tests—Standards—United States. I. American Psychological Association. II. National Council on Measurement in Education. III. Joint Committee on Standards for Educational and Psychological Testing (U.S.) IV. Title.
    LB3051.A693 2014
    371.26'0973—dc23
                        2014009333

CONTENTS

PART III
TESTING APPLICATIONS

PREFACE

This edition of *Standards for Educational and Psychological Testing* is sponsored by the American Educational Research Association (AERA), the American Psychological Association (APA), and the National Council on Measurement in Education (NCME). Earlier documents from the sponsoring organizations also guided the development and use of tests. The first was *Technical Recommendations for Psychological Tests and Diagnostic Techniques*, prepared by an APA committee and published by APA in 1954. The second was *Technical Recommendations for Achievement Tests*, prepared by a committee representing AERA and the National Council on Measurement Used in Education (NCMUE) and published by the National Education Association in 1955.

The third, which replaced the earlier two, was prepared by a joint committee representing AERA, APA, and NCME and was published by APA in 1966. It was the first edition of the *Standards for Educational and Psychological Testing*, also known as the *Standards*. Three subsequent editions of the *Standards* were prepared by joint committees representing AERA, APA, and NCME, published in 1974, 1985, and 1999.

The current *Standards* Management Committee was formed by AERA, APA, and NCME, the three sponsoring organizations, in 2005, consisting of one representative from each organization. The committee's responsibilities included determining whether the 1999 *Standards* needed revision and then creating the charge, budget, and work timeline for a joint committee; appointing joint committee co-chairs and members; overseeing finances and a development fund; and performing other tasks related to the revision and publication of the *Standards*.

Standards Management Committee

Wayne J. Camara (Chair), appointed by APA
David Frisbie (2008–present), appointed by NCME
Suzanne Lane, appointed by AERA
Barbara S. Plake (2005–2007), appointed by NCME

The present edition of the *Standards* was developed by the Joint Committee on the *Standards for Educational and Psychological Testing*, appointed by the *Standards* Management Committee in 2008. Members of the Joint Committee are members of at least one of the three sponsoring organizations, AERA, APA, and NCME. The Joint Committee was charged with the revision of the *Standards* and the preparation of a final document for publication. It held its first meeting in January 2009.

Joint Committee on the *Standards for Educational and Psychological Testing*

Barbara S. Plake (Co-Chair)
Lauress L. Wise (Co-Chair)
Linda L. Cook
Fritz Drasgow
Brian T. Gong
Laura S. Hamilton
Jo-Ida Hansen
Joan L. Herman
Michael T. Kane
Michael J. Kolen
Antonio E. Puente
Paul R. Sackett
Nancy T. Tippins
Walter D. Way
Frank C. Worrell

Each sponsoring organization appointed one or two liaisons, some of whom were members of the Joint Committee, to serve as the communication conduits between the sponsoring organizations and the committee during the revision process.

Liaisons to the Joint Committee

AERA: Joan L. Herman
APA: Michael J. Kolen and Frank C. Worrell
NCME: Steve Ferrara

Marianne Ernesto (APA) served as the project director for the Joint Committee, and Dianne L. Schneider (APA) served as the project coordinator. Gerald Sroufe (AERA) provided administrative support for the Management Committee. APA's legal counsel managed the external legal review of the *Standards*. Daniel R. Eignor and James C. Impara reviewed the *Standards* for technical accuracy and consistency across chapters.

In 2008, each of the three sponsoring organizations released a call for comments on the 1999 *Standards*. Based on a review of the comments received, the Management Committee identified four main content areas of focus for the revision: technological advances in testing, increased use of tests for accountability and education policy-setting, access for all examinee populations, and issues associated with workplace testing. In addition, the committee gave special attention to ensuring a common voice and consistent use of technical language across chapters.

In January 2011, a draft of the revised *Standards* was made available for public review and comment. Organizations that submitted comments on the draft and/or comments in response to the 2008 call for comments are listed below. Many individuals from each organization contributed comments, as did many individual members of AERA, APA, and NCME. The Joint Committee considered each comment in its revision of the *Standards*. These thoughtful reviews from a variety of professional vantage points helped the Joint Committee in drafting the final revisions of the present edition of the *Standards*.

Comments came from the following organizations:

Sponsoring Organizations

American Educational Research Association
American Psychological Association
National Council on Measurement in Education

Professional Associations

American Academy of Clinical Neuropsychology
American Board of Internal Medicine
American Counseling Association
American Institute of CPAs, Examinations Team
APA Board for the Advancement of Psychology in the Public Interest
APA Board of Educational Affairs
APA Board of Professional Affairs
APA Board of Scientific Affairs
APA Policy and Planning Board

APA Committee on Aging
APA Committee on Children, Youth, and Families
APA Committee on Ethnic Minority Affairs
APA Committee on International Relations in Psychology
APA Committee on Legal Issues
APA Committee on Psychological Tests and Assessment
APA Committee on Socioeconomic Status
APA Society for the Psychology of Women (Division 35)
APA Division of Evaluation, Measurement, and Statistics (Division 5)
APA Division of School Psychology (Division 16)
APA Ethics Committee
APA Society for Industrial and Organizational Psychology (Division 14)
APA Society of Clinical Child and Adolescent Psychology (Division 53)
APA Society of Counseling Psychology (Division 17)
Asian American Psychological Association
Association of Test Publishers
District of Columbia Psychological Association
Massachusetts Neuropsychological Society
Massachusetts Psychological Association
National Academy of Neuropsychology
National Association of School Psychologists
National Board of Medical Examiners
National Council of Teachers of Mathematics
NCME Board of Directors
NCME Diversity Issues and Testing Committee
NCME Standards and Test Use Committee

Testing Companies

ACT
Alpine Testing Solutions
The College Board
Educational Testing Service
Harcourt Assessment, Inc.
Hogan Assessment Systems
Pearson
Prometric
Vangent Human Capital Management
Wonderlic, Inc.

Academic and Research Institutions

Center for Educational Assessment, University of Massachusetts
George Washington University Center for Equity and Excellence in Education

Human Resources Research Organization (HumRRO)
National Center on Educational Outcomes,
    University of Minnesota

Credentialing Organizations

American Registry of Radiologic Technologists
National Board for Certified Counselors
National Board of Medical Examiners

Other Institutions

California Department of Education
Equal Employment Advisory Council
Fair Access Coalition on Testing
Instituto de Evaluación e Ingeniería of Avanzada,
    Mexico
Qualifications and Curriculum Authority, UK
    Department for Education
Performance Testing Council

When the Joint Committee completed its final revision of the *Standards,* it submitted the revision to the three sponsoring organizations for approval and endorsement. Each organization had its own governing body and mechanism for approval, as well as a statement on the meaning of its approval:

AERA: The AERA's approval of the *Standards* means that the Council adopts the document as AERA policy.

APA: The APA's approval of the *Standards* means that the Council of Representatives adopts the document as APA policy.

NCME: The *Standards for Educational and Psychological Testing* has been endorsed by NCME, and this endorsement carries with it an ethical imperative for all NCME members to abide by these standards in the practice of measurement.

Although the *Standards* is prescriptive, it does not contain enforcement mechanisms. The *Standards* was formulated with the intent of being consistent with other standards, guidelines, and codes of conduct published by the three sponsoring organizations.

Joint Committee on the *Standards for Educational and Psychological Testing*

INTRODUCTION

Educational and psychological testing and assessment are among the most important contributions of cognitive and behavioral sciences to our society, providing fundamental and significant sources of information about individuals and groups. Not all tests are well developed, nor are all testing practices wise or beneficial, but there is extensive evidence documenting the usefulness of well-constructed, well-interpreted tests. Well-constructed tests that are valid for their intended purposes have the potential to provide substantial benefits for test takers and test users. Their proper use can result in better decisions about individuals and programs than would result without their use and can also provide a route to broader and more equitable access to education and employment. The improper use of tests, on the other hand, can cause considerable harm to test takers and other parties affected by test-based decisions. The intent of the *Standards for Educational and Psychological Testing* is to promote sound testing practices and to provide a basis for evaluating the quality of those practices. The *Standards* is intended for professionals who specify, develop, or select tests and for those who interpret, or evaluate the technical quality of, test results.

The Purpose of the *Standards*

The purpose of the *Standards* is to provide criteria for the development and evaluation of tests and testing practices and to provide guidelines for assessing the validity of interpretations of test scores for the intended test uses. Although such evaluations should depend heavily on professional judgment, the *Standards* provides a frame of reference to ensure that relevant issues are addressed. All professional test developers, sponsors, publishers, and users should make reasonable efforts to satisfy and follow the *Standards* and should encourage others to do so. All applicable standards should be met by all tests and in all test uses unless a sound professional reason is available to show

why a standard is not relevant or technically feasible in a particular case.

The *Standards* makes no attempt to provide psychometric answers to questions of public policy regarding the use of tests. In general, the *Standards* advocates that, within feasible limits, the relevant technical information be made available so that those involved in policy decisions may be fully informed.

Legal Disclaimer

The *Standards* is not a statement of legal requirements, and compliance with the *Standards* is not a substitute for legal advice. Numerous federal, state, and local statutes, regulations, rules, and judicial decisions relate to some aspects of the use, production, maintenance, and development of tests and test results and impose standards that may be different for different types of testing. A review of these legal issues is beyond the scope of the *Standards*, the distinct purpose of which is to set forth the criteria for sound testing practices from the perspective of cognitive and behavioral science professionals. Where it appears that one or more standards address an issue on which established legal requirements may be particularly relevant, the standard, comment, or introductory material may make note of that fact. Lack of specific reference to legal requirements, however, does not imply the absence of a relevant legal requirement. When applying standards across international borders, legal differences may raise additional issues or require different treatment of issues.

In some areas, such as the collection, analysis, and use of test data and results for different subgroups, the law may both require participants in the testing process to take certain actions and prohibit those participants from taking other actions. Furthermore, because the science of testing is an evolving discipline, recent revisions to the *Standards* may not be reflected in existing legal authorities, including judicial decisions and agency guidelines. In all situations, participants in the testing process should obtain the advice of counsel concerning applicable legal requirements.

In addition, although the *Standards* is not enforceable by the sponsoring organizations, it has been repeatedly recognized by regulatory authorities and courts as setting forth the generally accepted professional standards that developers and users of tests and other selection procedures follow. Compliance or noncompliance with the *Standards* may be used as relevant evidence of legal liability in judicial and regulatory proceedings. The *Standards* therefore merits careful consideration by all participants in the testing process.

Nothing in the *Standards* is meant to constitute legal advice. Moreover, the publishers disclaim any and all responsibility for liability created by participation in the testing process.

Tests and Test Uses to Which These Standards Apply

A test is a device or procedure in which a sample of an examinee's behavior in a specified domain is obtained and subsequently evaluated and scored using a standardized process. Whereas the label *test* is sometimes reserved for instruments on which responses are evaluated for their correctness or quality, and the terms *scale* and *inventory* are used for measures of attitudes, interest, and dispositions, the *Standards* uses the single term test to refer to all such evaluative devices.

A distinction is sometimes made between tests and assessments. *Assessment* is a broader term than test, commonly referring to a process that integrates test information with information from other sources (e.g., information from other tests, inventories, and interviews; or the individual's social, educational, employment, health, or psychological history). The applicability of the *Standards* to an evaluation device or method is determined by substance and not altered by the label applied to it (e.g., test, assessment, scale, inventory). The *Standards* should not be used as a checklist, as is emphasized in the section "Cautions to Be Considered in Using the *Standards*" at the end of this chapter.

Tests differ on a number of dimensions: the mode in which test materials are presented (e.g., paper-and-pencil, oral, or computerized administration); the degree to which stimulus materials are standardized; the type of response format (selection of a response from a set of alternatives, as opposed to the production of a free-form response); and the degree to which test materials are designed to reflect or simulate a particular context. In all cases, however, tests standardize the process by which test takers' responses to test materials are evaluated and scored. As noted in prior versions of the *Standards*, the same general types of information are needed to judge the soundness of results obtained from using all varieties of tests.

The precise demarcation between measurement devices used in the fields of educational and psychological testing that do and do not fall within the purview of the *Standards* is difficult to identify. Although the *Standards* applies most directly to standardized measures generally recognized as "tests," such as measures of ability, aptitude, achievement, attitudes, interests, personality, cognitive functioning, and mental health, the *Standards* may also be usefully applied in varying degrees to a broad range of less formal assessment techniques. Rigorous application of the *Standards* to unstandardized employment assessments (such as some job interviews) or to the broad range of unstructured behavior samples used in some forms of clinical and school-based psychological assessment (e.g., an intake interview), or to instructor-made tests that are used to evaluate student performance in education and training, is generally not possible. It is useful to distinguish between devices that lay claim to the concepts and techniques of the field of educational and psychological testing and devices that represent unstandardized or less standardized aids to day-to-day evaluative decisions. Although the principles and concepts underlying the *Standards* can be fruitfully applied to day-to-day decisions—such as when a business owner interviews a job applicant, a manager evaluates the performance of subordinates, a teacher develops a classroom assessment to monitor student progress toward an educational goal, or a coach evaluates a prospective athlete—it would be overreaching to expect that the standards of the educational and psychological testing field be followed by those making such decisions. In contrast, a structured interviewing system developed by a psychologist and accompanied by claims that the system has been found to be predictive of job performance in a variety of other settings falls within the purview of the *Standards*. Adhering to the *Standards* becomes more critical as the stakes for the test taker and the need to protect the public increase.

Participants in the Testing Process

Educational and psychological testing and assessment involve and significantly affect individuals, institutions, and society as a whole. The individuals affected include students, parents, families, teachers, educational administrators, job applicants, employees, clients, patients, supervisors, executives, and evaluators, among others. The institutions affected include schools, colleges, businesses, industry, psychological clinics, and government agencies. Individuals and institutions benefit when testing helps them achieve their goals. Society, in turn, benefits when testing contributes to the achievement of individual and institutional goals.

There are many participants in the testing process, including, among others, (a) those who prepare and develop the test; (b) those who publish and market the test; (c) those who administer and score the test; (d) those who interpret test results for clients; (e) those who use the test results for some decision-making purpose (including policy makers and those who use data to inform social policy); (f) those who take the test by choice, direction, or necessity; (g) those who sponsor tests, such as boards that represent institutions or governmental agencies that contract with a test developer for a specific instrument or service; and (h) those who select or review tests, evaluating their comparative merits or suitability for the uses proposed. In general, those who are participants in the testing process should have appropriate knowledge of tests and assessments to allow them to make good decisions about which tests to use and how to interpret test results.

The interests of the various parties involved in the testing process may or may not be congruent. For example, when a test is given for counseling purposes or for job placement, the interests of the individual and the institution often coincide. In contrast, when a test is used to select from among many individuals for a highly competitive job or for entry into an educational or training program, the preferences of an applicant may be inconsistent with those of an employer or admissions officer. Similarly, when testing is mandated by a court, the interests of the test taker may be different from those of the party requesting the court order.

Individuals or institutions may serve several roles in the testing process. For example, in clinics the test taker is typically the intended beneficiary of the test results. In some situations the test administrator is an agent of the test developer, and sometimes the test administrator is also the test user. When an organization prepares its own employment tests, it is both the developer and the user. Sometimes a test is developed by a test author but published, marketed, and distributed by an independent publisher, although the publisher may play an active role in the test development process. Roles may also be further subdivided. For example, both an organization and a professional assessor may play a role in the provision of an assessment center. Given this intermingling of roles, it is often difficult to assign precise responsibility for addressing various standards to specific participants in the testing process. Uses of tests and testing practices are improved to the extent that those involved have adequate levels of assessment literacy.

Tests are designed, developed, and used in a wide variety of ways. In some cases, they are developed and "published" for use outside the organization that produces them. In other cases, as with state educational assessments, they are designed by the state educational agency and developed by contractors for exclusive and often one-time use by the state and not really "published" at all. Throughout the *Standards*, we use the general term *test developer*, rather than the more specific term *test publisher*, to denote those involved in the design and development of tests across the full range of test development scenarios.

The *Standards* is based on the premise that effective testing and assessment require that all professionals in the testing process possess the knowledge, skills, and abilities necessary to fulfill their roles, as well as an awareness of personal and contextual factors that may influence the testing process. For example, test developers and those selecting tests and interpreting test results need adequate knowledge of psychometric principles such as validity and reliability. They also should obtain any appropriate supervised experience and legislatively mandated practice credentials that are required to perform competently those aspects of the testing process in which they engage. All professionals in the testing process should follow the ethical guidelines of their profession.

Scope of the Revision

This volume serves as a revision of the 1999 *Standards for Educational and Psychological Testing*. The revision process started with the appointment of a Management Committee, composed of representatives of the three sponsoring organizations responsible for overseeing the general direction of the effort: the American Educational Research Association (AERA), the American Psychological Association (APA), and the National Council on Measurement in Education (NCME). To guide the revision, the Management Committee solicited and synthesized comments on the 1999 *Standards* from members of the sponsoring organizations and convened the Joint Committee for the Revision of the 1999 *Standards* in 2009 to do the actual revision. The Joint Committee also was composed of members of the three sponsoring organizations and was charged by the Management Committee with addressing five major areas: considering the accountability issues for use of tests in educational policy; broadening the concept of accessibility of tests for all examinees; representing more comprehensively the role of tests in the workplace; broadening the role of technology in testing; and providing for a better organizational structure for communicating the standards.

To be responsive to this charge, several actions were taken:

- The chapters "Educational Testing and Assessment" and "Testing in Program Evaluation and Public Policy," in the 1999 version, were rewritten to attend to the issues associated with the uses of tests for educational accountability purposes.

- A new chapter, "Fairness in Testing," was written to emphasize accessibility and fairness as fundamental issues in testing. Specific concerns for fairness are threaded throughout all of the chapters of the *Standards*.

- The chapter "Testing in Employment and Credentialing" (now "Workplace Testing and Credentialing") was reorganized to more clearly identify when a standard is relevant to employment and/or credentialing.

- The impact of technology was considered throughout the volume. One of the major technology issues identified was the tension between the use of proprietary algorithms and the need for test users to be able to evaluate complex applications in areas such as automated scoring of essays, administering and scoring of innovative item types, and computer-based testing. These issues are considered in the chapter "Test Design and Development."

- A content editor was engaged to help with the technical accuracy and clarity of each chapter and with consistency of language across chapters. As noted below, chapters in Part I ("Foundations") and Part II ("Operations") now have an "overarching standard" as well as themes under which the individual standards are organized. In addition, the glossary from the 1999 *Standards for Educational and Psychological Testing* was updated. As stated above, a major change in the organization of this volume involves the conceptualization of fairness. The 1999 edition had a part devoted to this topic, with separate chapters titled "Fairness in Testing and Test Use," "Testing Individuals of Diverse Linguistic Backgrounds," and "Testing Individuals With Disabilities." In the present edition, the topics addressed in those chapters are combined into a single, comprehensive chapter, and the chapter is located in Part I. This change was made to emphasize that fairness demands that all test takers be treated equitably. Fairness and accessibility, the unobstructed opportunity for all examinees to demonstrate their standing on the construct(s) being measured, are relevant for valid score interpretations for all individuals and subgroups in the intended population of test takers. Because issues related to fairness in testing are not restricted to individuals with diverse linguistic backgrounds or those with disabilities, the chapter was more broadly cast to support appropriate testing experiences for all individuals. Although the examples in the chapter often refer to individuals with diverse linguistic and cultural backgrounds and individuals with disabilities, they also include examples relevant to gender and to older adults, people of various ethnicities and racial backgrounds, and young children, to illustrate potential barriers to fair and equitable assessment for all examinees.

Organization of the Volume

Part I of the *Standards*, "Foundations," contains standards for validity (chap. 1); reliability/precision and errors of measurement (chap. 2); and fairness in testing (chap. 3). Part II, "Operations," addresses test design and development (chap. 4); scores, scales, norms, score linking, and cut scores (chap. 5); test administration, scoring, reporting, and interpretation (chap. 6); supporting documentation for tests (chap. 7); the rights and responsibilities of test takers (chap. 8); and the rights and responsibilities of test users (chap. 9). Part III, "Testing Applications," treats specific applications in psychological testing and assessment (chap. 10); workplace testing and credentialing (chap. 11); educational testing and assessment (chap. 12); and uses of tests for program evaluation, policy studies, and accountability (chap. 13). Also included is a glossary, which provides definitions for terms as they are used specifically in this volume.

Each chapter begins with introductory text that provides background for the standards that follow. Although the introductory text is at times prescriptive, it should not be interpreted as imposing additional standards.

Categories of Standards

The text of each standard and any accompanying commentary include the conditions under which a standard is relevant. Depending on the context and purpose of test development or use, some standards will be more salient than others. Moreover, some standards are broad in scope, setting forth concerns or requirements relevant to nearly all tests or testing contexts, and other standards are narrower in scope. However, all standards are important in the contexts to which they apply. Any classification that gives the appearance of elevating the general importance of some standards over others could invite neglect of certain standards that need to be addressed in particular situations. Rather than differentiate standards using priority labels, such as "primary," "secondary," or "conditional" (as were used in the 1985 *Standards*), this edition emphasizes that unless a standard is deemed clearly irrelevant, inappropriate, or technically infeasible for a particular use, all standards should be met, making all of them essentially "primary" for that context.

Unless otherwise specified in a standard or commentary, and with the caveats outlined below, standards should be met before operational test use. Each standard should be carefully considered to determine its applicability to the testing context under consideration. In a given case there may be a sound professional reason that adherence to the standard is inappropriate. There may also be occasions when technical feasibility influences whether a standard can be met prior to operational test use. For example, some standards may call for analyses of data that are not available at the point of initial operational test use. In other cases, traditional quantitative analyses may not be feasible due to small sample sizes. However, there may be other methodologies that could be used to gather information to support the standard, such as small sample methodologies, qualitative studies, focus groups, and even logical analysis. In such instances, test developers and users should make a good faith effort to provide the kinds of data called for in the standard to support the valid interpretations of the test results for their intended purposes. If test developers, users, and, when applicable, sponsors have deemed a standard to be inapplicable or technically infeasible, they should be able, if called upon, to explain the basis for their decision. However, there is no expectation that documentation of all such decisions be routinely available.

Presentation of Individual Standards

Individual standards are presented after an introductory text that presents some key concepts for interpreting and applying the standards. In many cases, the standards themselves are coupled with one or more comments. These comments are intended to amplify, clarify, or provide examples to aid in the interpretation of the meaning of the standards. The standards often direct a developer or user to implement certain actions. Depending on the type of test, it is sometimes not clear in the statement of a standard to whom the standard is directed. For example, Standard 1.2 in the chapter "Validity" states:

> A rationale should be presented for each intended interpretation of test scores for a given use, together with a summary of the evidence and theory bearing on the intended interpretation.

The party responsible for implementing this standard is the party or person who is articulating the recommended interpretation of the test scores. This may be a test user, a test developer, or someone who is planning to use the test scores for a particular purpose, such as making classification or licensure decisions. It often is not possible in the statement of a standard to specify who is responsible for such actions; it is intended that the party or person performing the action specified in the standard be the party responsible for adhering to the standard.

Some of the individual standards and introductory text refer to groups and subgroups. The term *group* is generally used to identify the full examinee population, referred to as the *intended examinee group,* the *intended test-taker group,* the *intended examinee population,* or the *population.* A *subgroup* includes members of the larger group who are identifiable in some way that is relevant to the standard being applied. When data or analyses are indicated for various subgroups, they are generally referred to as *subgroups within the intended examinee group, groups from the intended examinee population,* or *relevant subgroups.*

In applying the *Standards*, it is important to bear in mind that the intended referent subgroups for the individual standards are context specific. For example, referent ethnic subgroups to be considered during the design phase of a test would depend on the expected ethnic composition of the intended test group. In addition, many more subgroups could be relevant to a standard dealing with the design of fair test questions than to a standard dealing with adaptations of a test's format. Users of the *Standards* will need to exercise professional judgment when deciding which particular subgroups are relevant for the application of a specific standard.

In deciding which subgroups are relevant for a particular standard, the following factors, among others, may be considered: credible evidence that suggests a group may face particular construct-irrelevant barriers to test performance, statutes or regulations that designate a group as relevant to score interpretations, and large numbers of individuals in the group within the general population. Depending on the context, relevant subgroups might include, for example, males and females, individuals of differing socioeconomic status, individuals differing by race and/or ethnicity, individuals with different sexual orientations, individuals with diverse linguistic and cultural backgrounds (particularly when testing extends across international borders), individuals with disabilities, young children, or older adults.

Numerous examples are provided in the *Standards* to clarify points or to provide illustrations of how to apply a particular standard. Many of the examples are drawn from research with students with disabilities or persons from diverse language or cultural groups; fewer, from research with other identifiable groups, such as young children or adults. There was also a purposeful effort to provide examples for educational, psychological, and industrial settings.

The standards in each chapter in Parts I and II ("Foundations" and "Operations") are introduced by an overarching standard, designed to convey the central intent of the chapter. These overarching standards are always numbered with .0 following the chapter number. For example, the overarching standard in chapter 1 is numbered 1.0. The overarching standards summarize guiding principles that are applicable to all tests and test uses. Further, the themes and standards in each chapter are ordered to be consistent with the sequence of the material in the introductory text for the chapter. Because some users of the *Standards* may turn only to chapters directly relevant to a given application, certain standards are repeated in different chapters, particularly in Part III, "Testing Applications." When such repetition occurs, the essence of the standard is the same. Only the wording, area of application, or level of elaboration in the comment is changed.

Cautions to Be Considered in Using the *Standards*

In addition to the legal disclaimer set forth above, several cautions are important if we are to avoid misinterpretations, misapplications, and misuses of the *Standards*:

- Evaluating the acceptability of a test or test application does not rest on the literal satisfaction of every standard in this document, and the acceptability of a test or test application cannot be determined by using a checklist. Specific circumstances affect the importance of individual standards, and individual standards should not be considered in isolation. Therefore, evaluating acceptability depends on (a) professional judgment that is based on a knowledge of behavioral science, psychometrics, and the relevant standards in the professional field to which the test applies; (b) the degree to which the intent of the standard has been satisfied by the test developer and user; (c) the alternative measurement devices that are readily available; (d) research and experiential evidence regarding the feasibility of meeting the standard; and (e) applicable laws and regulations.

- When tests are at issue in legal proceedings and other situations requiring expert witness testimony, it is essential that professional judgment be based on the accepted corpus of knowledge in determining the relevance of particular standards in a given situation. The intent of the *Standards* is to offer guidance for such judgments.

- Claims by test developers or test users that a test, manual, or procedure satisfies or follows the standards in this volume should be made with care. It is appropriate for developers or users to state that efforts were made to adhere to the *Standards*, and to provide documents describing and supporting those efforts. Blanket claims without supporting evidence should not be made.

- The standards are concerned with a field that is rapidly evolving. Consequently, there is a continuing need to monitor changes in the field and to revise this document as knowledge develops. The use of older versions of the *Standards* may be a disservice to test users and test takers.

- Requiring the use of specific technical methods is not the intent of the *Standards*. For example, where specific statistical reporting requirements are mentioned, the phrase "or generally accepted equivalent" should always be understood.

I

Foundations

1. VALIDITY

BACKGROUND

Validity refers to the degree to which evidence and theory support the interpretations of test scores for proposed uses of tests. Validity is, therefore, the most fundamental consideration in developing tests and evaluating tests. The process of validation involves accumulating relevant evidence to provide a sound scientific basis for the proposed score interpretations. It is the interpretations of test scores for proposed uses that are evaluated, not the test itself. When test scores are interpreted in more than one way (e.g., both to describe a test taker's current level of the attribute being measured and to make a prediction about a future outcome), each intended interpretation must be validated. Statements about validity should refer to particular interpretations for specified uses. It is incorrect to use the unqualified phrase "the validity of the test."

Evidence of the validity of a given interpretation of test scores for a specified use is a necessary condition for the justifiable use of the test. Where sufficient evidence of validity exists, the decision as to whether to actually administer a particular test generally takes additional considerations into account. These include cost-benefit considerations, framed in different subdisciplines as utility analysis or as consideration of negative consequences of test use, and a weighing of any negative consequences against the positive consequences of test use.

Validation logically begins with an explicit statement of the proposed interpretation of test scores, along with a rationale for the relevance of the interpretation to the proposed use. The proposed interpretation includes specifying the construct the test is intended to measure. The term *construct* is used in the *Standards* to refer to the concept or characteristic that a test is designed to measure. Rarely, if ever, is there a single possible meaning that can be attached to a test score or a pattern of test responses. Thus, it is always incumbent on test developers and users to specify the construct interpretation that will be made on the basis of the score or response pattern.

Examples of constructs currently used in assessment include mathematics achievement, general cognitive ability, racial identity attitudes, depression, and self-esteem. To support test development, the proposed construct interpretation is elaborated by describing its scope and extent and by delineating the aspects of the construct that are to be represented. The detailed description provides a conceptual framework for the test, delineating the knowledge, skills, abilities, traits, interests, processes, competencies, or characteristics to be assessed. Ideally, the framework indicates how the construct as represented is to be distinguished from other constructs and how it should relate to other variables.

The conceptual framework is partially shaped by the ways in which test scores will be used. For instance, a test of mathematics achievement might be used to place a student in an appropriate program of instruction, to endorse a high school diploma, or to inform a college admissions decision. Each of these uses implies a somewhat different interpretation of the mathematics achievement test scores: that a student will benefit from a particular instructional intervention, that a student has mastered a specified curriculum, or that a student is likely to be successful with college-level work. Similarly, a test of conscientiousness might be used for psychological counseling, to inform a decision about employment, or for the basic scientific purpose of elaborating the construct of conscientiousness. Each of these potential uses shapes the specified framework and the proposed interpretation of the test's scores and also can have implications for test development and evaluation. Validation can be viewed as a process of constructing and evaluating arguments for and against the intended interpretation of test scores and their relevance to the proposed use. The conceptual framework points to the kinds of evidence that might be collected to evaluate the proposed interpretation in light of the purposes of testing. As validation proceeds, and new evidence regarding the interpretations that can and cannot be drawn from test scores becomes available, revisions may be needed in the test, in the conceptual framework that shapes it, and even in the construct underlying the test.

The wide variety of tests and circumstances makes it natural that some types of evidence will be especially critical in a given case, whereas other types will be less useful. Decisions about what types of evidence are important for the validation argument in each instance can be clarified by developing a set of propositions or claims that support the proposed interpretation for the particular purpose of testing. For instance, when a mathematics achievement test is used to assess readiness for an advanced course, evidence for the following propositions might be relevant: (a) that certain skills are prerequisite for the advanced course; (b) that the content domain of the test is consistent with these prerequisite skills; (c) that test scores can be generalized across relevant sets of items; (d) that test scores are not unduly influenced by ancillary variables, such as writing ability; (e) that success in the advanced course can be validly assessed; and (f) that test takers with high scores on the test will be more successful in the advanced course than test takers with low scores on the test. Examples of propositions in other testing contexts might include, for instance, the proposition that test takers with high general anxiety scores experience significant anxiety in a range of settings, the proposition that a child's score on an intelligence scale is strongly related to the child's academic performance, or the proposition that a certain pattern of scores on a neuropsychological battery indicates impairment that is characteristic of brain injury. The validation process evolves as these propositions are articulated and evidence is gathered to evaluate their soundness.

Identifying the propositions implied by a proposed test interpretation can be facilitated by considering rival hypotheses that may challenge the proposed interpretation. It is also useful to consider the perspectives of different interested parties, existing experience with similar tests and contexts, and the expected consequences of the proposed test use. A finding of unintended consequences of test use may also prompt a consideration of rival hypotheses. Plausible rival hypotheses can often be generated by considering whether a test measures less or more than its proposed construct. Such considerations are referred to as *construct underrepresentation* (or *construct deficiency*) and *construct-irrelevant variance* (or *construct contamination*), respectively.

Construct underrepresentation refers to the degree to which a test fails to capture important aspects of the construct. It implies a narrowed meaning of test scores because the test does not adequately sample some types of content, engage some psychological processes, or elicit some ways of responding that are encompassed by the intended construct. Take, for example, a test intended as a comprehensive measure of anxiety. A particular test might underrepresent the intended construct because it measures only physiological reactions and not emotional, cognitive, or situational components. As another example, a test of reading comprehension intended to measure children's ability to read and interpret stories with understanding might not contain a sufficient variety of reading passages or might ignore a common type of reading material.

Construct-irrelevance refers to the degree to which test scores are affected by processes that are extraneous to the test's intended purpose. The test scores may be systematically influenced to some extent by processes that are not part of the construct. In the case of a reading comprehension test, these might include material too far above or below the level intended to be tested, an emotional reaction to the test content, familiarity with the subject matter of the reading passages on the test, or the writing skill needed to compose a response. Depending on the detailed definition of the construct, vocabulary knowledge or reading speed might also be irrelevant components. On a test designed to measure anxiety, a response bias to underreport one's anxiety might be considered a source of construct-irrelevant variance. In the case of a mathematics test, it might include overreliance on reading comprehension skills that English language learners may be lacking. On a test designed to measure science knowledge, test-taker internalizing of gender-based stereotypes about women in the sciences might be a source of construct-irrelevant variance.

Nearly all tests leave out elements that some potential users believe should be measured and include some elements that some potential users consider inappropriate. Validation involves careful attention to possible distortions in meaning arising from inadequate representation of the construct and also to aspects of measurement, such as test format, administration conditions, or language level, that may materially limit or qualify the interpretation of test scores for various groups of test takers. That is, the process of validation may lead to revisions in the test, in the conceptual framework of the test, or both. Interpretations drawn from the revised test would again need validation.

When propositions have been identified that would support the proposed interpretation of test scores, one can proceed with validation by obtaining empirical evidence, examining relevant literature, and/or conducting logical analyses to evaluate each of the propositions. Empirical evidence may include both local evidence, produced within the contexts where the test will be used, and evidence from similar testing applications in other settings. Use of existing evidence from similar tests and contexts can enhance the quality of the validity argument, especially when data for the test and context in question are limited.

Because an interpretation for a given use typically depends on more than one proposition, strong evidence in support of one part of the interpretation in no way diminishes the need for evidence to support other parts of the interpretation. For example, when an employment test is being considered for selection, a strong predictor-criterion relationship in an employment setting is ordinarily not sufficient to justify use of the test. One should also consider the appropriateness and meaningfulness of the criterion measure, the appropriateness

of the testing materials and procedures for the full range of applicants, and the consistency of the support for the proposed interpretation across groups. Professional judgment guides decisions regarding the specific forms of evidence that can best support the intended interpretation for a specified use. As in all scientific endeavors, the quality of the evidence is paramount. A few pieces of solid evidence regarding a particular proposition are better than numerous pieces of evidence of questionable quality. The determination that a given test interpretation for a specific purpose is warranted is based on professional judgment that the preponderance of the available evidence supports that interpretation. The quality and quantity of evidence sufficient to reach this judgment may differ for test uses depending on the stakes involved in the testing. A given interpretation may not be warranted either as a result of insufficient evidence in support of it or as a result of credible evidence against it.

Validation is the joint responsibility of the test developer and the test user. The test developer is responsible for furnishing relevant evidence and a rationale in support of any test score interpretations for specified uses intended by the developer. The test user is ultimately responsible for evaluating the evidence in the particular setting in which the test is to be used. When a test user proposes an interpretation or use of test scores that differs from those supported by the test developer, the responsibility for providing validity evidence in support of that interpretation for the specified use is the responsibility of the user. It should be noted that important contributions to the validity evidence may be made as other researchers report findings of investigations that are related to the meaning of scores on the test.

Sources of Validity Evidence

The following sections outline various sources of evidence that might be used in evaluating the validity of a proposed interpretation of test scores for a particular use. These sources of evidence may illuminate different aspects of validity, but they do not represent distinct types of validity. Validity is a unitary concept. It is the degree to which all the accumulated evidence supports the intended interpretation of test scores for the proposed use. Like the 1999 *Standards*, this edition refers to types of validity evidence, rather than distinct types of validity. To emphasize this distinction, the treatment that follows does not follow historical nomenclature (i.e., the use of the terms *content validity* or *predictive validity*).

As the discussion in the prior section emphasizes, each type of evidence presented below is not required in all settings. Rather, support is needed for each proposition that underlies a proposed test interpretation for a specified use. A proposition that a test is predictive of a given criterion can be supported without evidence that the test samples a particular content domain. In contrast, a proposition that a test covers a representative sample of a particular curriculum may be supported without evidence that the test predicts a given criterion. However, a more complex set of propositions, e.g., that a test samples a specified domain and thus is predictive of a criterion reflecting a related domain, will require evidence supporting both parts of this set of propositions. Tests developers are also expected to make the case that the scores are not unduly influenced by construct-irrelevant variance (see chap. 3 for detailed treatment of issues related to construct-irrelevant variance). In general, adequate support for proposed interpretations for specific uses will require multiple sources of evidence.

The position developed above also underscores the fact that if a given test is interpreted in multiple ways for multiple uses, the propositions underlying these interpretations for different uses also are likely to differ. Support is needed for the propositions underlying each interpretation for a specific use. Evidence supporting the interpretation of scores on a mathematics achievement test for placing students in subsequent courses (i.e., evidence that the test interpretation is valid for its intended purpose) does not permit inferring validity for other purposes (e.g., promotion or teacher evaluation).

Evidence Based on Test Content

Important validity evidence can be obtained from an analysis of the relationship between the content of a test and the construct it is intended to measure. Test content refers to the themes, wording, and format of the items, tasks, or questions on a test. Administration and scoring may also be relevant to content-based evidence. Test developers often work from a specification of the content domain. The content specification carefully describes the content in detail, often with a classification of areas of content and types of items. Evidence based on test content can include logical or empirical analyses of the adequacy with which the test content represents the content domain and of the relevance of the content domain to the proposed interpretation of test scores. Evidence based on content can also come from expert judgments of the relationship between parts of the test and the construct. For example, in developing a licensure test, the major facets that are relevant to the purpose for which the occupation is regulated can be specified, and experts in that occupation can be asked to assign test items to the categories defined by those facets. These or other experts can then judge the representativeness of the chosen set of items.

Some tests are based on systematic observations of behavior. For example, a list of the tasks constituting a job domain may be developed from observations of behavior in a job, together with judgments of subject matter experts. Expert judgments can be used to assess the relative importance, criticality, and/or frequency of the various tasks. A job sample test can then be constructed from a random or stratified sampling of tasks rated highly on these characteristics. The test can then be administered under standardized conditions in an off-the-job setting.

The appropriateness of a given content domain is related to the specific inferences to be made from test scores. Thus, when considering an available test for a purpose other than that for which it was first developed, it is especially important to evaluate the appropriateness of the original content domain for the proposed new purpose. For example, a test given for research purposes to compare student achievement across states in a given domain may properly also cover material that receives little or no attention in the curriculum. Policy makers can then evaluate student achievement with respect to both content neglected and content addressed. On the other hand, when student mastery of a delivered curriculum is tested for purposes of informing decisions about individual students, such as promotion or graduation, the framework elaborating a content domain is appropriately limited to what students have had an opportunity to learn from the curriculum as delivered.

Evidence about content can be used, in part, to address questions about differences in the meaning or interpretation of test scores across relevant subgroups of test takers. Of particular concern is the extent to which construct underrepresentation or construct-irrelevance may give an unfair advantage or disadvantage to one or more subgroups of test takers. For example, in an employment test, the use of vocabulary more complex than needed on the job may be a source of construct-irrelevant variance for English language learners or others. Careful review of the construct and test content domain by a diverse panel of experts may point to potential sources of irrelevant difficulty (or easiness) that require further investigation.

Content-oriented evidence of validation is at the heart of the process in the educational arena known as *alignment*, which involves evaluating the correspondence between student learning standards and test content. Content-sampling issues in the alignment process include evaluating whether test content appropriately samples the domain set forward in curriculum standards, whether the cognitive demands of test items correspond to the level reflected in the student learning standards (e.g., content standards), and whether the test avoids the inclusion of features irrelevant to the standard that is the intended target of each test item.

Evidence Based on Response Processes

Some construct interpretations involve more or less explicit assumptions about the cognitive processes engaged in by test takers. Theoretical and empirical analyses of the response processes of test takers can provide evidence concerning the fit between the construct and the detailed nature of the performance or response actually engaged in by test takers. For instance, if a test is intended to assess mathematical reasoning, it becomes important to determine whether test takers are, in fact, reasoning about the material given instead of following a standard algorithm applicable only to the specific items on the test.

Evidence based on response processes generally comes from analyses of individual responses. Questioning test takers from various groups making up the intended test-taking population about their performance strategies or responses to particular items can yield evidence that enriches the definition of a construct. Maintaining records that monitor the development of a response to a writing task, through successive written drafts or electronically monitored revisions, for instance, also provides evidence of process. Documentation of other aspects of performance, like eye movements or response times, may also be relevant to some constructs. Inferences about processes involved in performance can also be developed by analyzing the relationship among parts of the test and between the test and other variables. Wide individual differences in process can be revealing and may lead to reconsideration of certain test formats.

Evidence of response processes can contribute to answering questions about differences in meaning or interpretation of test scores across relevant subgroups of test takers. Process studies involving test takers from different subgroups can assist in determining the extent to which capabilities irrelevant or ancillary to the construct may be differentially influencing test takers' test performance.

Studies of response processes are not limited to the test taker. Assessments often rely on observers or judges to record and/or evaluate test takers' performances or products. In such cases, relevant validity evidence includes the extent to which the processes of observers or judges are consistent with the intended interpretation of scores. For instance, if judges are expected to apply particular criteria in scoring test takers' performances, it is important to ascertain whether they are, in fact, applying the appropriate criteria and not being influenced by factors that are irrelevant to the intended interpretation (e.g., quality of handwriting is irrelevant to judging the content of an written essay). Thus, validation may include empirical studies of how observers or judges record and evaluate data along with analyses of the appropriateness of these processes to the intended interpretation or construct definition.

While evidence about response processes may be central in settings where explicit claims about response processes are made by test developers or where inferences about responses are made by test users, there are many other cases where claims about response processes are not part of the validity argument. In some cases, multiple response processes are available for solving the problems of interest, and the construct of interest is only concerned with whether the problem was solved correctly. As a simple example, there may be multiple possible routes to obtaining the correct solution to a mathematical problem.

Evidence Based on Internal Structure

Analyses of the internal structure of a test can indicate the degree to which the relationships among test items and test components conform to the construct on which the proposed test score interpretations are based. The conceptual framework for a test may imply a single dimension of behavior, or it may posit several components that are each expected to be homogeneous, but that are also distinct from each other. For example, a measure of discomfort on a health survey might assess both physical and emotional health. The extent to which item interrelationships bear out the presumptions of the framework would be relevant to validity.

The specific types of analyses and their interpretation depend on how the test will be used. For example, if a particular application posited a series of increasingly difficult test components, empirical evidence of the extent to which response patterns conformed to this expectation would be provided. A theory that posited unidimensionality would call for evidence of item homogeneity. In this case, the number of items and item interrela-

tionships form the basis for an estimate of score reliability, but such an index would be inappropriate for tests with a more complex internal structure.

Some studies of the internal structure of tests are designed to show whether particular items may function differently for identifiable subgroups of test takers (e.g., racial/ethnic or gender subgroups.) *Differential item functioning* occurs when different groups of test takers with similar overall ability, or similar status on an appropriate criterion, have, on average, systematically different responses to a particular item. This issue is discussed in chapter 3. However, differential item functioning is not always a flaw or weakness. Subsets of items that have a specific characteristic in common (e.g., specific content, task representation) may function differently for different groups of similarly scoring test takers. This indicates a kind of multidimensionality that may be unexpected or may conform to the test framework.

Evidence Based on Relations to Other Variables

In many cases, the intended interpretation for a given use implies that the construct should be related to some other variables, and, as a result, analyses of the relationship of test scores to variables external to the test provide another important source of validity evidence. External variables may include measures of some criteria that the test is expected to predict, as well as relationships to other tests hypothesized to measure the same constructs, and tests measuring related or different constructs. Measures other than test scores, such as performance criteria, are often used in employment settings. Categorical variables, including group membership variables, become relevant when the theory underlying a proposed test use suggests that group differences should be present or absent if a proposed test score interpretation is to be supported. Evidence based on relationships with other variables provides evidence about the degree to which these relationships are consistent with the construct underlying the proposed test score interpretations.

Convergent and discriminant evidence. Relationships between test scores and other measures intended to assess the same or similar constructs provide convergent evidence, whereas relationships between test scores and measures purportedly of different constructs provide discriminant evidence. For instance, within some theoretical frameworks, scores on a multiple-choice test of reading comprehension might be expected to relate closely (convergent evidence) to other measures of reading comprehension based on other methods, such as essay responses. Conversely, test scores might be expected to relate less closely (discriminant evidence) to measures of other skills, such as logical reasoning. Relationships among different methods of measuring the construct can be especially helpful in sharpening and elaborating score meaning and interpretation.

Evidence of relations with other variables can involve experimental as well as correlational evidence. Studies might be designed, for instance, to investigate whether scores on a measure of anxiety improve as a result of some psychological treatment or whether scores on a test of academic achievement differentiate between instructed and noninstructed groups. If performance increases due to short-term coaching are viewed as a threat to validity, it would be useful to investigate whether coached and uncoached groups perform differently.

Test-criterion relationships. Evidence of the relation of test scores to a relevant criterion may be expressed in various ways, but the fundamental question is always, how accurately do test scores predict criterion performance? The degree of accuracy and the score range within which accuracy is needed depends on the purpose for which the test is used.

The criterion variable is a measure of some attribute or outcome that is operationally distinct from the test. Thus, the test is not a measure of a criterion, but rather is a measure hypothesized as a potential predictor of that targeted criterion. Whether a test predicts a given criterion in a given context is a testable hypothesis. The criteria that are of interest are determined by test users, for example administrators in a school system or managers of a firm. The choice of the criterion and the measurement procedures used to obtain

criterion scores are of central importance. The credibility of a test-criterion study depends on the relevance, reliability, and validity of the interpretation based on the criterion measure for a given testing application.

Historically, two designs, often called predictive and concurrent, have been distinguished for evaluating test-criterion relationships. A predictive study indicates the strength of the relationship between test scores and criterion scores that are obtained at a later time. A concurrent study obtains test scores and criterion information at about the same time. When prediction is actually contemplated, as in academic admission or employment settings, or in planning rehabilitation regimens, predictive studies can retain the temporal differences and other characteristics of the practical situation. Concurrent evidence, which avoids temporal changes, is particularly useful for psychodiagnostic tests or in investigating alternative measures of some specified construct for which an accepted measurement procedure already exists. The choice of a predictive or concurrent research strategy in a given domain is also usefully informed by prior research evidence regarding the extent to which predictive and concurrent studies in that domain yield the same or different results.

Test scores are sometimes used in allocating individuals to different treatments in a way that is advantageous for the institution and/or for the individuals. Examples would include assigning individuals to different jobs within an organization, or determining whether to place a given student in a remedial class or a regular class. In that context, evidence is needed to judge the suitability of using a test when classifying or assigning a person to one job versus another or to one treatment versus another. Support for the validity of the classification procedure is provided by showing that the test is useful in determining which persons are likely to profit differentially from one treatment or another. It is possible for tests to be highly predictive of performance for different education programs or jobs without providing the information necessary to make a comparative judgment of the efficacy of assignments or treatments. In general, decision rules for selection or placement are also influenced by the number of persons to be accepted or the numbers that can be accommodated in alternative placement categories (see chap. 11).

Evidence about relations to other variables is also used to investigate questions of differential prediction for subgroups. For instance, a finding that the relation of test scores to a relevant criterion variable differs from one subgroup to another may imply that the meaning of the scores is not the same for members of the different groups, perhaps due to construct underrepresentation or construct-irrelevant sources of variance. However, the difference may also imply that the criterion has different meaning for different groups. The differences in test-criterion relationships can also arise from measurement error, especially when group means differ, so such differences do not necessarily indicate differences in score meaning. See the discussion of fairness in chapter 3 for more extended consideration of possible courses of action when scores have different meanings for different groups.

Validity generalization. An important issue in educational and employment settings is the degree to which validity evidence based on test-criterion relations can be generalized to a new situation without further study of validity in that new situation. When a test is used to predict the same or similar criteria (e.g., performance of a given job) at different times or in different places, it is typically found that observed test-criterion correlations vary substantially. In the past, this has been taken to imply that local validation studies are always required. More recently, a variety of approaches to generalizing evidence from other settings has been developed, with meta-analysis the most widely used in the published literature. In particular, meta-analyses have shown that in some domains, much of this variability may be due to statistical artifacts such as sampling fluctuations and variations across validation studies in the ranges of test scores and in the reliability of criterion measures. When these and other influences are taken into account, it may be found that the remaining variability in validity coefficients is rel-

atively small. Thus, statistical summaries of past validation studies in similar situations may be useful in estimating test-criterion relationships in a new situation. This practice is referred to as the study of validity generalization.

In some circumstances, there is a strong basis for using validity generalization. This would be the case where the meta-analytic database is large, where the meta-analytic data adequately represent the type of situation to which one wishes to generalize, and where correction for statistical artifacts produces a clear and consistent pattern of validity evidence. In such circumstances, the informational value of a local validity study may be relatively limited if not actually misleading, especially if its sample size is small. In other circumstances, the inferential leap required for generalization may be much larger. The meta-analytic database may be small, the findings may be less consistent, or the new situation may involve features markedly different from those represented in the meta-analytic database. In such circumstances, situation-specific validity evidence will be relatively more informative. Although research on validity generalization shows that results of a single local validation study may be quite imprecise, there are situations where a single study, carefully done, with adequate sample size, provides sufficient evidence to support or reject test use in a new situation. This highlights the importance of examining carefully the comparative informational value of local versus meta-analytic studies.

In conducting studies of the generalizability of validity evidence, the prior studies that are included may vary according to several situational facets. Some of the major facets are (a) differences in the way the predictor construct is measured, (b) the type of job or curriculum involved, (c) the type of criterion measure used, (d) the type of test takers, and (e) the time period in which the study was conducted. In any particular study of validity generalization, any number of these facets might vary, and a major objective of the study is to determine empirically the extent to which variation in these facets affects the test-criterion correlations obtained.

The extent to which predictive or concurrent validity evidence can be generalized to new situations is in large measure a function of accumulated research. Although evidence of generalization can often help to support a claim of validity in a new situation, the extent of available data limits the degree to which the claim can be sustained.

The above discussion focuses on the use of cumulative databases to estimate predictor-criterion relationships. Meta-analytic techniques can also be used to summarize other forms of data relevant to other inferences one may wish to draw from test scores in a particular application, such as effects of coaching and effects of certain alterations in testing conditions for test takers with specified disabilities. Gathering evidence about how well validity findings can be generalized across groups of test takers is an important part of the validation process. When the evidence suggests that inferences from test scores can be drawn for some subgroups but not for others, pursuing options such as those discussed in chapter 3 can reduce the risk of unfair test use.

Evidence for Validity and Consequences of Testing

Some consequences of test use follow directly from the interpretation of test scores for uses intended by the test developer. The validation process involves gathering evidence to evaluate the soundness of these proposed interpretations for their intended uses.

Other consequences may also be part of a claim that extends beyond the interpretation or use of scores intended by the test developer. For example, a test of student achievement might provide data for a system intended to identify and improve lower-performing schools. The claim that testing results, used this way, will result in improved student learning may rest on propositions about the system or intervention itself, beyond propositions based on the meaning of the test itself. Consequences may point to the need for evidence about components of the system that will go beyond the interpretation of test scores as a valid measure of student achievement.

Still other consequences are unintended, and are often negative. For example, school district or statewide educational testing on selected subjects may lead teachers to focus on those subjects at the expense of others. As another example, a test developed to measure knowledge needed for a given job may result in lower passing rates for one group than for another. Unintended consequences merit close examination. While not all consequences can be anticipated, in some cases factors such as prior experiences in other settings offer a basis for anticipating and proactively addressing unintended consequences. See chapter 12 for additional examples from educational settings. In some cases, actions to address one consequence bring about other consequences. One example involves the notion of "missed opportunities," as in the case of moving to computerized scoring of student essays to increase grading consistency, thus forgoing the educational benefits of addressing the same problem by training teachers to grade more consistently.

These types of consideration of consequences of testing are discussed further below.

Interpretation and uses of test scores intended by test developers. Tests are commonly administered in the expectation that some benefit will be realized from the interpretation and use of the scores intended by the test developers. A few of the many possible benefits that might be claimed are selection of efficacious therapies, placement of workers in suitable jobs, prevention of unqualified individuals from entering a profession, or improvement of classroom instructional practices. A fundamental purpose of validation is to indicate whether these specific benefits are likely to be realized. Thus, in the case of a test used in placement decisions, the validation would be informed by evidence that alternative placements, in fact, are differentially beneficial to the persons and the institution. In the case of employment testing, if a test publisher asserts that use of the test will result in reduced employee training costs, improved workforce efficiency, or some other benefit, then the validation would be informed by evidence in support of that proposition.

It is important to note that the validity of test score interpretations depends not only on the uses of the test scores but specifically on the claims that underlie the theory of action for these uses. For example, consider a school district that wants to determine children's readiness for kindergarten, and so administers a test battery and screens out students with low scores. If higher scores do, in fact, predict higher performance on key kindergarten tasks, the claim that use of the test scores for screening results in higher performance on these key tasks is supported and the interpretation of the test scores as a predictor of kindergarten readiness would be valid. If, however, the claim were made that use of the test scores for screening would result in the greatest benefit to students, the interpretation of test scores as indicators of readiness for kindergarten might not be valid because students with low scores might actually benefit more from access to kindergarten. In this case, different evidence is needed to support different claims that might be made about the same use of the screening test (for example, evidence that students below a certain cut score benefit more from another assignment than from assignment to kindergarten). The test developer is responsible for the validation of the interpretation that the test scores assess the indicated readiness skills. The school district is responsible for the validation of the proper interpretation of the readiness test scores and for evaluation of the policy of using the readiness test for placement/admissions decisions.

Claims made about test use that are not directly based on test score interpretations. Claims are sometimes made for benefits of testing that go beyond the direct interpretations or uses of the test scores themselves that are specified by the test developers. Educational tests, for example, may be advocated on the grounds that their use will improve student motivation to learn or encourage changes in classroom instructional practices by holding educators accountable for valued learning outcomes. Where such claims are central to the rationale advanced for testing, the direct examination of testing consequences necessarily assumes even greater importance. Those making the claims are responsible for evaluation of the claims. In some cases, such information can be drawn from

existing data collected for purposes other than test validation; in other cases new information will be needed to address the impact of the testing program.

Consequences that are unintended. Test score interpretation for a given use may result in unintended consequences. A key distinction is between consequences that result from a source of error in the intended test score interpretation for a given use and consequences that do not result from error in test score interpretation. Examples of each are given below.

As discussed at some length in chapter 3, one domain in which unintended negative consequences of test use are at times observed involves test score differences for groups defined in terms of race/ethnicity, gender, age, and other characteristics. In such cases, however, it is important to distinguish between evidence that is directly relevant to validity and evidence that may inform decisions about social policy but falls outside the realm of validity. For example, concerns have been raised about the effect of group differences in test scores on employment selection and promotion, the placement of children in special education classes, and the narrowing of a school's curriculum to exclude learning objectives that are not assessed. Although information about the consequences of testing may influence decisions about test use, such consequences do not, in and of themselves, detract from the validity of intended interpretations of the test scores. Rather, judgments of validity or invalidity in the light of testing consequences depend on a more searching inquiry into the sources of those consequences.

Take, as an example, a finding of different hiring rates for members of different groups as a consequence of using an employment test. If the difference is due solely to an unequal distribution of the skills the test purports to measure, and if those skills are, in fact, important contributors to job performance, then the finding of group differences per se does not imply any lack of validity for the intended interpretation. If, however, the test measured skill differences unrelated to job performance (e.g., a sophisticated reading test for a job that required only minimal functional literacy), or if the differences were due to the test's sensitivity to some test-taker characteristic not intended to be part of the test construct, then the intended interpretation of test scores as predicting job performance in a comparable manner for all groups of applicants would be rendered invalid, even if test scores correlated positively with some measure of job performance. If a test covers most of the relevant content domain but omits some areas, the content coverage might be judged adequate for some purposes. However, if it is found that excluding some components that could readily be assessed has a noticeable impact on selection rates for groups of interest (e.g., subgroup differences are found to be smaller on excluded components than on included components), the intended interpretation of test scores as predicting job performance in a comparable manner for all groups of applicants would be rendered invalid. Thus, evidence about consequences is relevant to validity when it can be traced to a source of invalidity such as construct underrepresentation or construct-irrelevant components. Evidence about consequences that cannot be so traced is not relevant to the validity of the intended interpretations of the test scores.

As another example, consider the case where research supports an employer's use of a particular test in the personality domain (i.e., the test proves to be predictive of an aspect of subsequent job performance), but it is found that some applicants form a negative opinion of the organization due to the perception that the test invades personal privacy. Thus, there is an unintended negative consequence of test use, but one that is not due to a flaw in the intended interpretation of test scores as predicting subsequent performance. Some employers faced with this situation may conclude that this negative consequence is grounds for discontinuing test use; others may conclude that the benefits gained by screening applicants outweigh this negative consequence. As this example illustrates, a consideration of consequences can influence a decision about test use, even though the consequence is independent of the validity of the intended test score interpretation. The example

also illustrates that different decision makers may make different value judgments about the impact of consequences on test use.

The fact that the validity evidence supports the intended interpretation of test scores for use in applicant screening does not mean that test use is thus required: Issues other than validity, including legal constraints, can play an important and, in some cases, a determinative role in decisions about test use. Legal constraints may also limit an employer's discretion to discard test scores from tests that have already been administered, when that decision is based on differences in scores for subgroups of different races, ethnicities, or genders.

Note that unintended consequences can also be positive. Reversing the above example of test takers who form a negative impression of an organization based on the use of a particular test, a different test may be viewed favorably by applicants, leading to a positive impression of the organization. A given test use may result in multiple consequences, some positive and some negative.

In short, decisions about test use are appropriately informed by validity evidence about intended test score interpretations for a given use, by evidence evaluating additional claims about consequences of test use that do not follow directly from test score interpretations, and by value judgments about unintended positive and negative consequences of test use.

Integrating the Validity Evidence

A sound validity argument integrates various strands of evidence into a coherent account of the degree to which existing evidence and theory support the intended interpretation of test scores for specific uses. It encompasses evidence gathered from new studies and evidence available from earlier reported research. The validity argument may indicate the need for refining the definition of the construct, may suggest revisions in the test or other aspects of the testing process, and may indicate areas needing further study.

It is commonly observed that the validation process never ends, as there is always additional information that can be gathered to more fully understand a test and the inferences that can be drawn from it. In this way an inference of validity is similar to any scientific inference. However, a test interpretation for a given use rests on evidence for a set of propositions making up the validity argument, and at some point validation evidence allows for a summary judgment of the intended interpretation that is well supported and defensible. At some point the effort to provide sufficient validity evidence to support a given test interpretation for a specific use does end (at least provisionally, pending the emergence of a strong basis for questioning that judgment). Legal requirements may necessitate that the validation study be updated in light of such factors as changes in the test population or newly developed alternative testing methods.

The amount and character of evidence required to support a provisional judgment of validity often vary between areas and also within an area as research on a topic advances. For example, prevailing standards of evidence may vary with the stakes involved in the use or interpretation of the test scores. Higher stakes may entail higher standards of evidence. As another example, in areas where data collection comes at a greater cost, one may find it necessary to base interpretations on fewer data than in areas where data collection comes with less cost.

Ultimately, the validity of an intended interpretation of test scores relies on all the available evidence relevant to the technical quality of a testing system. Different components of validity evidence are described in subsequent chapters of the *Standards*, and include evidence of careful test construction; adequate score reliability; appropriate test administration and scoring; accurate score scaling, equating, and standard setting; and careful attention to fairness for all test takers, as appropriate to the test interpretation in question.

STANDARDS FOR VALIDITY

The standards in this chapter begin with an overarching standard (numbered 1.0), which is designed to convey the central intent or primary focus of the chapter. The overarching standard may also be viewed as the guiding principle of the chapter, and is applicable to all tests and test users. All subsequent standards have been separated into three thematic clusters labeled as follows:

1. Establishing Intended Uses and Interpretations
2. Issues Regarding Samples and Settings Used in Validation
3. Specific Forms of Validity Evidence

Standard 1.0

Clear articulation of each intended test score interpretation for a specified use should be set forth, and appropriate validity evidence in support of each intended interpretation should be provided.

Cluster 1. Establishing Intended Uses and Interpretations

Standard 1.1

The test developer should set forth clearly how test scores are intended to be interpreted and consequently used. The population(s) for which a test is intended should be delimited clearly, and the construct or constructs that the test is intended to assess should be described clearly.

Comment: Statements about validity should refer to particular interpretations and consequent uses. It is incorrect to use the unqualified phrase "the validity of the test." No test permits interpretations that are valid for all purposes or in all situations. Each recommended interpretation for a given use requires validation. The test developer should specify in clear language the population for which the test is intended, the construct it is intended to measure, the contexts in which test scores are to

be employed, and the processes by which the test is to be administered and scored.

Standard 1.2

A rationale should be presented for each intended interpretation of test scores for a given use, together with a summary of the evidence and theory bearing on the intended interpretation.

Comment: The rationale should indicate what propositions are necessary to investigate the intended interpretation. The summary should combine logical analysis with empirical evidence to provide support for the test rationale. Evidence may come from studies conducted locally, in the setting where the test is to be used; from specific prior studies; or from comprehensive statistical syntheses of available studies meeting clearly specified study quality criteria. No type of evidence is inherently preferable to others; rather, the quality and relevance of the evidence to the intended test score interpretation for a given use determine the value of a particular kind of evidence. A presentation of empirical evidence on any point should give due weight to all relevant findings in the scientific literature, including those inconsistent with the intended interpretation or use. Test developers have the responsibility to provide support for their own recommendations, but test users bear ultimate responsibility for evaluating the quality of the validity evidence provided and its relevance to the local situation.

Standard 1.3

If validity for some common or likely interpretation for a given use has not been evaluated, or if such an interpretation is inconsistent with available evidence, that fact should be made clear and potential users should be strongly cautioned about making unsupported interpretations.

Comment: If past experience suggests that a test is likely to be used inappropriately for certain kinds of decisions or certain kinds of test takers, specific warnings against such uses should be given. Professional judgment is required to evaluate the extent to which existing validity evidence supports a given test use.

Standard 1.4

If a test score is interpreted for a given use in a way that has not been validated, it is incumbent on the user to justify the new interpretation for that use, providing a rationale and collecting new evidence, if necessary.

Comment: Professional judgment is required to evaluate the extent to which existing validity evidence applies in the new situation or to the new group of test takers and to determine what new evidence may be needed. The amount and kinds of new evidence required may be influenced by experience with similar prior test uses or interpretations and by the amount, quality, and relevance of existing data.

A test that has been altered or administered in ways that change the construct underlying the test for use with subgroups of the population requires evidence of the validity of the interpretation made on the basis of the modified test (see chap. 3). For example, if a test is adapted for use with individuals with a particular disability in a way that changes the underlying construct, the modified test should have its own evidence of validity for the intended interpretation.

Standard 1.5

When it is clearly stated or implied that a recommended test score interpretation for a given use will result in a specific outcome, the basis for expecting that outcome should be presented, together with relevant evidence.

Comment: If it is asserted, for example, that interpreting and using scores on a given test for employee selection will result in reduced employee errors or training costs, evidence in support of that assertion should be provided. A given claim may be supported by logical or theoretical argument as well as empirical data. Appropriate weight should be given to findings in the scientific literature that may be inconsistent with the stated expectation.

Standard 1.6

When a test use is recommended on the grounds that testing or the testing program itself will result in some indirect benefit, in addition to the utility of information from interpretation of the test scores themselves, the recommender should make explicit the rationale for anticipating the indirect benefit. Logical or theoretical arguments and empirical evidence for the indirect benefit should be provided. Appropriate weight should be given to any contradictory findings in the scientific literature, including findings suggesting important indirect outcomes other than those predicted.

Comment: For example, certain educational testing programs have been advocated on the grounds that they would have a salutary influence on classroom instructional practices or would clarify students' understanding of the kind or level of achievement they were expected to attain. To the extent that such claims enter into the justification for a testing program, they become part of the argument for test use. Evidence for such claims should be examined—in conjunction with evidence about the validity of intended test score interpretation and evidence about unintended negative consequences of test use—in making an overall decision about test use. Due weight should be given to evidence against such predictions, for example, evidence that under some conditions educational testing may have a negative effect on classroom instruction.

Standard 1.7

If test performance, or a decision made therefrom, is claimed to be essentially unaffected by practice and coaching, then the propensity for test performance to change with these forms of instruction should be documented.

Comment: Materials to aid in score interpretation should summarize evidence indicating the degree to which improvement with practice or coaching can be expected. Also, materials written for test takers should provide practical guidance about the value of test preparation activities, including coaching.

Cluster 2. Issues Regarding Samples and Settings Used in Validation

Standard 1.8

The composition of any sample of test takers from which validity evidence is obtained should be described in as much detail as is practical and permissible, including major relevant socio-demographic and developmental characteristics.

Comment: Statistical findings can be influenced by factors affecting the sample on which the results are based. When the sample is intended to represent a population, that population should be described, and attention should be drawn to any systematic factors that may limit the representativeness of the sample. Factors that might reasonably be expected to affect the results include self-selection, attrition, linguistic ability, disability status, and exclusion criteria, among others. If the participants in a validity study are patients, for example, then the diagnoses of the patients are important, as well as other characteristics, such as the severity of the diagnosed conditions. For tests used in employment settings, the employment status (e.g., applicants versus current job holders), the general level of experience and educational background, and the gender and ethnic composition of the sample may be relevant information. For tests used in credentialing, the status of those providing information (e.g., candidates for a credential versus already-credentialed individuals) is important for interpreting the resulting data. For tests used in educational settings, relevant information may include educational background, developmental level, community characteristics, or school admissions policies, as well as the gender and ethnic composition of the sample. Sometimes legal restrictions about privacy preclude obtaining or disclosing such population information or limit the level of particularity at which such data may be disclosed. The specific privacy laws, if any, governing the type of data should be considered, in order to ensure that any description of a population does not have the potential to identify an individual in a manner inconsistent with such standards. The extent of missing data, if any, and the methods for handling missing data (e.g., use of imputation procedures) should be described.

Standard 1.9

When a validation rests in part on the opinions or decisions of expert judges, observers, or raters, procedures for selecting such experts and for eliciting judgments or ratings should be fully described. The qualifications and experience of the judges should be presented. The description of procedures should include any training and instructions provided, should indicate whether participants reached their decisions independently, and should report the level of agreement reached. If participants interacted with one another or exchanged information, the procedures through which they may have influenced one another should be set forth.

Comment: Systematic collection of judgments or opinions may occur at many points in test construction (e.g., eliciting expert judgments of content appropriateness or adequate content representation), in the formulation of rules or standards for score interpretation (e.g., in setting cut scores), or in test scoring (e.g., rating of essay responses). Whenever such procedures are employed, the quality of the resulting judgments is important to the validation. Level of agreement should be specified clearly (e.g., whether percent agreement refers to agreement prior to or after a consensus discussion, and whether the criterion for agreement is exact agreement of ratings or agreement within a certain number of scale points.) The basis for specifying certain types of individuals (e.g., experienced teachers, experienced job incumbents, supervisors) as appropriate experts for the judgment or rating task should be articulated. It may be entirely appropriate to have experts work together to reach consensus, but it would not then be appropriate to treat their respective judgments as statistically independent. Different judges may be used for different purposes (e.g., one set may rate items for cultural sensitivity while another may rate for reading level) or for different portions of a test.

Standard 1.10

When validity evidence includes statistical analyses of test results, either alone or together with data on other variables, the conditions under which the data were collected should be described in enough detail that users can judge the relevance of the statistical findings to local conditions. Attention should be drawn to any features of a validation data collection that are likely to differ from typical operational testing conditions and that could plausibly influence test performance.

Comment: Such conditions might include (but would not be limited to) the following: test-taker motivation or prior preparation, the range of test scores over test takers, the time allowed for test takers to respond or other administrative conditions, the mode of test administration (e.g., unproctored online testing versus proctored on-site testing), examiner training or other examiner characteristics, the time intervals separating collection of data on different measures, or conditions that may have changed since the validity evidence was obtained.

Cluster 3. Specific Forms of Validity Evidence

(a) Content-Oriented Evidence

Standard 1.11

When the rationale for test score interpretation for a given use rests in part on the appropriateness of test content, the procedures followed in spec-

ifying and generating test content should be described and justified with reference to the intended population to be tested and the construct the test is intended to measure or the domain it is intended to represent. If the definition of the content sampled incorporates criteria such as importance, frequency, or criticality, these criteria should also be clearly explained and justified.

Comment: For example, test developers might provide a logical structure that maps the items on the test to the content domain, illustrating the relevance of each item and the adequacy with which the set of items represents the content domain. Areas of the content domain that are not included among the test items could be indicated as well. The match of test content to the targeted domain in terms of cognitive complexity and the accessibility of the test content to all members of the intended population are also important considerations.

(b) Evidence Regarding Cognitive Processes

Standard 1.12

If the rationale for score interpretation for a given use depends on premises about the psychological processes or cognitive operations of test takers, then theoretical or empirical evidence in support of those premises should be provided. When statements about the processes employed by observers or scorers are part of the argument for validity, similar information should be provided.

Comment: If the test specification delineates the processes to be assessed, then evidence is needed that the test items do, in fact, tap the intended processes.

(c) Evidence Regarding Internal Structure

Standard 1.13

If the rationale for a test score interpretation for a given use depends on premises about the relationships among test items or among parts of the test, evidence concerning the internal structure of the test should be provided.

Comment: It might be claimed, for example, that a test is essentially unidimensional. Such a claim could be supported by a multivariate statistical analysis, such as a factor analysis, showing that the score variability attributable to one major dimension was much greater than the score variability attributable to any other identified dimension, or showing that a single factor adequately accounts for the covariation among test items. When a test provides more than one score, the interrelationships of those scores should be shown to be consistent with the construct(s) being assessed.

Standard 1.14

When interpretation of subscores, score differences, or profiles is suggested, the rationale and relevant evidence in support of such interpretation should be provided. Where composite scores are developed, the basis and rationale for arriving at the composites should be given.

Comment: When a test provides more than one score, the distinctiveness and reliability of the separate scores should be demonstrated, and the interrelationships of those scores should be shown to be consistent with the construct(s) being assessed. Moreover, evidence for the validity of interpretations of two or more separate scores would not necessarily justify a statistical or substantive interpretation of the difference between them. Rather, the rationale and supporting evidence must pertain directly to the specific score, score combination, or score pattern to be interpreted for a given use. When subscores from one test or scores from different tests are combined into a composite, the basis for combining scores and for how scores are combined (e.g., differential weighting versus simple summation) should be specified.

Standard 1.15

When interpretation of performance on specific items, or small subsets of items, is suggested,

the rationale and relevant evidence in support of such interpretation should be provided. When interpretation of individual item responses is likely but is not recommended by the developer, the user should be warned against making such interpretations.

Comment: Users should be given sufficient guidance to enable them to judge the degree of confidence warranted for any interpretation for a use recommended by the test developer. Test manuals and score reports should discourage overinterpretation of information that may be subject to considerable error. This is especially important if interpretation of performance on isolated items, small subsets of items, or subtest scores is suggested.

(d) Evidence Regarding Relationships With Conceptually Related Constructs

Standard 1.16

When validity evidence includes empirical analyses of responses to test items together with data on other variables, the rationale for selecting the additional variables should be provided. Where appropriate and feasible, evidence concerning the constructs represented by other variables, as well as their technical properties, should be presented or cited. Attention should be drawn to any likely sources of dependence (or lack of independence) among variables other than dependencies among the construct(s) they represent.

Comment: The patterns of association between and among scores on the test under study and other variables should be consistent with theoretical expectations. The additional variables might be demographic characteristics, indicators of treatment conditions, or scores on other measures. They might include intended measures of the same construct or of different constructs. The reliability of scores from such other measures and the validity of intended interpretations of scores from these measures are an important part of the validity evidence for the test under study. If such variables include composite scores, the manner in which the composites were constructed should be explained (e.g., transformation or standardization of the variables, and weighting of the variables). In addition to considering the properties of each variable in isolation, it is important to guard against faulty interpretations arising from spurious sources of dependency among measures, including correlated errors or shared variance due to common methods of measurement or common elements.

(e) Evidence Regarding Relationships With Criteria

Standard 1.17

When validation relies on evidence that test scores are related to one or more criterion variables, information about the suitability and technical quality of the criteria should be reported.

Comment: The description of each criterion variable should include evidence concerning its reliability, the extent to which it represents the intended construct (e.g., task performance on the job), and the extent to which it is likely to be influenced by extraneous sources of variance. Special attention should be given to sources that previous research suggests may introduce extraneous variance that might bias the criterion for or against identifiable groups.

Standard 1.18

When it is asserted that a certain level of test performance predicts adequate or inadequate criterion performance, information about the levels of criterion performance associated with given levels of test scores should be provided.

Comment: For purposes of linking specific test scores with specific levels of criterion performance, regression equations are more useful than correlation coefficients, which are generally insufficient to fully describe patterns of association between tests and other variables. Means, standard deviations, and other statistical summaries are needed, as well as information about the distribution of criterion performances conditional upon a given test score. In the case of categorical rather than continuous variables, techniques appropriate to such data should be used (e.g., the use of logistic regression in the case of a dichotomous criterion). Evidence about the overall association between variables should be supplemented by information about the form of that association and about the variability of that association in different ranges of test scores. Note that data collections employing test takers selected for their extreme scores on one or more measures (extreme groups) typically cannot provide adequate information about the association.

Standard 1.19

If test scores are used in conjunction with other variables to predict some outcome or criterion, analyses based on statistical models of the predictor-criterion relationship should include those additional relevant variables along with the test scores.

Comment: In general, if several predictors of some criterion are available, the optimum combination of predictors cannot be determined solely from separate, pairwise examinations of the criterion variable with each separate predictor in turn, due to intercorrelation among predictors. It is often informative to estimate the increment in predictive accuracy that may be expected when each variable, including the test score, is introduced in addition to all other available variables. As empirically derived weights for combining predictors can capitalize on chance factors in a given sample, analyses involving multiple predictors should be verified by cross-validation or equivalent analysis whenever feasible, and the precision of estimated regression coefficients or other indices should be reported. Cross-validation procedures include formula estimates of validity in subsequent samples and empirical approaches such as deriving weights in one portion of a sample and applying them to an independent subsample.

Standard 1.20

When effect size measures (e.g., correlations between test scores and criterion measures, standardized mean test score differences between subgroups) are used to draw inferences that go beyond describing the sample or samples on which data have been collected, indices of the degree of uncertainty associated with these measures (e.g., standard errors, confidence intervals, or significance tests) should be reported.

Comment: Effect size measures are usefully paired with indices reflecting their sampling error to make meaningful evaluation possible. There are various possible measures of effect size, each applicable to different settings. In the presentation of indices of uncertainty, standard errors or confidence intervals provide more information and thus are preferred in place of, or as supplements to, significance testing.

Standard 1.21

When statistical adjustments, such as those for restriction of range or attenuation, are made, both adjusted and unadjusted coefficients, as well as the specific procedure used, and all statistics used in the adjustment, should be reported. Estimates of the construct-criterion relationship that remove the effects of measurement error on the test should be clearly reported as adjusted estimates.

Comment: The correlation between two variables, such as test scores and criterion measures, depends on the range of values on each variable. For example, the test scores and the criterion values of a selected subset of test takers (e.g., job applicants who have been selected for hire) will typically have a smaller range than the scores of all test takers (e.g., the entire applicant pool.) Statistical methods are available for adjusting the correlation to reflect the population of interest rather than the sample available. Such adjustments are often appropriate, as when results are compared across various situations. The correlation between two variables is also affected by measurement error, and methods are available

for adjusting the correlation to estimate the strength of the correlation net of the effects of measurement error in either or both variables. Reporting of an adjusted correlation should be accompanied by a statement of the method and the statistics used in making the adjustment.

Standard 1.22

When a meta-analysis is used as evidence of the strength of a test-criterion relationship, the test and the criterion variables in the local situation should be comparable with those in the studies summarized. If relevant research includes credible evidence that any other specific features of the testing application may influence the strength of the test-criterion relationship, the correspondence between those features in the local situation and in the meta-analysis should be reported. Any significant disparities that might limit the applicability of the meta-analytic findings to the local situation should be noted explicitly.

Comment: The meta-analysis should incorporate all available studies meeting explicitly stated inclusion criteria. Meta-analytic evidence used in test validation typically is based on a number of tests measuring the same or very similar constructs and criterion measures that likewise measure the same or similar constructs. A meta-analytic study may also be limited to multiple studies of a single test and a single criterion. For each study included in the analysis, the test-criterion relationship is expressed in some common metric, often as an effect size. The strength of the test-criterion relationship may be moderated by features of the situation in which the test and criterion measures were obtained (e.g., types of jobs, characteristics of test takers, time interval separating collection of test and criterion measures, year or decade in which the data were collected). If test-criterion relationships vary according to such moderator variables, then the meta-analysis should report separate estimated effect-size distributions conditional upon levels of these moderator variables when the number of studies available for analysis permits doing so. This might be accomplished, for example, by reporting separate distributions for subsets of studies or by estimating the magnitudes of the influences of situational features on effect sizes.

This standard addresses the responsibilities of the individual who is drawing on meta-analytic evidence to support a test score interpretation for a given use. In some instances, that individual may also be the one conducting the meta-analysis; in other instances, existing meta-analyses are relied on. In the latter instance, the individual drawing on meta-analytic evidence does not have control over how the meta-analysis was conducted or reported, and must evaluate the soundness of the meta-analysis for the setting in question.

Standard 1.23

Any meta-analytic evidence used to support an intended test score interpretation for a given use should be clearly described, including methodological choices in identifying and coding studies, correcting for artifacts, and examining potential moderator variables. Assumptions made in correcting for artifacts such as criterion unreliability and range restriction should be presented, and the consequences of these assumptions made clear.

Comment: The description should include documented information about each study used as input to the meta-analysis, thus permitting evaluation by an independent party. Note also that meta-analysis inevitably involves judgments regarding a number of methodological choices. The bases for these judgments should be articulated. In the case of choices involving some degree of uncertainty, such as artifact corrections based on assumed values, the uncertainty should be acknowledged and the degree to which conclusions about validity hinge on these assumptions should be examined and reported.

As in the case of Standard 1.22, the individual who is drawing on meta-analytic evidence to support a test score interpretation for a given use may or may not also be the one conducting the meta-analysis. As Standard 1.22 addresses the re-

porting of meta-analytic evidence, the individual drawing on existing meta-analytic evidence must evaluate the soundness of the meta-analysis for the setting in question.

Standard 1.24

If a test is recommended for use in assigning persons to alternative treatments, and if outcomes from those treatments can reasonably be compared on a common criterion, then, whenever feasible, supporting evidence of differential outcomes should be provided.

Comment: If a test is used for classification into alternative occupational, therapeutic, or educational programs, it is not sufficient just to show that the test predicts treatment outcomes. Support for the validity of the classification procedure is provided by showing that the test is useful in determining which persons are likely to profit differentially from one treatment or another. Treatment categories may have to be combined to assemble sufficient cases for statistical analysis. It is recognized, however, that such research may not be feasible, because ethical and legal constraints on differential assignments may forbid control groups.

(f) Evidence Based on Consequences of Tests

Standard 1.25

When unintended consequences result from test use, an attempt should be made to investigate whether such consequences arise from the test's sensitivity to characteristics other than those it is intended to assess or from the test's failure to fully represent the intended construct.

Comment: The validity of test score interpretations may be limited by construct-irrelevant components or construct underrepresentation. When unintended consequences appear to stem, at least in part, from the use of one or more tests, it is especially important to check that these consequences do not arise from construct-irrelevant components or construct underrepresentation. For example, although group differences, in and of themselves, do not call into question the validity of a proposed interpretation, they may increase the salience of plausible rival hypotheses that should be evaluated as part of the validation effort. A finding of unintended consequences may also lead to reconsideration of the appropriateness of the construct in question. Ensuring that unintended consequences are evaluated is the responsibility of those making the decision whether to use a particular test, although legal constraints may limit the test user's discretion to discard the results of a previously administered test, when that decision is based on differences in scores for subgroups of different races, ethnicities, or genders. These issues are discussed further in chapter 3.

2. RELIABILITY/PRECISION AND ERRORS OF MEASUREMENT

BACKGROUND

A test, broadly defined, is a set of tasks or stimuli designed to elicit responses that provide a sample of an examinee's behavior or performance in a specified domain. Coupled with the test is a scoring procedure that enables the scorer to evaluate the behavior or work samples and generate a score. In interpreting and using test scores, it is important to have some indication of their reliability.

The term *reliability* has been used in two ways in the measurement literature. First, the term has been used to refer to the reliability coefficients of classical test theory, defined as the correlation between scores on two equivalent forms of the test, presuming that taking one form has no effect on performance on the second form. Second, the term has been used in a more general sense, to refer to the consistency of scores across replications of a testing procedure, regardless of how this consistency is estimated or reported (e.g., in terms of standard errors, reliability coefficients per se, generalizability coefficients, error/tolerance ratios, item response theory (IRT) information functions, or various indices of classification consistency). To maintain a link to the traditional notions of reliability while avoiding the ambiguity inherent in using a single, familiar term to refer to a wide range of concepts and indices, we use the term *reliability/precision* to denote the more general notion of consistency of the scores across instances of the testing procedure, and the term *reliability coefficient* to refer to the reliability coefficients of classical test theory.

The reliability/precision of measurement is always important. However, the need for precision increases as the consequences of decisions and interpretations grow in importance. If a test score leads to a decision that is not easily reversed, such as rejection or admission of a candidate to a professional school, or a score-based clinical judgment (e.g., in a legal context) that a serious cognitive injury was sustained, a higher degree of reliability/precision is warranted. If a decision can and will be corroborated by information from other sources or if an erroneous initial decision can be easily corrected, scores with more modest reliability/precision may suffice.

Interpretations of test scores generally depend on assumptions that individuals and groups exhibit some degree of consistency in their scores across independent administrations of the testing procedure. However, different samples of performance from the same person are rarely identical. An individual's performances, products, and responses to sets of tasks or test questions vary in quality or character from one sample of tasks to another and from one occasion to another, even under strictly controlled conditions. Different raters may award different scores to a specific performance. All of these sources of variation are reflected in the examinees' scores, which will vary across instances of a measurement procedure.

The reliability/precision of the scores depends on how much the scores vary across replications of the testing procedure, and analyses of reliability/precision depend on the kinds of variability allowed in the testing procedure (e.g., over tasks, contexts, raters) and the proposed interpretation of the test scores. For example, if the interpretation of the scores assumes that the construct being assessed does not vary over occasions, the variability over occasions is a potential source of measurement error. If the test tasks vary over alternate forms of the test, and the observed performances are treated as a sample from a domain of similar tasks, the random variability in scores from one form to another would be considered error. If raters are used to assign scores to responses, the variability in scores over qualified raters is a source of error. Variations in a test taker's scores that are not consistent with the definition of the construct being assessed are attributed to errors of measurement.

A very basic way to evaluate the consistency of scores involves an analysis of the variation in each test taker's scores across replications of the testing procedure. The test is administered and then, after a brief period during which the examinee's standing on the variable being measured would not be expected to change, the test (or a distinct but equivalent form of the test) is administered a second time; it is assumed that the first administration has no influence on the second administration. Given that the attribute being measured is assumed to remain the same for each test taker over the two administrations and that the test administrations are independent of each other, more variation across the two administrations indicates more error in the test scores and therefore lower reliability/precision.

The impact of such measurement errors can be summarized in a number of ways, but typically, in educational and psychological measurement, it is conceptualized in terms of the standard deviation in the scores for a person over replications of the testing procedure. In most testing contexts, it is not possible to replicate the testing procedure repeatedly, and therefore it is not possible to estimate the standard error for each person's score via repeated measurement. Instead, using model-based assumptions, the average error of measurement is estimated over some population, and this average is referred to as the *standard error of measurement* (SEM). The SEM is an indicator of a lack of consistency in the scores generated by the testing procedure for some population. A relatively large SEM indicates relatively low reliability/precision. The *conditional standard error of measurement* for a score level is the standard error of measurement at that score level.

To say that a score includes error implies that there is a hypothetical error-free value that characterizes the variable being assessed. In classical test theory this error-free value is referred to as the person's *true score* for the test procedure. It is conceptualized as the hypothetical average score over an infinite set of replications of the testing procedure. In statistical terms, a person's true score is an unknown parameter, or constant, and the observed score for the person is a random

variable that fluctuates around the true score for the person.

Generalizability theory provides a different framework for estimating reliability/precision. While classical test theory assumes a single distribution for the errors in a test taker's scores, generalizability theory seeks to evaluate the contributions of different sources of error (e.g., items, occasions, raters) to the overall error. The *universe score* for a person is defined as the expected value over a universe of all possible replications of the testing procedure for the test taker. The universe score of generalizability theory plays a role that is similar to the role of true scores in classical test theory.

Item response theory (IRT) addresses the basic issue of reliability/precision using information functions, which indicate the precision with which observed task/item performances can be used to estimate the value of a latent trait for each test taker. Using IRT, indices analogous to traditional reliability coefficients can be estimated from the item information functions and distributions of the latent trait in some population.

In practice, the reliability/precision of the scores is typically evaluated in terms of various coefficients, including reliability coefficients, generalizability coefficients, and IRT information functions, depending on the focus of the analysis and the measurement model being used. The coefficients tend to have high values when the variability associated with the error is small compared with the observed variation in the scores (or score differences) to be estimated.

Implications for Validity

Although reliability/precision is discussed here as an independent characteristic of test scores, it should be recognized that the level of reliability/precision of scores has implications for validity. Reliability/precision of data ultimately bears on the generalizability or dependability of the scores and/or the consistency of classifications of individuals derived from the scores. To the extent that scores are not consistent across replications of the testing procedure (i.e., to the extent that they reflect random errors of measurement), their potential for accurate prediction of criteria, for beneficial examinee diagnosis, and for wise decision making is limited.

Specifications for Replications of the Testing Procedure

As indicated earlier, the general notion of reliability/precision is defined in terms of consistency over replications of the testing procedure. Reliability/precision is high if the scores for each person are consistent over replications of the testing procedure and is low if the scores are not consistent over replications. Therefore, in evaluating reliability/precision, it is important to be clear about what constitutes a replication of the testing procedure.

Replications involve independent administrations of the testing procedure, such that the attribute being measured would not be expected to change. For example, in assessing an attribute that is not expected to change over an extended period of time (e.g., in measuring a trait), scores generated on two successive days (using different test forms if appropriate) would be considered replications. For a state variable (e.g., mood or hunger), where fairly rapid changes are common, scores generated on two successive days would not be considered replications; the scores obtained on each occasion would be interpreted in terms of the value of the state variable on that occasion. For many tests of knowledge or skill, the administration of alternate forms of a test with different samples of items would be considered replications of the test; for survey instruments and some personality measures, it is expected that the same questions will be used every time the test is administered, and any substantial change in wording would constitute a different test form.

Standardized tests present the same or very similar test materials to all test takers, maintain close adherence to stipulated procedures for test administration, and employ prescribed scoring rules that can be applied with a high degree of consistency. Administering the same questions or commonly scaled questions to all test takers under the same conditions promotes fairness and facilitates comparisons of scores across individuals. Conditions of observation that are fixed or standardized for the testing procedure remain the same across replications. However, some aspects of any standardized testing procedure will be allowed to vary. The time and place of testing, as well as the persons administering the test, are generally allowed to vary to some extent. The particular tasks included in the test may be allowed to vary (as samples from a common content domain), and the persons who score the results can vary over some set of qualified scorers.

Alternate forms (or *parallel forms*) of a standardized test are designed to have the same general distribution of content and item formats (as described, for example, in detailed test specifications), the same administrative procedures, and at least approximately the same score means and standard deviations in some specified population or populations. Alternate forms of a test are considered interchangeable, in the sense that they are built to the same specifications, and are interpreted as measures of the same construct.

In classical test theory, strictly parallel tests are assumed to measure the same construct and to yield scores that have the same means and standard deviations in the populations of interest and have the same correlations with all other variables. A classical reliability coefficient is defined in terms of the correlation between scores from strictly parallel forms of the test, but it is estimated in terms of the correlation between alternate forms of the test that may not quite be strictly parallel.

Different approaches to the estimation of reliability/precision can be implemented to fit different data-collection designs and different interpretations and uses of scores. In some cases, it may be feasible to estimate the variability over replications directly (e.g., by having a number of qualified raters evaluate a sample of test performances for each test taker). In other cases, it may be necessary to use less direct estimates of the reliability coefficient. For example, internal-consistency estimates of reliability (e.g., split halves coefficient, KR–20, coefficient alpha) use the observed extent of agreement between different parts of one test to estimate the reliability associated with form-to-form variability. For the split-halves method, scores on two more-or-less parallel halves of the test (e.g., odd-numbered items and even-numbered items) are correlated, and the resulting half-test reliability coefficient is statistically adjusted to estimate reliability for the full-length test. However, when a test is designed to reflect rate of work, internal-consistency estimates of reliability (particularly by the odd-even method) are likely to yield inflated estimates of reliability for highly speeded tests.

In some cases, it may be reasonable to assume that a potential source of variability is likely to be negligible or that the user will be able to infer adequate reliability from other types of evidence. For example, if test scores are used mainly to predict some criterion scores and the test does an acceptable job in predicting the criterion, it can be inferred that the test scores are reliable/precise enough for their intended use.

The definition of what constitutes a standardized test or measurement procedure has broadened significantly over the last few decades. Various kinds of performance assessments, simulations, and portfolio-based assessments have been developed to provide measures of constructs that might otherwise be difficult to assess. Each step toward greater flexibility in the assessment procedures enlarges the scope of the variations allowed in replications of the testing procedure, and therefore tends to increase the measurement error. However, some of these sacrifices in reliability/precision may reduce construct irrelevance or construct underrepresentation and thereby improve the validity of the intended interpretations of the scores. For example, performance assessments that depend on ratings of extended responses tend to have lower reliability than more structured assessments (e.g., multiple-choice or short-answer tests), but they can sometimes provide more direct measures of the attribute of interest.

Random errors of measurement are viewed as unpredictable fluctuations in scores. They are conceptually distinguished from *systematic errors*, which may also affect the performances of individuals or groups but in a consistent rather than a random manner. For example, an incorrect answer key would contribute systematic error, as would

differences in the difficulty of test forms that have not been adequately equated or linked; examinees who take one form may receive higher scores on average than if they had taken the other form. Such systematic errors would not generally be included in the standard error of measurement, and they are not regarded as contributing to a lack of reliability/precision. Rather, systematic errors constitute construct-irrelevant factors that reduce validity but not reliability/precision.

Important sources of random error may be grouped in two broad categories: those rooted within the test takers and those external to them. Fluctuations in the level of an examinee's motivation, interest, or attention and the inconsistent application of skills are clearly internal sources that may lead to random error. Variations in testing conditions (e.g., time of day, level of distractions) and variations in scoring due to scorer subjectivity are examples of external sources that may lead to random error. The importance of any particular source of variation depends on the specific conditions under which the measures are taken, how performances are scored, and the interpretations derived from the scores.

Some changes in scores from one occasion to another are not regarded as error (random or systematic), because they result, in part, from changes in the construct being measured (e.g., due to learning or maturation that has occurred between the initial and final measures). In such cases, the changes in performance would constitute the phenomenon of interest and would not be considered errors of measurement.

Measurement error reduces the usefulness of test scores. It limits the extent to which test results can be generalized beyond the particulars of a given replication of the testing procedure. It reduces the confidence that can be placed in the results from any single measurement and therefore the reliability/precision of the scores. Because random measurement errors are unpredictable, they cannot be removed from observed scores. However, their aggregate magnitude can be summarized in several ways, as discussed below, and they can be controlled to some extent (e.g., by standardization or by averaging over multiple scores).

The standard error of measurement, as such, provides an indication of the expected level of random error over score points and replications for a specific population. In many cases, it is useful to have estimates of the standard errors for individual examinees (or for examinees with scores in certain score ranges). These conditional standard errors are difficult to estimate directly, but can be estimated indirectly. For example, the test information functions based on IRT models can be used to estimate standard errors for different values of a latent ability parameter and/or for different observed scores. In using any of these model-based estimates of conditional standard errors, it is important that the model assumptions be consistent with the data.

Evaluating Reliability/Precision

The ideal approach to the evaluation of reliability/precision would require many independent replications of the testing procedure on a large sample of test takers. The range of differences allowed in replications of the testing procedure and the proposed interpretation of the scores provide a framework for investigating reliability/precision.

For most testing programs, scores are expected to generalize over alternate forms of the test, occasions (within some period), testing contexts, and raters (if judgment is required in scoring). To the extent that the impact of any of these sources of variability is expected to be substantial, the variability should be estimated in some way. It is not necessary that the different sources of variance be estimated separately. The overall reliability/precision, given error variance due to the sampling of forms, occasions, and raters, can be estimated through a test-retest study involving different forms administered on different occasions and scored by different raters.

The interpretation of reliability/precision analyses depends on the population being tested. For example, reliability or generalizability coefficients derived from scores of a nationally representative sample may differ significantly from those obtained from a more homogeneous sample drawn from one gender, one ethnic group, or one community.

Therefore, to the extent feasible (i.e., if sample sizes are large enough), reliability/precision should be estimated separately for all relevant subgroups (e.g., defined in terms of race/ethnicity, gender, language proficiency) in the population. (Also see chap. 3, "Fairness in Testing.")

Reliability/Generalizability Coefficients

In classical test theory, the consistency of test scores is evaluated mainly in terms of reliability coefficients, defined in terms of the correlation between scores derived from replications of the testing procedure on a sample of test takers. Three broad categories of reliability coefficients are recognized: (a) coefficients derived from the administration of alternate forms in independent testing sessions (*alternate-form coefficients*); (b) coefficients obtained by administration of the same form on separate occasions (*test-retest coefficients*); and (c) coefficients based on the relationships/interactions among scores derived from individual items or subsets of the items within a test, all data accruing from a single administration (*internal-consistency coefficients*). In addition, where test scoring involves a high level of judgment, indices of scorer consistency are commonly obtained. In formal treatments of classical test theory, reliability can be defined as the ratio of true-score variance to observed score variance, but it is estimated in terms of reliability coefficients of the kinds mentioned above.

In generalizability theory, these different reliability analyses are treated as special cases of a more general framework for estimating error variance in terms of the variance components associated with different sources of error. A *generalizability coefficient* is defined as the ratio of universe score variance to observed score variance. Unlike traditional approaches to the study of reliability, generalizability theory encourages the researcher to specify and estimate components of true score variance, error score variance, and observed score variance, and to calculate coefficients based on these estimates. Estimation is typically accomplished by the application of analysis-of-variance techniques. The separate numerical estimates of the components of variance (e.g., variance components for items, occasions, and raters, and for the interactions among these potential sources of error) can be used to evaluate the contribution of each source of error to the overall measurement error; the variance-component estimates can be helpful in identifying an effective strategy for controlling overall error variance.

Different reliability (and generalizability) coefficients may appear to be interchangeable, but the different coefficients convey different information. A coefficient may encompass one or more sources of error. For example, a coefficient may reflect error due to scorer inconsistencies but not reflect the variation over an examinee's performances or products. A coefficient may reflect only the internal consistency of item responses within an instrument and fail to reflect measurement error associated with day-to-day changes in examinee performance.

It should not be inferred, however, that alternate-form or test-retest coefficients based on test administrations several days or weeks apart are always preferable to internal-consistency coefficients. In cases where we can assume that scores are not likely to change, based on past experience and/or theoretical considerations, it may be reasonable to assume invariance over occasions (without conducting a test-retest study). Another limitation of test-retest coefficients is that, when the same form of the test is used, the correlation between the first and second scores could be inflated by the test taker's recall of initial responses.

The test information function, an important result of IRT, summarizes how well the test discriminates among individuals at various levels of ability on the trait being assessed. Under the IRT conceptualization for dichotomously scored items, the *item characteristic curve* or *item response function* is used as a model to represent the increasing proportion of correct responses to an item at increasing levels of the ability or trait being measured. Given appropriate data, the parameters of the characteristic curve for each item in a test can be estimated. The test information function can then be calculated from the parameter estimates for the set of items in the test and can be used to derive coefficients with interpretations similar to reliability coefficients.

The information function may be viewed as a mathematical statement of the precision of measurement at each level of the given trait. The IRT information function is based on the results obtained on a specific occasion or in a specific context, and therefore it does not provide an indication of generalizability over occasions or contexts.

Coefficients (e.g., reliability, generalizability, and IRT-based coefficients) have two major advantages over standard errors. First, as indicated above, they can be used to estimate standard errors (overall and/or conditional) in cases where it would not be possible to do so directly. Second, coefficients (e.g., reliability and generalizability coefficients), which are defined in terms of ratios of variances for scores on the same scale, are invariant over linear transformations of the score scale and can be useful in comparing different testing procedures based on different scales. However, such comparisons are rarely straightforward, because they can depend on the variability of the groups on which the coefficients are based, the techniques used to obtain the coefficients, the sources of error reflected in the coefficients, and the lengths and contents of the instruments being compared.

Factors Affecting Reliability/Precision

A number of factors can have significant effects on reliability/precision, and in some cases, these factors can lead to misinterpretations of the results, if not taken into account.

First, any evaluation of reliability/precision applies to a particular assessment procedure and is likely to change if the procedure is changed in any substantial way. In general, if the assessment is shortened (e.g., by decreasing the number of items or tasks), the reliability is likely to decrease; and if the assessment is lengthened with comparable tasks or items, the reliability is likely to increase. In fact, lengthening the assessment, and thereby increasing the size of the sample of tasks/items (or raters or occasions) being employed, is an effective and commonly used method for improving reliability/precision.

Second, if the variability associated with raters is estimated for a select group of raters who have been especially well trained (and were perhaps involved in the development of the procedures), but raters are not as well trained in some operational contexts, the error associated with rater variability in these operational settings may be much higher than is indicated by the reported interrater reliability coefficients. Similarly, if raters are still refining their performance in the early days of an extended scoring window, the error associated with rater variability may be greater for examinees testing early in the window than for examinees who test later.

Reliability/precision can also depend on the population for which the procedure is being used. In particular, if variability in the construct of interest in the population for which scores are being generated is substantially different from what it is in the population for which reliability/precision was evaluated, the reliability/precision can be quite different in the two populations. When the variability in the construct being measured is low, reliability and generalizability coefficients tend to be small, and when the variability in the construct being measured is higher, the coefficients tend to be larger. Standard errors of measurement are less dependent than reliability and generalizability coefficients on the variability in the sample of test takers.

In addition, reliability/precision can vary from one population to another, even if the variability in the construct of interest in the two populations is the same. The reliability can vary from one population to another because particular sources of error (rater effects, familiarity with formats and instructions, etc.) have more impact in one population than they do in the other. In general, if any aspects of the assessment procedures or the population being assessed are changed in an operational setting, the reliability/precision may change.

Standard Errors of Measurement

The standard error of measurement can be used to generate confidence intervals around reported scores. It is therefore generally more informative than a reliability or generalizability coefficient, once a measurement procedure has been adopted

and the interpretation of scores has become the user's primary concern.

Estimates of the standard errors at different score levels (that is, conditional standard errors) are usually a valuable supplement to the single statistic for all score levels combined. Conditional standard errors of measurement can be much more informative than a single average standard error for a population. If decisions are based on test scores and these decisions are concentrated in one area or a few areas of the score scale, then the conditional errors in those areas are of special interest.

Like reliability and generalizability coefficients, standard errors may reflect variation from many sources of error or only a few. A more comprehensive standard error (i.e., one that includes the most relevant sources of error, given the definition of the testing procedure and the proposed interpretation) tends to be more informative than a less comprehensive standard error. However, practical constraints often preclude the kinds of studies that would yield information on all potential sources of error, and in such cases, it is most informative to evaluate the sources of error that are likely to have the greatest impact.

Interpretations of test scores may be broadly categorized as *relative* or *absolute*. Relative interpretations convey the standing of an individual or group within a reference population. Absolute interpretations relate the status of an individual or group to defined performance standards. The standard error is not the same for the two types of interpretations. Any source of error that is the same for all individuals does not contribute to the relative error but may contribute to the absolute error.

Traditional norm-referenced reliability coefficients were developed to evaluate the precision with which test scores estimate the relative standing of examinees on some scale, and they evaluate reliability/precision in terms of the ratio of true-score variance to observed-score variance. As the range of uses of test scores has expanded and the contexts of use have been extended (e.g., diagnostic categorization, the evaluation of educational programs), the range of indices that are used to evaluate reliability/precision has also grown to include indices for various kinds of change scores and difference scores, indices of decision consistency, and indices appropriate for evaluating the precision of group means.

Some indices of precision, especially standard errors and conditional standard errors, also depend on the scale in which they are reported. An index stated in terms of raw scores or the trait-level estimates of IRT may convey a very different perception of the error if restated in terms of scale scores. For example, for the raw-score scale, the conditional standard error may appear to be high at one score level and low at another, but when the conditional standard errors are restated in units of scale scores, quite different trends in comparative precision may emerge.

Decision Consistency

Where the purpose of measurement is classification, some measurement errors are more serious than others. Test takers who are far above or far below the cut score established for pass/fail or for eligibility for a special program can have considerable error in their observed scores without any effect on their classification decisions. Errors of measurement for examinees whose true scores are close to the cut score are more likely to lead to classification errors. The choice of techniques used to quantify reliability/precision should take these circumstances into account. This can be done by reporting the conditional standard error in the vicinity of the cut score or the decision-consistency/accuracy indices (e.g., percentage of correct decisions, Cohen's kappa), which vary as functions of both score reliability/precision and the location of the cut score.

Decision consistency refers to the extent to which the observed classifications of examinees would be the same across replications of the testing procedure. *Decision accuracy* refers to the extent to which observed classifications of examinees based on the results of a single replication would agree with their true classification status. Statistical methods are available to calculate indices for both decision consistency and decision accuracy. These methods evaluate the consistency or accuracy of classifications rather than the consistency in scores

per se. Note that the degree of consistency or agreement in examinee classification is specific to the cut score employed and its location within the score distribution.

Reliability/Precision of Group Means

Estimates of mean (or average) scores of groups (or proportions in certain categories) involve sources of error that are different from those that operate at the individual level. Such estimates are often used as measures of program effectiveness (and, under some educational accountability systems, may be used to evaluate the effectiveness of schools and teachers).

In evaluating group performance by estimating the mean performance or mean improvement in performance for samples from the group, the variation due to the sampling of persons can be a major source of error, especially if the sample sizes are small. To the extent that different samples from the group of interest (e.g., all students who use certain educational materials) yield different results, conclusions about the expected outcome over all students in the group (including those who might join the group in the future) are uncertain. For large samples, the variability due to the sampling of persons in the estimates of the group means may be quite small. However, in cases where the samples of persons are not very large (e.g., in evaluating the mean achievement of students in a single classroom or the average expressed satisfaction of samples of clients in a clinical program), the error associated with the sampling of persons may be a major component of overall error. It can be a significant source of error in inferences about programs even if there is a high degree of precision in individual test scores.

Standard errors for individual scores are not appropriate measures of the precision of group averages. A more appropriate statistic is the standard error for the estimates of the group means.

Documenting Reliability/Precision

Typically, developers and distributors of tests have primary responsibility for obtaining and reporting evidence for reliability/precision (e.g., appropriate standard errors, reliability or generalizability coefficients, or test information functions). The test user must have such data to make an informed choice among alternative measurement approaches and will generally be unable to conduct adequate reliability/precision studies prior to operational use of an instrument.

In some instances, however, local users of a test or assessment procedure must accept at least partial responsibility for documenting the precision of measurement. This obligation holds when one of the primary purposes of measurement is to classify students using locally developed performance standards, or to rank examinees within the local population. It also holds when users must rely on local scorers who are trained to use the scoring rubrics provided by the test developer. In such settings, local factors may materially affect the magnitude of error variance and observed score variance. Therefore, the reliability/precision of scores may differ appreciably from that reported by the developer.

Reported evaluations of reliability/precision should identify the potential sources of error for the testing program, given the proposed uses of the scores. These potential sources of error can then be evaluated in terms of previously reported research, new empirical studies, or analyses of the reasons for assuming that a potential source of error is likely to be negligible and therefore can be ignored.

The reporting of indices of reliability/precision alone—with little detail regarding the methods used to estimate the indices reported, the nature of the group from which the data were derived, and the conditions under which the data were obtained—constitutes inadequate documentation. General statements to the effect that a test is "reliable" or that it is "sufficiently reliable to permit interpretations of individual scores" are rarely, if ever, acceptable. It is the user who must take responsibility for determining whether scores are sufficiently trustworthy to justify anticipated uses and interpretations for particular uses. Nevertheless, test constructors and publishers are obligated to provide sufficient data to make informed judgments possible.

If scores are to be used for classification, indices of decision consistency are useful in addition to estimates of the reliability/precision of the scores. If group means are likely to play a substantial role in the use of the scores, the reliability/precision of these mean scores should be reported.

As the foregoing comments emphasize, there is no single, preferred approach to quantification of reliability/precision. No single index adequately conveys all of the relevant information. No one method of investigation is optimal in all situations, nor is the test developer limited to a single approach for any instrument. The choice of estimation techniques and the minimum acceptable level for any index remain a matter of professional judgment.

STANDARDS FOR RELIABILITY/PRECISION

The standards in this chapter begin with an overarching standard (numbered 2.0), which is designed to convey the central intent or primary focus of the chapter. The overarching standard may also be viewed as the guiding principle of the chapter, and is applicable to all tests and test users. All subsequent standards have been separated into eight thematic clusters labeled as follows:

1. Specifications for Replications of the Testing Procedure
2. Evaluating Reliability/Precision
3. Reliability/Generalizability Coefficients
4. Factors Affecting Reliability/Precision
5. Standard Errors of Measurement
6. Decision Consistency
7. Reliability/Precision of Group Means
8. Documenting Reliability/Precision

Standard 2.0

Appropriate evidence of reliability/precision should be provided for the interpretation for each intended score use.

Comment: The form of the evidence (reliability or generalizability coefficient, information function, conditional standard error, index of decision consistency) for reliability/precision should be appropriate for the intended uses of the scores, the population involved, and the psychometric models used to derive the scores. A higher degree of reliability/precision is required for score uses that have more significant consequences for test takers. Conversely, a lower degree may be acceptable where a decision based on the test score is reversible or dependent on corroboration from other sources of information.

Cluster 1. Specifications for Replications of the Testing Procedure

Standard 2.1

The range of replications over which reliability/precision is being evaluated should be clearly stated, along with a rationale for the choice of this definition, given the testing situation.

Comment: For any testing program, some aspects of the testing procedure (e.g., time limits and availability of resources such as books, calculators, and computers) are likely to be fixed, and some aspects will be allowed to vary from one administration to another (e.g., specific tasks or stimuli, testing contexts, raters, and, possibly, occasions). Any test administration that maintains fixed conditions and involves acceptable samples of the conditions that are allowed to vary would be considered a legitimate replication of the testing procedure. As a first step in evaluating the reliability/precision of the scores obtained with a testing procedure, it is important to identify the range of conditions of various kinds that are allowed to vary, and over which scores are to be generalized.

Standard 2.2

The evidence provided for the reliability/precision of the scores should be consistent with the domain of replications associated with the testing procedures, and with the intended interpretations for use of the test scores.

Comment: The evidence for reliability/precision should be consistent with the design of the testing procedures and with the proposed interpretations for use of the test scores. For example, if the test can be taken on any of a range of occasions, and the interpretation presumes that the scores are invariant over these occasions, then any variability in scores over these occasions is a potential source of error. If the tasks or stimuli are allowed to vary over alternate forms of the test, and the observed performances are treated as a sample from a domain of similar tasks, the variability in scores from one form to another would be considered error. If raters are used to assign scores to responses, the variability in scores over qualified raters is a source of error. Different sources of error can be evaluated in a single coefficient or standard error, or they can be evaluated separately, but they should all be addressed in some way. Reports of reliability/precision should specify the potential sources of error included in the analyses.

Cluster 2. Evaluating Reliability/Precision

Standard 2.3

For each total score, subscore, or combination of scores that is to be interpreted, estimates of relevant indices of reliability/precision should be reported.

Comment: It is not sufficient to report estimates of reliabilities and standard errors of measurement only for total scores when subscores are also interpreted. The form-to-form and day-to-day consistency of total scores on a test may be acceptably high, yet subscores may have unacceptably low reliability, depending on how they are defined and used. Users should be supplied with reliability data for all scores to be interpreted, and these data should be detailed enough to enable the users to judge whether the scores are precise enough for the intended interpretations for use. Composites formed from selected subtests within a test battery are frequently proposed for predictive and diagnostic purposes. Users need information about the reliability of such composites.

Standard 2.4

When a test score interpretation emphasizes differences between two observed scores of an individual or two averages of a group, reliability/precision data, including standard errors, should be provided for such differences.

Comment: Observed score differences are used for a variety of purposes. Achievement gains are frequently of interest for groups as well as individuals. In some cases, the reliability/precision of change scores can be much lower than the reliabilities of the separate scores involved. Differences between verbal and performance scores on tests of intelligence and scholastic ability are often employed in the diagnosis of cognitive impairment and learning problems. Psychodiagnostic inferences are frequently drawn from the differences between subtest scores. Aptitude and achievement batteries, interest inventories, and personality assessments are commonly used to identify and quantify the relative strengths and weaknesses, or the pattern of trait levels, of a test taker. When the interpretation of test scores centers on the peaks and valleys in the examinee's test score profile, the reliability of score differences is critical.

Standard 2.5

Reliability estimation procedures should be consistent with the structure of the test.

Comment: A single total score can be computed on tests that are multidimensional. The total score on a test that is substantially multidimensional should be treated as a composite score. If an internal-consistency estimate of total score reliability is obtained by the split-halves procedure, the halves should be comparable in content and statistical characteristics.

In adaptive testing procedures, the set of tasks included in the test and the sequencing of tasks are tailored to the test taker, using model-based algorithms. In this context, reliability/precision can be estimated using simulations based on the model. For adaptive testing, model-based conditional standard errors may be particularly useful and appropriate in evaluating the technical adequacy of the procedure.

Cluster 3. Reliability/Generalizability Coefficients

Standard 2.6

A reliability or generalizability coefficient (or standard error) that addresses one kind of variability should not be interpreted as interchangeable with indices that address other kinds of variability, unless their definitions of measurement error can be considered equivalent.

Comment: Internal-consistency, alternate-form, and test-retest coefficients should not be considered equivalent, as each incorporates a unique definition of measurement error. Error variances derived via item response theory are generally not equivalent to error variances estimated via other approaches. Test developers should state the sources of error that are reflected in, and those that are ignored by, the reported reliability or generalizability coefficients.

Standard 2.7

When subjective judgment enters into test scoring, evidence should be provided on both interrater consistency in scoring and within-examinee consistency over repeated measurements. A clear distinction should be made among reliability data based on (a) independent panels of raters scoring the same performances or products, (b) a single panel scoring successive performances or new products, and (c) independent panels scoring successive performances or new products.

Comment: Task-to-task variations in the quality of an examinee's performance and rater-to-rater inconsistencies in scoring represent independent sources of measurement error. Reports of reliability/precision studies should make clear which of these sources are reflected in the data. Generalizability studies and variance component analyses can be helpful in estimating the error variances arising from each source of error. These analyses can provide separate error variance estimates for tasks, for judges, and for occasions within the

time period of trait stability. Information should be provided on the qualifications and training of the judges used in reliability studies. Interrater or interobserver agreement may be particularly important for ratings and observational data that involve subtle discriminations. It should be noted, however, that when raters evaluate positively correlated characteristics, a favorable or unfavorable assessment of one trait may color their opinions of other traits. Moreover, high interrater consistency does not imply high examinee consistency from task to task. Therefore, interrater agreement does not guarantee high reliability of examinee scores.

Cluster 4. Factors Affecting Reliability/Precision

Standard 2.8

When constructed-response tests are scored locally, reliability/precision data should be gathered and reported for the local scoring when adequate-size samples are available.

Comment: For example, many statewide testing programs depend on local scoring of essays, constructed-response exercises, and performance tasks. Reliability/precision analyses can indicate that additional training of scorers is needed and, hence, should be an integral part of program monitoring. Reliability/precision data should be released only when sufficient to yield statistically sound results and consistent with applicable privacy obligations.

Standard 2.9

When a test is available in both long and short versions, evidence for reliability/precision should be reported for scores on each version, preferably based on independent administration(s) of each version with independent samples of test takers.

Comment: The reliability/precision of scores on each version is best evaluated through an independent administration of each, using the designated time limits. Psychometric models can be used to estimate the reliability/precision of a shorter (or longer) version of an existing test, based on data from an administration of the existing test. However, these models generally make assumptions that may not be met (e.g., that the items in the existing test and the items to be added or dropped are all randomly sampled from a single domain). Context effects are commonplace in tests of maximum performance, and the short version of a standardized test often comprises a nonrandom sample of items from the full-length version. As a result, the predicted value of the reliability/precision may not provide a very good estimate of the actual value, and therefore, where feasible, the reliability/precision of both forms should be evaluated directly and independently.

Standard 2.10

When significant variations are permitted in tests or test administration procedures, separate reliability/precision analyses should be provided for scores produced under each major variation if adequate sample sizes are available.

Comment: To make a test accessible to all examinees, test publishers or users might authorize, or might be legally required to authorize, accommodations or modifications in the procedures that are specified for the administration of a test. For example, audio or large print versions may be used for test takers who are visually impaired. Any alteration in standard testing materials or procedures may have an impact on the reliability/precision of the resulting scores, and therefore, to the extent feasible, the reliability/precision should be examined for all versions of the test and testing procedures.

Standard 2.11

Test publishers should provide estimates of reliability/precision as soon as feasible for each relevant subgroup for which the test is recommended.

Comment: Reporting estimates of reliability/precision for relevant subgroups is useful in many contexts, but it is especially important if the inter-

pretation of scores involves within-group inferences (e.g., in terms of subgroup norms). For example, test users who work with a specific linguistic and cultural subgroup or with individuals who have a particular disability would benefit from an estimate of the standard error for the subgroup. Likewise, evidence that preschool children tend to respond to test stimuli in a less consistent fashion than do older children would be helpful to test users interpreting scores across age groups.

When considering the reliability/precision of test scores for relevant subgroups, it is useful to evaluate and report the standard error of measurement as well as any coefficients that are estimated. Reliability and generalizability coefficients can differ substantially when subgroups have different variances on the construct being assessed. Differences in within-group variability tend to have less impact on the standard error of measurement.

Standard 2.12

If a test is proposed for use in several grades or over a range of ages, and if separate norms are provided for each grade or each age range, reliability/precision data should be provided for each age or grade-level subgroup, not just for all grades or ages combined.

Comment: A reliability or generalizability coefficient based on a sample of examinees spanning several grades or a broad range of ages in which average scores are steadily increasing will generally give a spuriously inflated impression of reliability/precision. When a test *is* intended to discriminate within age or grade populations, reliability or generalizability coefficients and standard errors should be reported separately for each subgroup.

Cluster 5. Standard Errors of Measurement

Standard 2.13

The standard error of measurement, both overall and conditional (if reported), should be provided in units of each reported score.

Comment: The standard error of measurement (overall or conditional) that is reported should be consistent with the scales that are used in reporting scores. Standard errors in scale-score units for the scales used to report scores and/or to make decisions are particularly helpful to the typical test user. The data on examinee performance should be consistent with the assumptions built into any statistical models used to generate scale scores and to estimate the standard errors for these scores.

Standard 2.14

When possible and appropriate, conditional standard errors of measurement should be reported at several score levels unless there is evidence that the standard error is constant across score levels. Where cut scores are specified for selection or classification, the standard errors of measurement should be reported in the vicinity of each cut score.

Comment: Estimation of conditional standard errors is usually feasible with the sample sizes that are used for analyses of reliability/precision. If it is assumed that the standard error *is* constant over a broad range of score levels, the rationale for this assumption should be presented. The model on which the computation of the conditional standard errors is based should be specified.

Standard 2.15

When there is credible evidence for expecting that conditional standard errors of measurement or test information functions will differ substantially for various subgroups, investigation of the extent and impact of such differences should be undertaken and reported as soon as is feasible.

Comment: If differences are found, they should be clearly indicated in the appropriate documentation. In addition, if substantial differences do exist, the test content and scoring models should be examined to see if there are legally acceptable alternatives that do not result in such differences.

Cluster 6. Decision Consistency

Standard 2.16

When a test or combination of measures is used to make classification decisions, estimates should be provided of the percentage of test takers who would be classified in the same way on two replications of the procedure.

Comment: When a test score or composite score is used to make classification decisions (e.g., pass/fail, achievement levels), the standard error of measurement at or near the cut scores has important implications for the trustworthiness of these decisions. However, the standard error cannot be translated into the expected percentage of consistent or accurate decisions without strong assumptions about the distributions of measurement errors and true scores. Although decision consistency is typically estimated from the administration of a single form, it can and should be estimated directly through the use of a test-retest approach, if consistent with the requirements of test security, and if the assumption of no change in the construct is met and adequate samples are available.

Cluster 7. Reliability/Precision of Group Means

Standard 2.17

When average test scores for groups are the focus of the proposed interpretation of the test results, the groups tested should generally be regarded as a sample from a larger population, even if all examinees available at the time of measurement are tested. In such cases the standard error of the group mean should be reported, because it reflects variability due to sampling of examinees as well as variability due to individual measurement error.

Comment: The overall levels of performance in various groups tend to be the focus in program evaluation and in accountability systems, and the groups that are of interest include all students/clients who could participate in the program over some period. Therefore, the students in a particular class or school at the current time, the current clients of a social service agency, and analogous groups exposed to a program of interest typically constitute a sample in a longitudinal sense. Presumably, comparable groups from the same population will recur in future years, given static conditions. The factors leading to uncertainty in conclusions about program effectiveness arise from the sampling of persons as well as from individual measurement error.

Standard 2.18

When the purpose of testing is to measure the performance of groups rather than individuals, subsets of items can be assigned randomly to different subsamples of examinees. Data are aggregated across subsamples and item subsets to obtain a measure of group performance. When such procedures are used for program evaluation or population descriptions, reliability/precision analyses must take the sampling scheme into account.

Comment: This type of measurement program is termed *matrix sampling*. It is designed to reduce the time demanded of individual examinees and yet to increase the total number of items on which data can be obtained. This testing approach provides the same type of information about group performances that would be obtained if all examinees had taken all of the items. Reliability/precision statistics should reflect the sampling plan used with respect to examinees and items.

Cluster 8. Documenting Reliability/Precision

Standard 2.19

Each method of quantifying the reliability/precision of scores should be described clearly and expressed in terms of statistics appropriate to the method. The sampling procedures used to select test takers for reliability/precision analyses and the descriptive statistics on these samples, subject to privacy obligations where applicable, should be reported.

Comment: Information on the method of data collection, sample sizes, means, standard deviations, and demographic characteristics of the groups tested helps users judge the extent to which reported data apply to their own examinee populations. If the test-retest or alternate-form approach is used, the interval between administrations should be indicated.

Because there are many ways of estimating reliability/precision, and each is influenced by different sources of measurement error, it is unacceptable to say simply, "The reliability/precision of scores on test X is .90." A better statement would be, "The reliability coefficient of .90 reported for scores on test X was obtained by correlating scores from forms A and B, administered on successive days. The data were based on a sample of 400 10th-grade students from five middle-class suburban schools in New York State. The demographic breakdown of this group was as follows: . . ." In some cases, for example, when small sample sizes or particularly sensitive data are involved, applicable legal restrictions governing privacy may limit the level of information that should be disclosed.

Standard 2.20

If reliability coefficients are adjusted for restriction of range or variability, the adjustment procedure and both the adjusted and unadjusted coefficients should be reported. The standard deviations of the group actually tested and of the target population, as well as the rationale for the adjustment, should be presented.

Comment: Application of a correction for restriction in variability presumes that the available sample is not representative (in terms of variability) of the test-taker population to which users might be expected to generalize. The rationale for the correction should consider the appropriateness of such a generalization. Adjustment formulas that presume constancy in the standard error across score levels should not be used unless constancy can be defended.

3. FAIRNESS IN TESTING

BACKGROUND

This chapter addresses the importance of fairness as a fundamental issue in protecting test takers and test users in all aspects of testing. The term *fairness* has no single technical meaning and is used in many different ways in public discourse. It is possible that individuals endorse fairness in testing as a desirable social goal, yet reach quite different conclusions about the fairness of a given testing program. A full consideration of the topic would explore the multiple functions of testing in relation to its many goals, including the broad goal of achieving equality of opportunity in our society. It would consider the technical properties of tests, the ways in which test results are reported and used, the factors that affect the validity of score interpretations, and the consequences of test use. A comprehensive analysis of fairness in testing also would examine the regulations, statutes, and case law that govern test use and the remedies for harmful testing practices. The *Standards* cannot hope to deal adequately with all of these broad issues, some of which have occasioned sharp disagreement among testing specialists and others interested in testing. Our focus must be limited here to delineating the aspects of tests, testing, and test use that relate to fairness as described in this chapter, which are the responsibility of those who develop, use, and interpret the results of tests, and upon which there is general professional and technical agreement.

Fairness is a fundamental validity issue and requires attention throughout all stages of test development and use. In previous versions of the *Standards*, fairness and the assessment of individuals from specific subgroups of test takers, such as individuals with disabilities and individuals with diverse linguistic and cultural backgrounds, were presented in separate chapters. In the current version of the *Standards*, these issues are presented in a single chapter to emphasize that fairness to all individuals in the intended population of test takers is an overriding, foundational concern, and that common principles apply in responding to test-taker characteristics that could interfere with the validity of test score interpretation. This is not to say that the response to test-taker characteristics is the same for individuals from diverse subgroups such as those defined by race, ethnicity, gender, culture, language, age, disability or socioeconomic status, but rather that these responses should be sensitive to individual characteristics that otherwise would compromise validity. Nonetheless, as discussed in the Introduction, it is important to bear in mind, when using the *Standards,* that applicability depends on context. For example, potential threats to test validity for examinees with limited English proficiency are different from those for examinees with disabilities. Moreover, threats to validity may differ even for individuals within the same subgroup. For example, individuals with diverse specific disabilities constitute the subgroup of "individuals with disabilities," and examinees classified as "limited English proficient" represent a range of language proficiency levels, educational and cultural backgrounds, and prior experiences. Further, the equivalence of the construct being assessed is a central issue in fairness, whether the context is, for example, individuals with diverse special disabilities, individuals with limited English proficiency, or individuals across countries and cultures.

As in the previous versions of the *Standards*, the current chapter addresses measurement bias as a central threat to fairness in testing. However, it also adds two major concepts that have emerged in the literature, particularly in literature regarding education, for minimizing bias and thereby increasing fairness. The first concept is *accessibility,* the notion that all test takers should have an unobstructed opportunity to demonstrate their standing on the construct(s) being measured. For example, individuals with limited English proficiency may not be adequately diagnosed on the target construct of a clinical examination if the assessment requires a level of English proficiency that they do not possess. Similarly, standard print and some electronic formats can disadvantage examinees with visual impairments and some older adults who need magnification for reading, and the disadvantage is considered unfair if visual acuity is irrelevant to the construct being measured. These examples show how access to the construct the test is measuring can be impeded by characteristics and/or skills that are unrelated to the intended construct and thereby can limit the validity of score interpretations for intended uses for certain individuals and/or subgroups in the intended test-taking population. Accessibility is a legal requirement in some testing contexts.

The second new concept contained in this chapter is that of *universal design*. Universal design is an approach to test design that seeks to maximize accessibility for all intended examinees. Universal design, as described more thoroughly later in this chapter, demands that test developers be clear on the construct(s) to be measured, including the target of the assessment, the purpose for which scores will be used, the inferences that will be made from the scores, and the characteristics of examinees and subgroups of the intended test population that could influence access. Test items and tasks can then be purposively designed and developed from the outset to reflect the intended construct, to minimize construct-irrelevant features that might otherwise impede the performance of intended examinee groups, and to maximize, to the extent possible, access for as many examinees as possible in the intended population regardless of race, ethnicity, age, gender, socioeconomic status, disability, or language or cultural background.

Even so, for some individuals in some test contexts and for some purposes—as is described later—there may be need for additional test adaptations to respond to individual characteristics that otherwise would limit access to the construct as measured. Some examples are creating a braille version of a test, allowing additional testing time, and providing test translations or language simplification. Any test adaption must be carefully considered, as some adaptations may alter a test's intended construct. Responding to individual characteristics that would otherwise impede access and improving the validity of test score interpretations for intended uses are dual considerations for supporting fairness.

In summary, this chapter interprets fairness as responsiveness to individual characteristics and testing contexts so that test scores will yield valid interpretations for intended uses. The *Standards'* definition of fairness is often broader than what is legally required. A test that is fair within the meaning of the *Standards* reflects the same construct(s) for all test takers, and scores from it have the same meaning for all individuals in the intended population; a fair test does not advantage or disadvantage some individuals because of characteristics irrelevant to the intended construct. To the degree possible, characteristics of all individuals in the intended test population, including those associated with race, ethnicity, gender, age, socioeconomic status, or linguistic or cultural background, must be considered throughout all stages of development, administration, scoring, interpretation, and use so that barriers to fair assessment can be reduced. At the same time, test scores must yield valid interpretations for intended uses, and different test contexts and uses may call for different approaches to fairness. For example, in tests used for selection purposes, adaptations to standardized procedures that increase accessibility for some individuals but change the construct being measured could reduce the validity of score inferences for the intended purposes and unfairly advantage those who qualify for adaptation relative to those who do not. In contrast, for diagnostic purposes in medicine and education, adapting a test to increase accessibility for some individuals could increase the accuracy of the diagnosis.

These issues are discussed in the sections below and are represented in the standards that follow the chapter introduction.

General Views of Fairness

The first view of fairness in testing described in this chapter establishes the principle of fair and equitable treatment of all test takers during the testing process. The second, third, and fourth views presented here emphasize issues of fairness in measurement quality: fairness as the lack or absence of measurement bias, fairness as access to the constructs measured, and fairness as validity of individual test score interpretations for the intended use(s).

Fairness in Treatment During the Testing Process

Regardless of the purpose of testing, the goal of fairness is to maximize, to the extent possible, the opportunity for test takers to demonstrate their standing on the construct(s) the test is intended to measure. Traditionally, careful standardization of tests, administration conditions, and scoring procedures have helped to ensure that test takers have comparable contexts in which to demonstrate the abilities or attributes to be measured. For example, uniform directions, specified time limits, specified room arrangements, use of proctors, and use of consistent security procedures are implemented so that differences in administration conditions will not inadvertently influence the performance of some test takers relative to others. Similarly, concerns for equity in treatment may require, for some tests, that all test takers have qualified test administrators with whom they can communicate and feel comfortable to the extent practicable. Where technology is involved, it is important that examinees have had similar prior exposure to the technology and that the equipment provided to all test takers be of similar processing speed and provide similar clarity and size for images and other media. Procedures for the standardized administration of a test should be carefully documented by the test developer and followed carefully by the test administrator.

Although standardization has been a fundamental principle for assuring that all examinees have the same opportunity to demonstrate their standing on the construct that a test is intended to measure, sometimes flexibility is needed to provide essentially equivalent opportunities for some test takers. In these cases, aspects of a standardized testing process that pose no particular challenge for most test takers may prevent specific groups or individuals from accurately demonstrating their standing with respect to the construct of interest. For example, challenges may arise due to an examinee's disability, cultural background, linguistic background, race, ethnicity, socioeconomic status, limitations that may come with aging, or some combination of these or other factors. In some instances, greater comparability of scores may be attained if standardized procedures are changed to address the needs of specific groups or individuals without any adverse effects on the validity or reliability of the results obtained. For example, a braille test form, a large-print answer sheet, or a screen reader may be provided to enable those with some visual impairments to obtain more equitable access to test content. Legal considerations may also influence how to address individualized needs.

Fairness as Lack of Measurement Bias

Characteristics of the test itself that are not related to the construct being measured, or the manner in which the test is used, may sometimes result in different meanings for scores earned by members of different identifiable subgroups. For example, *differential item functioning* (DIF) is said to occur when equally able test takers differ in their probabilities of answering a test item correctly as a function of group membership. DIF can be evaluated in a variety of ways. The detection of DIF does not always indicate bias in an item; there needs to be a suitable, substantial explanation for the DIF to justify the conclusion that the item is biased. *Differential test functioning* (DTF) refers to differences in the functioning of tests (or sets of items) for different specially defined groups. When DTF occurs, individuals from different groups who have the same standing on the characteristic assessed by the test do not have the same expected test score.

The term *predictive bias* may be used when evidence is found that differences exist in the patterns of associations between test scores and other variables for different groups, bringing with it concerns about bias in the inferences drawn from the use of test scores. Differential prediction is examined using regression analysis. One approach examines slope and intercept differences between two targeted groups (e.g., African American examinees and Caucasian examinees), while another examines systematic deviations from a common regression line for any number of groups of interest. Both approaches provide valuable information when examining differential prediction. Correlation coefficients provide inadequate evidence for or against a differential prediction hypothesis if groups are found to have unequal means and variances on the test and the criterion.

When credible evidence indicates potential bias in measurement (i.e., lack of consistent construct meaning across groups, DIF, DTF) or bias in predictive relations, these potential sources of bias should be independently investigated because the presence or absence of one form of such bias may have no relationship with other forms of bias. For example, a predictor test may show no significant levels of DIF, yet show group differences in regression lines in predicting a criterion. Although it is important to guard against the possibility of measurement bias for the subgroups that have been defined as relevant in the intended test population, it may not be feasible to fully investigate all possibilities, particularly in the employment context. For example, the number of subgroup members in the field test or norming population may limit the possibility of standard empirical analyses. In these cases, previous research, a construct-based rationale, and/or data from similar tests may address concerns related to potential bias in measurement. In addition, and especially where credible evidence of potential bias exists, small sample methodologies should be considered. For example, potential bias for relevant subgroups may be examined through small-scale tryouts that use cognitive labs and/or interviews or focus groups to solicit evidence on the validity of interpretations made from the test scores.

A related issue is the extent to which the construct being assessed has equivalent meaning across the individuals and groups within the intended population of test takers. This is especially important when the assessment crosses international borders and cultures. Evaluation of the underlying construct and properties of the test within one country or culture may not generalize across borders or cultures. This can lead to invalid test score interpretations. Careful attention to bias in score interpretations should be practiced in such contexts.

Fairness in Access to the Construct(s) as Measured

The goal that all intended test takers have a full opportunity to demonstrate their standing on the construct being measured has given rise to concerns about accessibility in testing. Accessible testing situations are those that enable all test takers in the intended population, to the extent feasible, to show their status on the target construct(s) without being unduly advantaged or disadvantaged by individual characteristics (e.g., characteristics related to age, disability, race/ethnicity, gender, or language) that are irrelevant to the construct(s) the test is intended to measure. Accessibility is actually a test bias issue because obstacles to accessibility can result in different interpretations of test scores for individuals from different groups. Accessibility also has important ethical and legal ramifications.

Accessibility can best be understood by contrasting the knowledge, skills, and abilities that reflect the construct(s) the test is intended to measure with the knowledge, skills, and abilities that are not the target of the test but are required to respond to the test tasks or test items. For some test takers, factors related to individual characteristics such as age, race, ethnicity, socioeconomic status, cultural background, disability, and/or English language proficiency may restrict accessibility and thus interfere with the measurement of the construct(s) of interest. For example, a test taker with impaired vision may not be able to access the printed text of a personality test. If the test were provided in large print, the test questions could be more accessible to the test taker and would be more likely to lead to a valid measurement of the test taker's personality characteristics. It is important to be aware of test characteristics that may inadvertently render test questions less accessible for some subgroups of the intended testing population. For example, a test question that employs idiomatic phrases unrelated to the construct being measured could have the effect of making the test less accessible for test takers who are not native speakers of English. The accessibility of a test could also be decreased by questions that use regional vocabulary unrelated to the target construct or use stimulus contexts that are less familiar to individuals from some cultural subgroups than others.

As discussed later in this chapter, some test-taker characteristics that impede access are related to the construct being measured, for example, dyslexia in the context of tests of reading. In these cases, providing individuals with access to the construct and getting some measure of it may require some adaptation of the construct as well. In situations like this, it may not be possible to develop a measurement that is comparable across adapted and unadapted versions of the test; however, the measure obtained by the adapted test will most likely provide a more accurate assessment of the individual's skills and/or abilities (although perhaps not of the full intended construct) than that obtained without using the adaptation.

Providing access to a test construct becomes particularly challenging for individuals with more than one characteristic that could interfere with test performance; for example, older adults who are not fluent in English or English learners who have moderate cognitive disabilities.

Fairness as Validity of Individual Test Score Interpretations for the Intended Uses

It is important to keep in mind that fairness concerns the validity of individual score interpretations for intended uses. In attempting to ensure fairness, we often generalize across groups of test takers such as individuals with disabilities, older adults, individuals who are learning English, or those from different racial or ethnic groups or different cultural and/or socioeconomic backgrounds; however, this is done for convenience and is not meant to imply that these groups are homogeneous or that, consequently, all members of a group should be treated similarly when making interpretations of test scores for individuals (unless there is validity evidence to support such generalizations). It is particularly important, when drawing inferences about an examinee's skills or abilities,

to take into account the individual characteristics of the test taker and how these characteristics may interact with the contextual features of the testing situation.

The complex interplay of language proficiency and context provides one example of the challenges to valid interpretation of test scores for some testing purposes. Proficiency in English not only affects the interpretation of an English language learner's test scores on tests administered in English but, more important, also may affect the individual's developmental and academic progress. Individuals who differ culturally and linguistically from the majority of the test takers are at risk for inaccurate score interpretations because of multiple factors associated with the assumption that, absent language proficiency issues, these individuals have developmental trajectories comparable to those of individuals who have been raised in an environment mediated by a single language and culture. For instance, consider two sixth-grade children who entered school as limited English speakers. The first child entered school in kindergarten and has been instructed in academic courses in English; the second also entered school in kindergarten but has been instructed in his or her native language. The two will have a different developmental pattern. In the former case, the interrupted native language development has an attenuating effect on learning and academic performance, but the individual's English proficiency may not be a significant barrier to testing. In contrast, the examinee who has had instruction in his or her native language through the sixth grade has had the opportunity for fully age-appropriate cognitive, academic, and language development; but, if tested in English, the examinee will need the test administered in such a way as to minimize the language barrier if proficiency in English is not part of the construct being measured.

As the above examples show, adaptation to individual characteristics and recognition of the heterogeneity within subgroups may be important to the validity of individual interpretations of test results in situations where the intent is to understand and respond to individual performance. Professionals may be justified in deviating from standardized procedures to gain a more accurate measurement of the intended construct and to provide more appropriate individual decisions. However, for other contexts and uses, deviations from standardized procedures may be inappropriate because they change the construct being measured, compromise the comparability of scores or use of norms, and/or unfairly advantage some individuals.

In closing this section on the meanings of fairness, note that the *Standards'* measurement perspective explicitly excludes one common view of fairness in public discourse: fairness as the equality of testing outcomes for relevant test-taker subgroups. Certainly, most testing professionals agree that group differences in testing outcomes should trigger heightened scrutiny for possible sources of test bias. Examination of group differences also may be important in generating new hypotheses about bias, fair treatment, and the accessibility of the construct as measured; and in fact, there may be legal requirements to investigate certain differences in the outcomes of testing among subgroups. However, group differences in outcomes do not in themselves indicate that a testing application is biased or unfair.

In many cases, it is not clear whether the differences are due to real differences between groups in the construct being measured or to some source of bias (e.g., construct-irrelevant variance or construct underrepresentation). In most cases, it may be some combination of real differences and bias. A serious search for possible sources of bias that comes up empty provides reassurance that the potential for bias is limited, but even a very extensive research program cannot rule the possibility out. It is always possible that something was missed, and therefore, prudence would suggest that an attempt be made to minimize the differences. For example, some racial and ethnic subgroups have lower mean scores on some standardized tests than do other subgroups. Some of the factors that contribute to these differences are understood (e.g., large differences in family income and other resources, differences in school quality and students' opportunity to learn the material to be assessed), but even where serious efforts have been made to eliminate possible sources of bias in test content

and formats, the potential for some score bias cannot be completely ruled out. Therefore, continuing efforts in test design and development to eliminate potential sources of bias without compromising validity, and consistent with legal and regulatory standards, are warranted.

Threats to Fair and Valid Interpretations of Test Scores

A prime threat to fair and valid interpretation of test scores comes from aspects of the test or testing process that may produce construct-irrelevant variance in scores that systematically lowers or raises scores for identifiable groups of test takers and results in inappropriate score interpretations for intended uses. Such construct-irrelevant components of scores may be introduced by inappropriate sampling of test content, aspects of the test context such as lack of clarity in test instructions, item complexities that are unrelated to the construct being measured, and/or test response expectations or scoring criteria that may favor one group over another. In addition, opportunity to learn (i.e., the extent to which an examinee has been exposed to instruction or experiences assumed by the test developer and/or user) can influence the fair and valid interpretations of test scores for their intended uses.

Test Content

One potential source of construct-irrelevant variance in test scores arises from inappropriate test content, that is, test content that confounds the measurement of the target construct and differentially favors individuals from some subgroups over others. A test intended to measure critical reading, for example, should not include words and expressions especially associated with particular occupations, disciplines, cultural backgrounds, socioeconomic status, racial/ethnic groups, or geographical locations, so as to maximize the measurement of the construct (the ability to read critically) and to minimize confounding of this measurement with prior knowledge and experience that are likely to advantage, or disadvantage, test takers from particular subgroups.

Differential engagement and motivational value may also be factors in exacerbating construct-irrelevant components of content. Material that is likely to be differentially interesting should be balanced to appeal broadly to the full range of the targeted testing population (except where the interest level is part of the construct being measured). In testing, such balance extends to representation of individuals from a variety of subgroups within the test content itself. For example, applied problems can feature children and families from different racial/ethnic, socioeconomic, and language groups. Also, test content or situations that are offensive or emotionally disturbing to some test takers and may impede their ability to engage with the test should not appear in the test unless the use of the offensive or disturbing content is needed to measure the intended construct. Examples of this type of content are graphic descriptions of slavery or the Holocaust, when such descriptions are not specifically required by the construct.

Depending on the context and purpose of tests, it is both common and advisable for test developers to engage an independent and diverse panel of experts to review test content for language, illustrations, graphics, and other representations that might be differentially familiar or interpreted differently by members of different groups and for material that might be offensive or emotionally disturbing to some test takers.

Test Context

The term *test context,* as used here, refers to multiple aspects of the test and testing environment that may affect the performance of an examinee and consequently give rise to construct-irrelevant variance in the test scores. As research on contextual factors (e.g., stereotype threat) is ongoing, test developers and test users should pay attention to the emerging empirical literature on these topics so that they can use this information if and when the preponderance of evidence dictates that it is appropriate to do so. Construct-irrelevant variance may result from a lack of clarity in test instructions, from unrelated complexity or language demands in test tasks, and/or from other characteristics of

test items that are unrelated to the construct but lead some individuals to respond in particular ways. For example, examinees from diverse racial/ethnic, linguistic, or cultural backgrounds or who differ by gender may be poorly assessed by a vocational interest inventory whose questions disproportionately ask about competencies, activities, and interests that are stereotypically associated with particular subgroups.

When test settings have an interpersonal context, the interaction of examiner with test taker can be a source of construct-irrelevant variance or bias. Users of tests should be alert to the possibility that such interactions may sometimes affect test fairness. Practitioners administering the test should be aware of the possibility of complex interactions with test takers and other situational variables. Factors that may affect the performance of the test taker include the race, ethnicity, gender, and linguistic and cultural background of both examiner and test taker, the test taker's experience with formal education, the testing style of the examiner, the level of acculturation of the test taker and examiner, the test taker's primary language, the language used for test administration (if it is not the primary language of the test taker), and the use of a bilingual or bicultural interpreter.

Testing of individuals who are bilingual or multilingual poses special challenges. An individual who knows two or more languages may not test well in one or more of the languages. For example, children from homes whose families speak Spanish may be able to understand Spanish but express themselves best in English or vice versa. In addition, some persons who are bilingual use their native language in most social situations and use English primarily for academic and work-related activities; the use of one or both languages depends on the nature of the situation. Non-native English speakers who give the impression of being fluent in conversational English may be slower or not completely competent in taking tests that require English comprehension and literacy skills. Thus, in some settings, an understanding of an individual's type and degree of bilingualism or multilingualism is important for testing the individual appropriately. Note that this concern may not apply when the construct of interest is defined as a particular kind of language proficiency (e.g., academic language of the kind found in text books, language and vocabulary specific to workplace and employment testing).

Test Response

In some cases, construct-irrelevant variance may arise because test items elicit varieties of responses other than those intended or because items can be solved in ways that were not intended. To the extent that such responses are more typical of some subgroups than others, biased score interpretations may result. For example, some clients responding to a neuropsychological test may attempt to provide the answers they think the test administrator expects, as opposed to the answers that best describe themselves.

Construct-irrelevant components in test scores may also be associated with test response formats that pose particular difficulties or are differentially valued by particular individuals. For example, test performance may rely on some capability (e.g., English language proficiency or fine-motor coordination) that is irrelevant to the target construct(s) but nonetheless poses impediments to the test responses for some test takers not having the capability. Similarly, different values associated with the nature and degree of verbal output can influence test-taker responses. Some individuals may judge verbosity or rapid speech as rude, whereas others may regard those speech patterns as indications of high mental ability or friendliness. An individual of the first type who is evaluated with values appropriate to the second may be considered taciturn, withdrawn, or of low mental ability. Another example is a person with memory or language problems or depression; such a person's ability to communicate or show interest in communicating verbally may be constrained, which may result in interpretations of the outcomes of the assessment that are invalid and potentially harmful to the person being tested.

In the development and use of scoring rubrics, it is particularly important that credit be awarded for response characteristics central to the construct being measured and not for response characteristics that are irrelevant or tangential to the construct. Scoring rubrics may inadvertently advantage some individuals over others. For example, a scoring rubric for a constructed response item might reserve the highest score level for test takers who provide more information or elaboration than was actually requested. In this situation, test takers who simply follow instructions, or test takers who value succinctness in responses, will earn lower scores; thus, characteristics of the individuals become construct-irrelevant components of the test scores. Similarly, the scoring of open-ended responses may introduce construct-irrelevant variance for some test takers if scorers and/or automated scoring routines are not sensitive to the full diversity of ways in which individuals express their ideas. With the advent of automated scoring for complex performance tasks, for example, it is important to examine the validity of the automated scoring results for relevant subgroups in the test-taking population.

Opportunity to Learn

Finally, *opportunity to learn*—the extent to which individuals have had exposure to instruction or knowledge that affords them the opportunity to learn the content and skills targeted by the test—has several implications for the fair and valid interpretation of test scores for their intended uses. Individuals' prior opportunity to learn can be an important contextual factor to consider in interpreting and drawing inferences from test scores. For example, a recent immigrant who has had little prior exposure to school may not have had the opportunity to learn concepts assumed to be common knowledge by a personality inventory or ability measure, even if that measure is administered in the native language of the test taker. Similarly, as another example, there has been considerable public discussion about potential inequities in school resources available to students from traditionally disadvantaged groups, for example, racial, ethnic, language, and cultural minorities and rural students. Such inequities affect the quality of education received. To the extent that inequity exists, the validity of inferences about student ability drawn from achievement test scores may be compromised. Not taking into account prior opportunity to learn could lead to misdiagnosis, inappropriate placement, and/or inappropriate assignment of services, which could have significant consequences for an individual.

Beyond its impact on the validity of test score interpretations for intended uses, opportunity to learn has important policy and legal ramifications in education. Opportunity to learn is a fairness issue when an authority provides differential access to opportunity to learn for some individuals and then holds those individuals who have not been provided that opportunity accountable for their test performance. This problem may affect high-stakes competency tests in education, for example, when educational authorities require a certain level of test performance for high school graduation. Here, there is a fairness concern that students not be held accountable for, or face serious permanent negative consequences from, their test results when their school experiences have not provided them the opportunity to learn the subject matter covered by the test. In such cases, students' low scores may accurately reflect what they know and can do, so that, technically, the interpretation of the test results for the purpose of measuring how much the students have learned may not be biased. However, it may be considered unfair to severely penalize students for circumstances that are not under their control, that is, for not learning content that their schools have not taught. It is generally accepted that before high-stakes consequences can be imposed for failing an examination in educational settings, there must be evidence that students have been provided curriculum and instruction that incorporates the constructs addressed by the test.

Several important issues arise when opportunity to learn is considered as a component of fairness. First, it is difficult to define opportunity to learn in educational practice, particularly at the individual level. Opportunity is generally a matter of degree and is difficult to quantify; moreover, the measurement of some important learning outcomes may require students to work with materials that they have not seen before. Second, even if it is possible to document the topics included in the curriculum for a group of students, specific content

coverage for any one student may be impossible to determine. Third, granting a diploma to a low-scoring examinee on the grounds that the student had insufficient opportunity to learn the material tested means certificating someone who has not attained the degree of proficiency the diploma is intended to signify.

It should be noted that concerns about opportunity to learn do not necessarily apply to situations where the same authority is not responsible for both the delivery of instruction and the testing and/or interpretation of results. For example, in college admissions decisions, opportunity to learn may be beyond the control of the test users and it may not influence the validity of test interpretations for their intended use (e.g., selection and/or admissions decisions). Chapter 12, "Educational Testing and Assessment," provides additional perspective on opportunity to learn.

Minimizing Construct-Irrelevant Components Through Test Design and Testing Adaptations

Standardized tests should be designed to facilitate accessibility and minimize construct-irrelevant barriers for all test takers in the target population, as far as practicable. Before considering the need for any assessment adaptations for test takers who may have special needs, the assessment developer first must attempt to improve accessibility within the test itself. Some of these basic principles are included in the test design process called universal design. By using universal design, test developers begin the test development process with an eye toward maximizing fairness. Universal design emphasizes the need to develop tests that are as usable as possible for all test takers in the intended test population, regardless of characteristics such as gender, age, language background, culture, socioeconomic status, or disability.

Principles of universal design include defining constructs precisely, so that what is being measured can be clearly differentiated from test-taker characteristics that are irrelevant to the construct but that could otherwise interfere with some test takers' ability to respond. Universal design avoids, where possible, item characteristics and formats, or test characteristics (for example, inappropriate test speededness), that may bias scores for individuals or subgroups due to construct-irrelevant characteristics that are specific to these test takers.

Universal design processes strive to minimize access challenges by taking into account test characteristics that may impede access to the construct for certain test takers, such as the choice of content, test tasks, response procedures, and testing procedures. For example, the content of tests can be made more accessible by providing user-selected font sizes in a technology-based test, by avoiding item contexts that would likely be unfamiliar to individuals because of their cultural background, by providing extended administration time when speed is not relevant to the construct being measured, or by minimizing the linguistic load of test items intended to measure constructs other than competencies in the language in which the test is administered.

Although the principles of universal design for assessment provide a useful guide for developing assessments that reduce construct-irrelevant variance, researchers are still in the process of gathering empirical evidence to support some of these principles. It is important to note that not all tests can be made accessible for everyone by attention to design changes such as those discussed above. Even when tests are developed to maximize fairness through the use of universal design and other practices to increase access, there will still be situations where the test is not appropriate for all test takers in the intended population. Therefore, some test adaptations may be needed for those individuals whose characteristics would otherwise impede their access to the examination.

Adaptations are changes to the original test design or administration to increase access to the test for such individuals. For example, a person who is blind may read only in braille format, and an individual with hemiplegia may be unable to hold a pencil and thus have difficulty completing a standard written exam. Students with limited English proficiency may be proficient in physics but may not be able to demonstrate their knowledge

if the physics test is administered in English. Depending on testing circumstances and purposes of the test, as well as individual characteristics, such adaptations might include changing the content or presentation of the test items, changing the administration conditions, and/or changing the response processes. The term adaptation is used to refer to any such change. It is important, however, to differentiate between changes that result in comparable scores and changes that may not produce scores that are comparable to those from the original test. Although the terms may have different meanings under applicable laws, as used in the *Standards* the term *accommodation* is used to denote changes with which the comparability of scores is retained, and the term *modification* is used to denote changes that affect the construct measured by the test. With a modification, the changes affect the construct being measured and consequently lead to scores that differ in meaning from those from the original test.[1]

It is important to keep in mind that attention to design and the provision of altered tests do not always ensure that test results will be fair and valid for all examinees. Those who administer tests and interpret test scores need to develop a full understanding of the usefulness and limitations of test design procedures for accessibility and any alterations that are offered.

A Range of Test Adaptations

Rather than a simple dichotomy, potential test adaptations reflect a broad range of test changes. At one end of the range are test accommodations. As the term is used in the *Standards,* accommodations consist of relatively minor changes to the presentation and/or format of the test, test ad-

---

[1]The Americans with Disabilities Act (ADA) uses the terms *accommodation* and *modification* differently from the *Standards*. Title I of the ADA uses the term *reasonable accommodation* to refer to changes that enable qualified individuals with disabilities to obtain employment to perform their jobs. Titles II and III use the term *reasonable modification* in much the same way. Under the ADA, an accommodation or modification to a test that fundamentally alters the construct being measured would not be called something different; rather it would probably be found not "reasonable."

ministration, or response procedures that maintain the original construct and result in scores comparable to those on the original test. For example, text magnification might be an accommodation for a test taker with a visual impairment who otherwise would have difficulty deciphering test directions or items. English–native language glossaries are an example of an accommodation that might be provided for limited English proficient test takers on a construction safety test to help them understand what is being asked. The glossaries would contain words that, while not directly related to the construct being measured, would help limited English test takers understand the context of the question or task being posed.

At the other end of the range are adaptations that transform the construct being measured, including the test content and/or testing conditions, to get a reasonable measure of a somewhat different but appropriate construct for designated test takers. For example, in educational testing, different tests addressing alternate achievement standards are designed for students with severe cognitive disabilities for the same subjects in which students without disabilities are assessed. Clearly, scores from these different tests cannot be considered comparable to those resulting from the general assessment, but instead represent scores from a new test that requires the same rigorous development and validation processes as would be carried out for any new assessment. (An expanded discussion of the use of such alternate assessments is found in chap. 12; alternate assessments will not be treated further in the present chapter.) Other adaptations change the intended construct to make it accessible for designated students while retaining as much of the original construct as possible. For example, a reading test adaptation might provide a dyslexic student with a screen reader that reads aloud the passages and the test questions measuring reading comprehension. If the construct is intentionally defined as requiring both the ability to decode and the ability to comprehend written language, the adaptation would require a different interpretation of the test scores as a measure of reading comprehension. Clearly, this adaptation changes the construct being meas-

ured, because the student does not have to decode the printed text; but without the adaptation, the student may not be able to demonstrate any standing on the construct of reading comprehension. On the other hand, if the purpose of the reading test is to evaluate comprehension without concern for decoding ability, the adaptation might be judged to support more valid interpretations of some students' reading comprehension and the essence of the relevant parts of the construct might be judged to be intact. The challenge for those who report, interpret, and/or use test scores from adapted tests is to recognize which adaptations provide scores that are comparable to the scores from the original, unadapted assessment and which adaptations do not. This challenge becomes even more difficult when evidence to support the comparability of scores is not available.

Test Accommodations: Comparable Measures That Maintain the Intended Construct

Comparability of scores enables test users to make comparable inferences based on the scores for all test takers. Comparability also is the defining feature for a test adaptation to be considered an accommodation. Scores from the accommodated version of the test must yield inferences comparable to those from the standard version; to make this happen is a challenging proposition. On the one hand, common, uniform procedures are a basic underpinning for score validity and comparability. On the other hand, accommodations by their very nature mean that something in the testing circumstance has been changed because adhering to the original standardized procedures would interfere with valid measurement of the intended construct(s) for some individuals.

The comparability of inferences made from accommodated test scores rests largely on whether the scores represent the same constructs as those from the original test. This determination requires a very clear definition of the intended construct(s). For example, when non-native speakers of the language of the test take a survey of their health and nutrition knowledge, one may not know whether the test score is, in whole or in part, a measure of the ability to read in the language of the test rather than a measure of the intended construct. If the test is not intended to also be a measure of the ability to read in English, then test scores do not represent the same construct(s) for examinees who may have poor reading skills, such as limited English proficient test takers, as they do for those who are fully proficient in reading English. An adaptation that improves the accessibility of the test for non-native speakers of English by providing direct or indirect linguistic supports may yield a score that is uncontaminated by the ability to understand English.

At the same time, construct underrepresentation is a primary threat to the validity of test accommodations. For example, extra time is a common accommodation, but if speed is part of the intended construct, it is inappropriate to allow for extra time in the test administration. Scores obtained on the test with extended administration time may underrepresent the construct measured by the strictly timed test because speed will not be part of the construct measured by the extended-time test. Similarly, translating a reading comprehension test used for selection into an organization's training program is inappropriate if reading comprehension in English is important to successful participation in the program.

Claims that accommodated versions of a test yield interpretations comparable to those based on scores from the original test and that the construct being measured has not been changed need to be evaluated and substantiated with evidence. Although score comparability is easiest to establish when different test forms are constructed following identical procedures and then equated statistically, such procedures usually are not possible for accommodated and nonaccommodated versions of tests. Instead, relevant evidence can take a variety of forms, from experimental studies to assess construct equivalence to smaller, qualitative studies and/or use of professional judgment and expert review. Whatever the case, test developers and/or users should seek evidence of the comparability of the accommodated and original assessments.

A variety of strategies for accommodating tests and testing procedures have been implemented to be responsive to the needs of test takers with

disabilities and those with diverse linguistic and cultural backgrounds. Similar approaches may be adapted for other subgroups. Specific strategies depend on the purpose of the test and the construct(s) the test is intended to measure. Some strategies require changing test administration procedures (e.g., instructions, response format), whereas others alter testing medium, timing, settings, or format. Depending on the linguistic background or the nature and extent of the disability, one or more testing changes may be appropriate for a particular individual.

Regardless of the individual's characteristics that make accommodations necessary, it is important that test accommodations address the specific access issue(s) that otherwise would bias an individual's test results. For example, accommodations provided to limited English proficient test takers should be designed to address appropriate linguistic support needs; those provided to test takers with visual impairments should address the inability to see test material. Accommodations should be effective in removing construct-irrelevant barriers to an individual's test performance without providing an unfair advantage over individuals who do not receive the accommodation. Admittedly, achieving both objectives can be challenging.

Adaptations involving test translations merit special consideration. Simply translating a test from one language to another does not ensure that the translation produces a version of the test that is comparable in content and difficulty level to the original version of the test, or that the translated test produces scores that are equally reliable/precise and valid as those from the original test. Furthermore, one cannot assume that the relevant acculturation, clinical, or educational experiences are similar for test takers taking the translated version and for the target group used to develop the original version. In addition, it cannot be assumed that translation into the native language is always a preferred accommodation. Research in educational testing, for example, shows that translated content tests are not effective unless test takers have been instructed using the language of the translated test. Whenever tests are translated from one language to a second language, evidence of the validity, reliability/precision, and comparability of scores on the different versions of the tests should be collected and reported.

When the testing accommodation employs the use of an interpreter, it is desirable, where feasible, to obtain someone who has a basic understanding of the process of psychological and educational assessment, is fluent in the language of the test and the test taker's native language, and is familiar with the test taker's cultural background. The interpreter ideally needs to understand the importance of following standardized procedures, the importance of accurately conveying to the examiner a test taker's actual responses, and the role and responsibilities of the interpreter in testing. The interpreter must be careful not to provide any assistance to the candidate that might potentially compromise the validity of the interpretation for intended uses of the assessment results.

Finally, it is important to standardize procedures for implementing accommodations, as far as possible, so that comparability of scores is maintained. Standardized procedures for test accommodations must include rules for determining who is eligible for an accommodation, as well as precisely how the accommodation is to be administered. Test users should monitor adherence to the rules for eligibility and for appropriate administration of the accommodated test.

Test Modifications: Noncomparable Measures That Change the Intended Construct

There may be times when additional flexibility is required to obtain even partial measurement of the construct; that is, it may be necessary to consider a modification to a test that will result in changing the intended construct to provide even limited access to the construct that is being measured. For example, an individual with dyscalculia may have limited ability to do computations without a calculator; however, if provided a calculator, the individual may be able to do the calculations required in the assessment. If the construct being assessed involves broader mathematics skill, the individual may have limited access to the construct being measured without the use of a calculator; with the modi-

fication, however, the individual may be able to demonstrate mathematics problem-solving skills, even if he or she is not able to demonstrate computation skills. Because modified assessments are measuring a different construct from that measured by the standardized assessment, it is important to interpret the assessment scores as resulting from a new test and to gather whatever evidence is necessary to evaluate the validity of the interpretations for intended uses of the scores. For norm-based score interpretations, any modification that changes the construct will invalidate the norms for score interpretations. Likewise, if the construct is changed, criterion-based score interpretations from the modified assessment (for example, making classification decisions such as "pass/fail" or assigning categories of mastery such as "basic," "proficient," or "advanced" using cut scores determined on the original assessment) will not be valid.

Reporting Scores From Accommodated and Modified Tests

Typically, test administrators and testing professionals document steps used in making test accommodations or modifications in the test report; clinicians may also include a discussion of the validity of the interpretations of the resulting scores for intended uses. This practice of reporting the nature of accommodations and modifications is consistent with implied requirements to communicate information as to the nature of the assessment process if these changes may affect the reliability/precision of test scores or the validity of interpretations drawn from test scores.

The flagging of test score reports can be a controversial issue and subject to legal requirements. When there is clear evidence that scores from regular and altered tests or test administrations are not comparable, consideration should be given to informing score users, potentially by flagging the test results to indicate their special nature, to the extent permitted by law. Where there is credible evidence that scores from regular and altered tests are comparable, then flagging generally is not appropriate. There is little agreement in the field on how to proceed when credible evidence on comparability does not exist. To the extent possible, test developers and/or users should collect evidence to examine the comparability of regular and altered tests or administration procedures for the test's intended purposes.

Appropriate Use of Accommodations or Modifications

Depending on the construct to be measured and the test's purpose, there are some testing situations where accommodations as defined by the *Standards* are not needed or modifications as defined by the *Standards* are not appropriate. First, the reason for the possible alteration, such as English language skills or a disability, may in fact be directly relevant to the focal construct. In employment testing, it would be inappropriate to make changes to the test if the test is designed to assess essential skills required for the job and the test changes would fundamentally alter the constructs being measured. For example, despite increased automation and use of recording devices, some court reporter jobs require individuals to be able to work quickly and accurately. Speed is an important aspect of the construct that cannot be adapted. As another example, a work sample for a customer service job that requires fluent communication in English would not be translated into another language.

Second, an adaptation for a particular disability is inappropriate when the purpose of a test is to diagnose the presence and degree of that disability.

For example, allowing extra time on a timed test to determine distractibility and speed-of-processing difficulties associated with attention deficit disorder would make it impossible to determine the extent to which the attention and processing-speed difficulties actually exist.

Third, it is important to note that not all individuals within a general class of examinees, such as those with diverse linguistic or cultural backgrounds or with disabilities, may require special provisions when taking tests. The language skills, cultural knowledge, or specific disabilities that these individuals possess, for example, might not influence their performance on a particular type of test. Hence, for these individuals, no changes are needed.

The effectiveness of a given accommodation also plays a role in determinations of appropriate use. If a given accommodation or modification does not increase access to the construct as measured, there is little point in using it. Evidence of effectiveness may be gathered through quantitative or qualitative studies. Professional judgment necessarily plays a substantial role in decisions about changes to the test or testing situation.

In summary, fairness is a fundamental issue for valid test score interpretation, and it should therefore be the goal for all testing applications. Fairness is the responsibility of all parties involved in test development, administration, and score interpretation for the intended purposes of the test.

STANDARDS FOR FAIRNESS

The standards in this chapter begin with an overarching standard (numbered 3.0), which is designed to convey the central intent or primary focus of the chapter. The overarching standard may also be viewed as the guiding principle of the chapter, and is applicable to all tests and test users. All subsequent standards have been separated into four thematic clusters labeled as follows:

1. Test Design, Development, Administration, and Scoring Procedures That Minimize Barriers to Valid Score Interpretations for the Widest Possible Range of Individuals and Relevant Subgroups
2. Validity of Test Score Interpretations for Intended Uses for the Intended Examinee Population
3. Accommodations to Remove Construct-Irrelevant Barriers and Support Valid Interpretations of Scores for Their Intended Uses
4. Safeguards Against Inappropriate Score Interpretations for Intended Uses

Standard 3.0

All steps in the testing process, including test design, validation, development, administration, and scoring procedures, should be designed in such a manner as to minimize construct-irrelevant variance and to promote valid score interpretations for the intended uses for all examinees in the intended population.

Comment: The central idea of fairness in testing is to identify and remove construct-irrelevant barriers to maximal performance for any examinee. Removing these barriers allows for the comparable and valid interpretation of test scores for all examinees. Fairness is thus central to the validity and comparability of the interpretation of test scores for intended uses.

Cluster 1. Test Design, Development, Administration, and Scoring Procedures That Minimize Barriers to Valid Score Interpretations for the Widest Possible Range of Individuals and Relevant Subgroups

Standard 3.1

Those responsible for test development, revision, and administration should design all steps of the testing process to promote valid score interpretations for intended score uses for the widest possible range of individuals and relevant subgroups in the intended population.

Comment: Test developers must clearly delineate both the constructs that are to be measured by the test and the characteristics of the individuals and subgroups in the intended population of test takers. Test tasks and items should be designed to maximize access and be free of construct-irrelevant barriers as far as possible for all individuals and relevant subgroups in the intended test-taker population. One way to accomplish these goals is to create the test using principles of universal design, which take account of the characteristics of all individuals for whom the test is intended and include such elements as precisely defining constructs and avoiding, where possible, characteristics and formats of items and tests (for example, test speededness) that may compromise valid score interpretations for individuals or relevant subgroups. Another principle of universal design is to provide simple, clear, and intuitive testing procedures and instructions. Ultimately, the goal is to design a testing process that will, to the extent practicable, remove potential barriers to the measurement of the intended construct for all individuals, including those individuals requiring accommodations. Test developers need to be knowledgeable about group differences that may interfere with the precision of scores and the validity of test score inferences, and they need to be able to take steps to reduce bias.

Standard 3.2

Test developers are responsible for developing tests that measure the intended construct and for minimizing the potential for tests' being affected by construct-irrelevant characteristics, such as linguistic, communicative, cognitive, cultural, physical, or other characteristics.

Comment: Unnecessary linguistic, communicative, cognitive, cultural, physical, and/or other characteristics in test item stimulus and/or response requirements can impede some individuals in demonstrating their standing on intended constructs. Test developers should use language in tests that is consistent with the purposes of the tests and that is familiar to as wide a range of test takers as possible. Avoiding the use of language that has different meanings or different connotations for relevant subgroups of test takers will help ensure that test takers who have the skills being assessed are able to understand what is being asked of them and respond appropriately. The level of language proficiency, physical response, or other demands required by the test should be kept to the minimum required to meet work and credentialing requirements and/or to represent the target construct(s). In work situations, the modality in which language proficiency is assessed should be comparable to that required on the job, for example, oral and/or written, comprehension and/or production. Similarly, the physical and verbal demands of response requirements should be consistent with the intended construct.

Standard 3.3

Those responsible for test development should include relevant subgroups in validity, reliability/precision, and other preliminary studies used when constructing the test.

Comment: Test developers should include individuals from relevant subgroups of the intended testing population in pilot or field test samples used to evaluate item and test appropriateness for construct interpretations. The analyses that are carried out using pilot and field testing data should seek to detect aspects of test design, content, and format that might distort test score interpretations for the intended uses of the test scores for particular groups and individuals. Such analyses could employ a range of methodologies, including those appropriate for small sample sizes, such as expert judgment, focus groups, and cognitive labs. Both qualitative and quantitative sources of evidence are important in evaluating whether items are psychometrically sound and appropriate for all relevant subgroups.

If sample sizes permit, it is often valuable to carry out separate analyses for relevant subgroups of the population. When it is not possible to include sufficient numbers in pilot and/or field test samples in order to do separate analyses, operational test results may be accumulated and used to conduct such analyses when sample sizes become large enough to support the analyses.

If pilot or field test results indicate that items or tests function differentially for individuals from, for example, relevant age, cultural, disability, gender, linguistic and/or racial/ethnic groups in the population of test takers, test developers should investigate aspects of test design, content, and format (including response formats) that might contribute to the differential performance of members of these groups and, if warranted, eliminate these aspects from future test development practices.

Expert and sensitivity reviews can serve to guard against construct-irrelevant language and images, including those that may offend some individuals or subgroups, and against construct-irrelevant context that may be more familiar to some than others. Test publishers often conduct sensitivity reviews of all test material to detect and remove sensitive material from tests (e.g., text, graphics, and other visual representations within the test that could be seen as offensive to some groups and possibly affect the scores of individuals from these groups). Such reviews should be conducted before a test becomes operational.

Standard 3.4

Test takers should receive comparable treatment during the test administration and scoring process.

Comment: Those responsible for testing should adhere to standardized test administration, scoring, and security protocols so that test scores will reflect the construct(s) being assessed and will not be unduly influenced by idiosyncrasies in the testing process. Those responsible for test administration should mitigate the possibility of personal predispositions that might affect the test administration or interpretation of scores.

Computerized and other forms of technology-based testing add extra concerns for standardization in administration and scoring. Examinees must have access to technology so that aspects of the technology itself do not influence scores. Examinees working on older, slower equipment may be unfairly disadvantaged relative to those working on newer equipment. If computers or other devices differ in speed of processing or movement from one screen to the next, in the fidelity of the visuals, or in other important ways, it is possible that construct-irrelevant factors may influence test performance.

Issues related to test security and fidelity of administration can also threaten the comparability of treatment of individuals and the validity and fairness of test score interpretations. For example, unauthorized distribution of items to some examinees but not others, or unproctored test administrations where standardization cannot be ensured, could provide an advantage to some test takers over others. In these situations, test results should be interpreted with caution.

Standard 3.5

Test developers should specify and document provisions that have been made to test administration and scoring procedures to remove construct-irrelevant barriers for all relevant subgroups in the test-taker population.

Comment: Test developers should specify how construct-irrelevant barriers were minimized in the test development process for individuals from all relevant subgroups in the intended test population. Test developers and/or users should also document any studies carried out to examine the reliability/precision of scores and validity of scorer interpretations for relevant subgroups of the intended population of test takers for the intended uses of the test scores. Special test administration, scoring, and reporting procedures should be documented and made available to test users.

Cluster 2. Validity of Test Score Interpretations for Intended Uses for the Intended Examinee Population

Standard 3.6

Where credible evidence indicates that test scores may differ in meaning for relevant subgroups in the intended examinee population, test developers and/or users are responsible for examining the evidence for validity of score interpretations for intended uses for individuals from those subgroups. What constitutes a significant difference in subgroup scores and what actions are taken in response to such differences may be defined by applicable laws.

Comment: Subgroup mean differences do not in and of themselves indicate lack of fairness, but such differences should trigger follow-up studies, where feasible, to identify the potential causes of such differences. Depending on whether subgroup differences are discovered during the development or use phase, either the test developer or the test user is responsible for initiating follow-up inquiries and, as appropriate, relevant studies. The inquiry should investigate construct underrepresentation and sources of construct-irrelevant variance as potential causes of subgroup differences, investigated as feasible, through quantitative and/or qualitative studies. The kinds of validity evidence considered may include analysis of test content, internal structure of test responses, the relationship of test scores to other variables, or the response processes employed by the individual examinees. When sample sizes are sufficient, studies of score precision and accuracy for relevant subgroups also should be conducted. When sample sizes are small, data may sometimes be accumulated over operational administrations of the test so that suitable quantitative analyses by subgroup can be performed after the test has been in use for a period of time. Qualitative studies also are relevant to the supporting validity arguments (e.g., expert reviews, focus groups, cognitive labs). Test developers should closely consider findings from quantitative and/or qualitative analyses in documenting the interpretations for the intended score uses, as well as in subsequent test revisions.

Analyses, where possible, may need to take into account the level of heterogeneity within relevant subgroups, for example, individuals with different disabilities, or linguistic minority examinees at different levels of English proficiency. Differences within these subgroups may influence the appropriateness of test content, the internal structure of the test responses, the relation of test scores to other variables, or the response processes employed by individual examinees.

Standard 3.7

When criterion-related validity evidence is used as a basis for test score–based predictions of future performance and sample sizes are sufficient, test developers and/or users are responsible for evaluating the possibility of differential prediction for relevant subgroups for which there is prior evidence or theory suggesting differential prediction.

Comment: When sample sizes are sufficient, differential prediction is often examined using regression analysis. One approach to regression analysis examines slope and intercept differences between targeted groups (e.g., Black and White samples), while another examines systematic deviations from a common regression line for the groups of interest. Both approaches can account for the possibility of predictive bias and/or differences in heterogeneity between groups and provide valuable information for the examination of dif-

ferential predictions. In contrast, correlation coefficients provide inadequate evidence for or against a differential prediction hypothesis if groups or treatments are found to have unequal means and variances on the test and the criterion. It is particularly important in the context of testing for high-stakes purposes that test developers and/or users examine differential prediction and avoid the use of correlation coefficients in situations where groups or treatments result in unequal means or variances on the test and criterion.

Standard 3.8

When tests require the scoring of constructed responses, test developers and/or users should collect and report evidence of the validity of score interpretations for relevant subgroups in the intended population of test takers for the intended uses of the test scores.

Comment: Subgroup differences in examinee responses and/or the expectations and perceptions of scorers can introduce construct-irrelevant variance in scores from constructed response tests. These, in turn, could seriously affect the reliability/precision, validity, and comparability of score interpretations for intended uses for some individuals. Different methods of scoring could differentially influence the construct representation of scores for individuals from some subgroups.

For human scoring, scoring procedures should be designed with the intent that the scores reflect the examinee's standing relative to the tested construct(s) and are not influenced by the perceptions and personal predispositions of the scorers. It is essential that adequate training and calibration of scorers be carried out and monitored throughout the scoring process to support the consistency of scorers' ratings for individuals from relevant subgroups. Where sample sizes permit, the precision and accuracy of scores for relevant subgroups also should be calculated.

Automated scoring algorithms may be used to score complex constructed responses, such as essays, either as the sole determiner of the score or in conjunction with a score provided by a human scorer. Scoring algorithms need to be reviewed for potential sources of bias. The precision of scores and validity of score interpretations resulting from automated scoring should be evaluated for all relevant subgroups of the intended population.

Cluster 3. Accommodations to Remove Construct-Irrelevant Barriers and Support Valid Interpretations of Scores for Their Intended Uses

Standard 3.9

Test developers and/or test users are responsible for developing and providing test accommodations, when appropriate and feasible, to remove construct-irrelevant barriers that otherwise would interfere with examinees' ability to demonstrate their standing on the target constructs.

Comment: Test accommodations are designed to remove construct-irrelevant barriers related to individual characteristics that otherwise would interfere with the measurement of the target construct and therefore would unfairly disadvantage individuals with these characteristics. These accommodations include changes in administration setting, presentation, interface/engagement, and response requirements, and may include the addition of individuals to the administration process (e.g., readers, scribes).

An appropriate accommodation is one that responds to specific individual characteristics but does so in a way that does not change the construct the test is measuring or the meaning of scores. Test developers and/or test users should document the basis for the conclusion that the accommodation does not change the construct that the test is measuring. Accommodations must address individual test takers' specific needs (e.g., cognitive, linguistic, sensory, physical) and may be required by law. For example, individuals who are not fully proficient in English may need linguistic accommodations that address their language status, while visually impaired individuals may need text magnification. In many cases when a test is used to evaluate the academic progress of an individual, the accommodation that will best eliminate construct irrelevance will match the accommodation used for instruction.

Test modifications that change the construct that the test is measuring may be needed for some examinees to demonstrate their standing on some aspect of the intended construct. If an assessment is modified to improve access to the intended construct for designated individuals, the modified assessment should be treated like a newly developed assessment that needs to adhere to the test standards for validity, reliability/precision, fairness, and so forth.

Standard 3.10

When test accommodations are permitted, test developers and/or test users are responsible for documenting standard provisions for using the accommodation and for monitoring the appropriate implementation of the accommodation.

Comment: Test accommodations should be used only when the test taker has a documented need for the accommodation, for example, an Individualized Education Plan (IEP) or documentation by a physician, psychologist, or other qualified professional. The documentation should be prepared in advance of the test-taking experience and reviewed by one or more experts qualified to make a decision about the relevance of the documentation to the requested accommodation.

Test developers and/or users should provide individuals requiring accommodations in a testing situation with information about the availability of accommodations and the procedures for requesting them prior to the test administration. In settings where accommodations are routinely provided for individuals with documented needs (e.g., educational settings), the documentation should describe permissible accommodations and include standardized protocols and/or procedures for identifying examinees eligible for accommodations, identifying and assigning appropriate accommodations for these individuals, and administering accommodations, scoring, and reporting in accordance with standardized rules.

Test administrators and users should also provide those who have a role in determining and administering accommodations with sufficient information and expertise to appropriately use accommodations that may be applied to the assessment. Instructions for administering any changes in the test or testing procedures should be clearly documented and, when necessary, test administrators should be trained to follow these procedures. The test administrator should administer the accommodations in a standardized manner as documented by the test developer. Administration procedures should include procedures for recording which accommodations were used for specific individuals and, where relevant, for recording any deviation from standardized procedures for administering the accommodations.

The test administrator or appropriate representative of the test user should document any use of accommodations. For large-scale education assessments, test users also should monitor the appropriate use of accommodations.

Standard 3.11

When a test is changed to remove barriers to the accessibility of the construct being measured, test developers and/or users are responsible for obtaining and documenting evidence of the validity of score interpretations for intended uses of the changed test, when sample sizes permit.

Comment: It is desirable, where feasible and appropriate, to pilot and/or field test any test alterations with individuals representing each relevant subgroup for whom the alteration is intended. Validity studies typically should investigate both the efficacy of the alteration for intended subgroup(s) and the comparability of score inferences from the altered and original tests.

In some circumstances, developers may not be able to obtain sufficient samples of individuals, for example, those with the same disability or similar levels of a disability, to conduct standard empirical analyses of reliability/precision and validity. In these situations, alternative ways should be sought to evaluate the validity of the changed test for relevant subgroups, for example through small-sample qualitative studies or professional judgments that examine the comparability of the original and altered tests and/or that investigate alternative explanations for performance on the changed tests.

Evidence should be provided for recommended alterations. If a test developer recommends different time limits, for example, for individuals with disabilities or those from diverse linguistic and cultural backgrounds, pilot or field testing should be used, whenever possible, to establish these particular time limits rather than simply allowing test takers a multiple of the standard time without examining the utility of the arbitrary implementation of multiples of the standard time. When possible, fatigue and other time-related issues should be investigated as potentially important factors when time limits are extended.

When tests are linguistically simplified to remove construct-irrelevant variance, test developers and/or users are responsible for documenting evidence of the comparability of scores from the linguistically simplified tests to the original test, when sample sizes permit.

Standard 3.12

When a test is translated and adapted from one language to another, test developers and/or test users are responsible for describing the methods used in establishing the adequacy of the adaptation and documenting empirical or logical evidence for the validity of test score interpretations for intended use.

Comment: The term *adaptation* is used here to describe changes made to tests translated from one language to another to reduce construct-irrelevant variance that may arise due to individual or subgroup characteristics. In this case the translation/adaptation process involves not only translating the language of the test so that it is suitable for the subgroup taking the test, but also addressing any construct-irrelevant linguistic and cultural subgroup characteristics that may interfere with measurement of the intended construct(s). When multiple language versions of a test are intended to provide comparable scores, test developers should describe in detail the methods used for test translation and adaptation and should report evidence of test score validity pertinent to the linguistic and cultural groups for whom the test is intended and pertinent to the scores' intended uses. Evidence of validity may include empirical studies and/or professional judgment documenting that the different language versions measure comparable or similar constructs and that the score interpretations from the two versions have comparable validity for their intended uses. For example, if a test is translated and adapted into Spanish for use with Central American, Cuban, Mexican, Puerto Rican, South American, and Spanish populations, the validity of test score interpretations for specific uses should be evaluated with members of each of these groups separately, where feasible. Where sample sizes permit, evidence of score accuracy and precision should be provided for each group, and test properties for each subgroup should be included in test manuals.

Standard 3.13

A test should be administered in the language that is most relevant and appropriate to the test purpose.

Comment: Test users should take into account the linguistic and cultural characteristics and relative language proficiencies of examinees who are bilingual or use multiple languages. Identifying the most appropriate language(s) for testing also requires close consideration of the context and purpose for testing. Except in cases where the purpose of testing is to determine test takers' level of proficiency in a particular language, the test takers should be tested in the language in which they are most proficient. In some cases, test takers' most proficient language in general may not be the language in which they were instructed or trained in relation to tested constructs, and in these cases it may be more appropriate to administer the test in the language of instruction.

Professional judgment needs to be used to determine the most appropriate procedures for establishing relative language proficiencies. Such procedures may range from self-identification by examinees to formal language proficiency testing. Sensitivity to linguistic and cultural characteristics may require the sole use of one language in testing or use of multiple languages to minimize the introduction of construct-irrelevant components into the measurement process.

Determination of a test taker's most proficient language for test administration does not automatically guarantee validity of score inferences for the intended use. For example, individuals may be more proficient in one language than another, but not necessarily developmentally proficient in either; disconnects between the language of construct acquisition and that of assessment also can compromise appropriate interpretation of the test taker's scores.

Standard 3.14

When testing requires the use of an interpreter, the interpreter should follow standardized procedures and, to the extent feasible, be sufficiently fluent in the language and content of the test and the examinee's native language and culture to translate the test and related testing materials and to explain the examinee's test responses, as necessary.

Comment: Although individuals with limited proficiency in the language of the test (including deaf and hard-of-hearing individuals whose native language may be sign language) should ideally be tested by professionally trained bilingual/bicultural examiners, the use of an interpreter may be necessary in some situations. If an interpreter is required, the test user is responsible for selecting an interpreter with reasonable qualifications, experience, and preparation to assist appropriately in the administration of the test. As with other aspects of standardized testing, procedures for administering a test when an interpreter is used should be standardized and documented. It is necessary for the interpreter to understand the importance of following standardized procedures for this test, the importance of accurately conveying to the examiner an examinee's actual responses, and the role and responsibilities of the interpreter in testing. When the translation of technical terms is important to accurately assess the construct, the interpreter should be familiar with the meaning of these terms and corresponding vocabularies in the respective languages.

Unless a test has been standardized and normed with the use of interpreters, their use may need to be viewed as an alteration that could change the measurement of the intended construct, in particular because of the introduction of a third party during testing, as well as the modification of the standardized protocol. Differences in word meaning, familiarity, frequency, connotations, and associations make it difficult to directly compare scores from any non-standardized translations to English-language norms.

When a test is likely to require the use of interpreters, the test developer should provide clear guidance on how interpreters should be selected and their role in administration.

Cluster 4. Safeguards Against Inappropriate Score Interpretations for Intended Uses

Standard 3.15

Test developers and publishers who claim that a test can be used with examinees from specific subgroups are responsible for providing the necessary information to support appropriate test score interpretations for their intended uses for individuals from these subgroups.

Comment: Test developers should include in test manuals and instructions for score interpretation explicit statements about the applicability of the test for relevant subgroups. Test developers should provide evidence of the applicability of the test for relevant subgroups and make explicit cautions against foreseeable (based on prior experience or other relevant sources such as research literature) misuses of test results.

Standard 3.16

When credible research indicates that test scores for some relevant subgroups are differentially affected by construct-irrelevant characteristics of the test or of the examinees, when legally permissible, test users should use the test only for those subgroups for which there is sufficient evidence of validity to support score interpretations for the intended uses.

Comment: A test may not measure the same construct(s) for individuals from different relevant subgroups because different characteristics of test content or format influence scores of test takers from one subgroup to another. Any such differences may inadvertently advantage or disadvantage individuals from these subgroups. The decision whether to use a test with any given relevant subgroup necessarily involves a careful analysis of the validity evidence for the subgroup, as is called for in Standard 1.4. The decision also requires consideration of applicable legal requirements and the exercise of thoughtful professional judgment regarding the significance of any construct-irrelevant components. In cases where there is credible evidence of differential validity, developers should provide clear guidance to the test user about when and whether valid interpretations of scores for their intended uses can or cannot be drawn for individuals from these subgroups.

There may be occasions when examinees request or demand to take a version of the test other than that deemed most appropriate by the developer or user. For example, an individual with a disability may decline an altered format and request the standard form. Acceding to such requests, after fully informing the examinee about the characteristics of the test, the accommodations that are available, and how the test scores will be used, is not a violation of this standard and in some instances may be required by law.

In some cases, such as when a test will distribute benefits or burdens (such as qualifying for an honors class or denial of a promotion in a job), the law may limit the extent to which a test user may evaluate some groups under the test and other groups under a different test.

Standard 3.17

When aggregate scores are publicly reported for relevant subgroups—for example, males and females, individuals of differing socioeconomic status, individuals differing by race/ethnicity, individuals with different sexual orientations, individuals with diverse linguistic and cultural backgrounds, individuals with disabilities, young children or older adults—test users are responsible for providing evidence of comparability and for including cautionary statements whenever credible research or theory indicates that test scores may not have comparable meaning across these subgroups.

Comment: Reporting scores for relevant subgroups is justified only if the scores have comparable meaning across these groups and there is sufficient sample size per group to protect individual identity and warrant aggregation. This standard is intended to be applicable to settings where scores are implicitly or explicitly presented as comparable in meaning across subgroups. Care should be taken that the terms used to describe reported subgroups are clearly defined, consistent with common usage, and clearly understood by those interpreting test scores.

Terminology for describing specific subgroups for which valid test score inferences can and cannot be drawn should be as precise as possible, and categories should be consistent with the intended uses of the results. For example, the terms *Latino* or *Hispanic* can be ambiguous if not specifically defined, in that they may denote individuals of Cuban, Mexican, Puerto Rican, South or Central American, or other Spanish-culture origin, regardless of race/ethnicity, and may combine those who are recent immigrants with those who are U.S. native born, those who may not be proficient in English, and those of diverse socioeconomic background. Similarly, the term "individuals with disabilities" encompasses a wide range of specific conditions and background characteristics.

Even references to specific categories of individuals with disabilities, such as hearing impaired, should be accompanied by an explanation of the meaning of the term and an indication of the variability of individuals within the group.

Standard 3.18

In testing individuals for diagnostic and/or special program placement purposes, test users should not use test scores as the sole indicators to characterize an individual's functioning, competence, attitudes, and/or predispositions. Instead, multiple sources of information should be used, alternative explanations for test performance should be considered, and the professional judgment of someone familiar with the test should be brought to bear on the decision.

Comment: Many test manuals point out variables that should be considered in interpreting test scores, such as clinically relevant history, medications, school record, vocational status, and test-taker motivation. Influences associated with variables such as age, culture, disability, gender, and linguistic or racial/ethnic characteristics may also be relevant.

Opportunity to learn is another variable that may need to be taken into account in educational and/or clinical settings. For instance, if recent immigrants being tested on a personality inventory or an ability measure have little prior exposure to school, they may not have had the opportunity to learn concepts that the test assumes are common knowledge or common experience, even if the test is administered in the native language. Not taking into account prior opportunity to learn can lead to misdiagnoses, inappropriate placements and/or services, and unintended negative consequences.

Inferences about test takers' general language proficiency should be based on tests that measure a range of language features, not a single linguistic skill. A more complete range of communicative abilities (e.g., word knowledge, syntax as well as cultural variation) will typically need to be assessed. Test users are responsible for interpreting individual scores in light of alternative explanations and/or relevant individual variables noted in the test manual.

Standard 3.19

In settings where the same authority is responsible for both provision of curriculum and high-stakes decisions based on testing of examinees' curriculum mastery, examinees should not suffer permanent negative consequences if evidence indicates that they have not had the opportunity to learn the test content.

Comment: In educational settings, students' opportunity to learn the content and skills assessed by an achievement test can seriously affect their test performance and the validity of test score interpretations for intended use for high-stakes individual decisions. If there is not a good match between the content of curriculum and instruction and that of tested constructs for some students, those students cannot be expected to do well on the test and can be unfairly disadvantaged by high-stakes individual decisions, such as denying high school graduation, that are made based on test results. When an authority, such as a state or district, is responsible for prescribing and/or delivering curriculum and instruction, it should not penalize individuals for test performance on content that the authority has not provided.

Note that this standard is not applicable in situations where different authorities are responsible for curriculum, testing, and/or interpretation and use of results. For example, opportunity to learn may be beyond the knowledge or control of test users, and it may not influence the validity of test interpretations such as predictions of future performance.

Standard 3.20

When a construct can be measured in different ways that are equal in their degree of construct representation and validity (including freedom from construct-irrelevant variance), test users should consider, among other factors, evidence of subgroup differences in mean scores or in percentages of examinees whose scores exceed the cut scores, in deciding which test and/or cut scores to use.

Comment: Evidence of differential subgroup performance is one important factor influencing the choice between one test and another. However, other factors, such as cost, testing time, test security, and logistical issues (e.g., the need to screen very large numbers of examinees in a very short time), must also enter into professional judgments about test selection and use. If the scores from two tests lead to equally valid interpretations and impose similar costs or other burdens, legal considerations may require selecting the test that minimizes subgroup differences.

II

Operations

4. TEST DESIGN AND DEVELOPMENT

BACKGROUND

Test development is the process of producing a measure of some aspect of an individual's knowledge, skills, abilities, interests, attitudes, or other characteristics by developing questions or tasks and combining them to form a test, according to a specified plan. The steps and considerations for this process are articulated in the test design plan. Test design begins with consideration of expected interpretations for intended uses of the scores to be generated by the test. The content and format of the test are then specified to provide evidence to support the interpretations for intended uses. Test design also includes specification of test administration and scoring procedures, and of how scores are to be reported. Questions or tasks (hereafter referred to as *items*) are developed following the test specifications and screened using criteria appropriate to the intended uses of the test. Procedures for scoring individual items and the test as a whole are also developed, reviewed, and revised as needed. Test design is commonly iterative, with adjustments and revisions made in response to data from tryouts and operational use.

Test design and development procedures must support the validity of the interpretations of test scores for their intended uses. For example, current educational assessments often are used to indicate students' proficiency with regard to standards for the knowledge and skill a student should exhibit; thus, the relationship between the test content and the established content standards is key. In this case, content specifications must clearly describe the content and/or cognitive categories to be covered so that evidence of the alignment of the test questions to these categories can be gathered. When normative interpretations are intended, development procedures should include a precise definition of the reference population and plans to collect appropriate normative data. Many tests, such as employment or college selection tests, rely on predictive validity evidence. Specifi-cations for such tests should include descriptions of the outcomes the test is designed to predict and plans to collect evidence of the effectiveness of test scores in predicting these outcomes.

Issues bearing on validity, reliability, and fairness are interwoven within the stages of test development. Each of these topics is addressed comprehensively in other chapters of the *Standards*: validity in chapter 1, reliability in chapter 2, and fairness in chapter 3. Additional material on test administration and scoring, and on reporting and interpretation of scores and results, is provided in chapter 6. Chapter 5 discusses score scales, and chapter 7 covers documentation requirements.

In addition, test developers should respect the rights of participants in the development process, including pretest participants. In particular, developers should take steps to ensure proper notice and consent from participants and to protect participants' personally identifiable information consistent with applicable legal and professional requirements. The rights of test takers are discussed in chapter 8.

This chapter describes four phases of the test development process leading from the original statement of purpose(s) to the final product: (a) development and evaluation of the test specifications; (b) development, tryout, and evaluation of the items; (c) assembly and evaluation of new test forms; and (d) development of procedures and materials for administration and scoring. What follows is a description of typical test development procedures, although there may be sound reasons that some of the steps covered in the description are followed in some settings and not in others.

Test Specifications

General Considerations

In nearly all cases, test development is guided by a set of test specifications. The nature of these specifications and the way in which they are created may vary widely as a function of the nature of the test and its intended uses. The term *test specifications* is sometimes limited to description of the content and format of the test. In the *Standards*, test specifications are defined more broadly to also include documentation of the purpose and intended uses of the test, as well as detailed decisions about content, format, test length, psychometric characteristics of the items and test, delivery mode, administration, scoring, and score reporting.

Responsibility for developing test specifications also varies widely across testing programs. For most commercial tests, test specifications are created by the test developer. In other contexts, such as tests used for educational accountability, many aspects of the test specifications are established through a public policy process. As discussed in the introduction, the generic term *test developer* is used in this chapter in preference to other terms, such as *test publisher*, to cover both those responsible for developing and those responsible for implementing test specifications across a wide range of test development processes.

Statement of Purpose and Intended Uses

The process of developing educational and psychological tests should begin with a statement of the purpose(s) of the test, the intended users and uses, the construct or content domain to be measured, and the intended examinee population. Tests of the same construct or domain can differ in important ways because factors such as purpose, intended uses, and examinee population may vary. In addition, tests intended for diverse examinee populations must be developed to minimize construct-irrelevant factors that may unfairly depress or inflate some examinees' performance. In many cases, accommodations and/or alternative versions of tests may need to be specified to remove irrelevant barriers to performance for particular subgroups in the intended examinee population.

Specification of intended uses will include an indication of whether the test score interpretations will be primarily *norm-referenced* or *criterion-referenced*. When scores are norm-referenced, relative score interpretations are of primary interest. A score for an individual or for a definable group is ranked within a distribution of scores or compared with the average performance of test takers in a reference population (e.g., based on age, grade, diagnostic category, or job classification). When interpretations are criterion-referenced, absolute score interpretations are of primary interest. The meaning of such scores does not depend on rank information. Rather, the test score conveys directly a level of competence in some defined criterion domain. Both relative and absolute interpretations are often used with a given test, but the test developer determines which approach is most relevant to specific uses of the test.

Content Specifications

The first step in developing test specifications is to extend the original statement of purpose(s), and the construct or content domain being considered, into a framework for the test that describes the extent of the domain, or the scope of the construct to be measured. *Content specifications,* sometimes referred to as *content frameworks,* delineate the aspects (e.g., content, skills, processes, and diagnostic features) of the construct or domain to be measured. The specifications should address questions about what is to be included, such as "Does eighth-grade mathematics include algebra?" "Does verbal ability include text comprehension as well as vocabulary?" "Does self-esteem include both feelings and acts?" The delineation of the content specifications can be guided by theory or by an analysis of the content domain (e.g., an analysis of job requirements in the case of many credentialing and employment tests). The content specifications serve as a guide to subsequent test evaluation. The chapter on validity provides a more thorough discussion of the relationships among the construct or content domain, the test framework, and the purpose(s) of the test.

Format Specifications

Once decisions have been made about what the test is to measure and what meaning its scores are intended to convey, the next step is to create format specifications. Format specifications delineate the format of items (i.e., tasks or questions); the response format or conditions for responding; and the type of scoring procedures. Although format decisions are often driven by considerations of expediency, such as ease of responding or cost of scoring, validity considerations must not be overlooked. For example, if test questions require test takers to possess significant linguistic skill to interpret them but the test is not intended as a measure of linguistic skill, the complexity of the questions may lead to construct-irrelevant variance in test scores. This would be unfair to test takers with limited linguistic skills, thereby reducing the validity of the test scores as a measure of the intended content. Format specifications should include a rationale for how the chosen format supports the validity, reliability, and fairness of intended uses of the resulting scores.

The nature of the item and response formats that may be specified depends on the purposes of the test, the defined domain of the test, and the testing platform. Selected-response formats, such as true-false or multiple-choice items, are suitable for many purposes of testing. Computer-based testing allows different ways of indicating responses, such as drag-and-drop. Other purposes may be more effectively served by a short-answer format. Short-answer items require a response of no more than a few words. Extended-response formats require the test taker to write a more extensive response of one or more sentences or paragraphs. Performance assessments often seek to emulate the context or conditions in which the intended knowledge or skills are actually applied. One type of performance assessment, for example, is the standardized job or work sample where a task is presented to the test taker in a standardized format under standardized conditions. Job or work samples might include the assessment of a medical practitioner's ability to make an accurate diagnosis and recommend treatment for a defined condition, a manager's ability to articulate goals for an organization, or a student's proficiency in performing a science laboratory experiment.

Accessibility of item formats. As described in chapter 3, designing tests to be accessible and valid for all intended examinees, to the maximum extent possible, is critical. Formats that may be unfamiliar to some groups of test takers or that place inappropriate demands should be avoided. The principles of *universal design* describe the use of test formats that allow tests to be taken without adaptation by as broad a range of individuals as possible, but they do not necessarily eliminate the need for adaptations. Format specifications should include consideration of alternative formats that might also be needed to remove irrelevant barriers to performance, such as large print or braille for examinees who are visually impaired or, where appropriate to the construct being measured, bilingual dictionaries for test takers who are more proficient in a language other than the language of the test. The number and types of adaptations to be specified depend on both the nature of the construct being assessed and the targeted population of test takers.

Complex item formats. Some testing programs employ more complex item formats. Examples include performance assessments, simulations, and portfolios. Specifications for more complex item formats should describe the domain from which the items or tasks are sampled, components of the domain to be assessed by the tasks or items, and critical features of the items that should be replicated in creating items for alternate forms. Special considerations for complex item formats are illustrated through the following discussion of performance assessments, simulations, and portfolios.

Performance assessments. Performance assessments require examinees to demonstrate the ability to perform tasks that are often complex in nature and generally require the test takers to demonstrate their abilities or skills in settings that closely resemble real-life situations. One distinction between performance assessments and other forms of tests is the type of response that is required from the test takers. Performance assessments require the test takers to carry out a process such as playing a musical instrument or tuning a car's engine or creating a product such as a written essay. An assessment of a clinical psychologist in training may require the test taker to interview a client, choose appropriate tests, arrive at a diagnosis, and plan for therapy.

Because performance assessments typically consist of a small number of tasks, establishing the extent to which the results can be generalized to a broader domain described in the test specifications is particularly important. The test specifications should indicate critical dimensions to be measured (e.g., skills and knowledge, cognitive processes, context for performing the tasks) so that tasks selected for testing will systematically represent the critical dimensions, leading to a comprehensive coverage of the domain as well as consistent coverage across test forms. Specification of the domain to be covered is also important for clarifying potentially irrelevant sources of variation in performance. Further, both theoretical and empirical *evidence* are important for documenting the extent to which performance assessments—tasks as well as scoring criteria—reflect the processes or skills that are specified by the domain definition. When tasks are designed to elicit complex cognitive processes, detailed analyses of the tasks and scoring criteria and both theoretical and empirical analyses of the test takers' performances on the tasks provide necessary validity evidence.

Simulations. Simulation assessments are similar to performance assessments in that they require the examinee to engage in a complex set of behaviors for a specified period of time. Simulations are sometimes a substitute for performance assessments, when actual task performance might be costly or dangerous. Specifications for simulation tasks should describe the domain of activities to be covered by the tasks, critical dimensions of performance to be reflected in each task, and specific format considerations such as the number or duration of the tasks and essentials of how the user interacts with the tasks. Specifications should be sufficient to allow experts to judge the comparability of different sets of simulation tasks included in alternate forms.

Portfolios. Portfolios are systematic collections of work or educational products, typically gathered over time. The design of a portfolio assessment,

like that of other assessment procedures, must flow from the purpose of the assessment. Typical purposes include judgment of improvement in job or educational performance and evaluation of eligibility for employment, promotion, or graduation. Portfolio specifications indicate the nature of the work that is to be included in the portfolio. The portfolio may include entries such as representative products, the best work of the test taker, or indicators of progress. For example, in an employment setting involving promotion decisions, employees may be instructed to include their best work or products. Alternatively, if the purpose is to judge students' educational growth, the students may be asked to provide evidence of improvement with respect to particular competencies or skills. Students may also be asked to provide justifications for their choices or a cover piece reflecting on the work presented and what the student has learned from it. Still other methods may call for the use of videos, exhibitions, or demonstrations.

The specifications for the portfolio indicate who is responsible for selecting its contents. For example, the specifications must state whether the test taker, the examiner, or both parties working together should be involved in the selection of the contents of the portfolio. The particular responsibilities of each party are delineated in the specifications. In employment settings, employees may be involved in the selection of their work and products that demonstrate their competencies for promotion purposes. Analogously, in educational applications, students may participate in the selection of some of their work and the products to be included in their portfolios.

Specifications for how portfolios are scored and by whom will vary as a function of the use of the portfolio scores. Centralized evaluation of portfolios is common where portfolios are used in high-stakes decisions. The more standardized the contents and procedures for collecting and scoring material, the more comparable the scores from the resulting portfolios will be. Regardless of the methods used, all performance assessments, simulations, and portfolios are evaluated by the same standards of technical quality as other forms of tests.

Test Length

Test developers frequently follow *test blueprints* that specify the number of items for each content area to be included in each test form. Specifications for test length must balance testing time requirements with the precision of the resulting scores, with longer tests generally leading to more precise scores. Test developers frequently follow test blueprints that provide guidance on the number or percentage of items for each area of content and that may also include specification of the distribution of items by cognitive requirements or by item format. Test length and blueprint specifications are often updated based on data from tryouts on time requirements, content coverage, and score precision. When tests are administered adaptively, test length (the number of items administered to each examinee) is determined by stopping rules, which may be based on a fixed number of test questions or may be based on a desired level of score precision.

Psychometric Specifications

Psychometric specifications indicate desired statistical properties of items (e.g., difficulty, discrimination, and inter-item correlations) as well as the desired statistical properties of the whole test, including the nature of the reporting scale, test difficulty and precision, and the distribution of items across content or cognitive categories. When psychometric indices of the items are estimated using item response theory (IRT), the fit of the model to the data is also evaluated. This is accomplished by evaluating the extent to which the assumptions underlying the item response model (e.g., unidimensionality and local independence) are satisfied.

Scoring Specifications

Test specifications will describe how individual test items are to be scored and how item scores are to be combined to yield one or more overall test scores. All types of items require some indication of how to score the responses. For selected-response items, one of the response options is considered the correct response in some testing programs. In other testing programs, each response option may

yield a different item score. For short-answer items, a list of acceptable responses may suffice, although more general scoring instructions are sometimes required. Extended-response items require more detailed rules for scoring, sometimes called *scoring rubrics*. Scoring rubrics specify the criteria for evaluating performance and may vary in the degree of judgment entailed, the number of score levels employed, and the ways in which criteria for each score level are described. It is common practice for test developers to provide scorers with examples of performances at each of the score levels to help clarify the criteria.

For extended-response items, including performance tasks, simulations, and portfolios, two major types of scoring procedures are used: analytic and holistic. Both of the procedures require explicit performance criteria that reflect the test framework. However, the approaches lead to some differences in the scoring specifications. Under the analytic scoring procedure, each critical dimension of the performance criteria is judged independently, and separate scores are obtained for each of these dimensions in addition to an overall score. Under the holistic scoring procedure, the same performance criteria may implicitly be considered, but only one overall score is provided. Because the analytic procedure can provide information on a number of critical dimensions, it potentially provides valuable information for diagnostic purposes and lends itself to evaluating strengths and weaknesses of test takers. However, validation will be required for diagnostic interpretations for particular uses of the separate scores. In contrast, the holistic procedure may be preferable when an overall judgment is desired and when the skills being assessed are complex and highly interrelated. Regardless of the type of scoring procedure, designing the items and developing the scoring rubrics and procedures is an integrated process.

When scoring procedures require human judgment, the scoring specifications should describe essential scorer qualifications, how scorers are to be trained and monitored, how scoring discrepancies are to be identified and resolved, and how the absence of bias in scorer judgment is to be checked. In some cases, computer algorithms are used to score complex examinee responses, such as essays. In such cases, scoring specifications should indicate how scores are generated by these algorithms and how they are to be checked and validated.

Scoring specifications will also include whether test scores are simple sums of item scores, involve differential weighting of items or sections, or are based on a more complex measurement model. If an IRT model is used, specifications should indicate the form of the model, how model parameters are to be estimated, and how model fit is to be evaluated.

Test Administration Specifications

Test administration specifications describe how the test is to be administered. Administration procedures include mode of test delivery (e.g., paper-and-pencil or computer based), time limits, accommodation procedures, instructions and materials provided to examiners and examinees, and procedures for monitoring test taking and ensuring test security. For tests administered by computer, administration specifications will also include a description of any hardware and software requirements, including connectivity considerations for Web-based testing.

Refining the Test Specifications

There is often a subtle interplay between the process of conceptualizing a construct or content domain and the development of a test of that construct or domain. The specifications for the test provide a description of how the construct or domain will be represented and may need to be refined as development proceeds. The procedures used to develop items and scoring rubrics and to examine item and test characteristics may often contribute to clarifying the specifications. The extent to which the construct is fully defined a priori is dependent on the testing application. In many testing applications, well-defined and detailed test specifications guide the development of items and their associated scoring rubrics and procedures. In some areas of psychological measurement, test development may be less dependent on an a priori defined framework and may rely more on a data-based approach that results in an empirically derived definition of the construct being measured. In such instances, items are selected primarily on the basis of their empirical relationship with an external criterion, their relationships with one another, or the degree to which they discriminate among groups of individuals. For example, items for a test for sales personnel might be selected based on the correlations of item scores with productivity measures of current sales personnel. Similarly, an inventory to help identify different patterns of psychopathology might be developed using patients from different diagnostic subgroups. When test development relies on a data-based approach, some items will likely be selected based on chance occurrences in the data. Cross-validation studies are routinely conducted to determine the tendency to select items by chance, which involves administering the test to a comparable sample that was not involved in the original test development effort.

In other testing applications, however, the test specifications are fixed in advance and guide the development of items and scoring procedures. Empirical relationships may then be used to inform decisions about retaining, rejecting, or modifying items. Interpretations of scores from tests developed by this process have the advantage of a theoretical and an empirical foundation for the underlying dimensions represented by the test.

Considerations for Adaptive Testing

In adaptive testing, test items or sets of items are selected as the test is being administered based on the test taker's responses to prior items. Specification of item selection algorithms may involve consideration of content coverage as well as increasing the precision of the score estimate. When several items are tied to a single passage or task, more complex algorithms for selecting the next passage or task are needed. In some instances, a larger number of items are developed for each passage or task and the selection algorithm chooses specific items to administer based on content and precision considerations. Specifications must also indicate whether a fixed number of items are to be administered or whether the test is to continue until precision or content coverage criteria are met.

The use of adaptive testing and related computer-based testing models also involves special considerations related to item development. When a pool of operational items is developed for a computerized adaptive test, the specifications refer both to the item pool and to the rules or procedures by which an individualized set of items is selected for each test taker. Some of the appealing features of computerized adaptive tests, such as tailoring the difficulty level of the items to the test taker's ability, place additional constraints on the design of such tests. In most cases, large numbers of items are needed in constructing a computerized adaptive test to ensure that the set of items administered to each test taker meets all of the requirements of the test specifications. Further, tests often are developed in the context of larger systems or programs. Multiple pools of items, for example, may be created for use with different groups of test takers or on different testing dates. Test security concerns are heightened when limited availability of equipment makes it impossible to test all examinees at the same time. A number of issues, including test security, the complexity of content coverage requirements, required score precision levels, and whether test takers might be allowed to retest using the same pool, must be considered when specifying the size of item pools associated with each form of the adaptive test.

The development of items for adaptive testing typically requires a greater proportion of items to be developed at high or low levels of difficulty relative to the targeted testing population. Tryout data for items developed for use in adaptive tests should be examined for possible context effects to assess how much item parameters might shift when items are administered in different orders. In addition, if items are associated with a common passage or stimulus, development should be informed by an understanding of how item selection will work. For example, the approach to developing items associated with a passage may differ depending on whether the item selection algorithm selects all of the available items related to the passage or is able to choose subsets of the available items related to the passage. Because of the issues that arise when items or tasks are nested within common passages or stimuli, variations on adaptive testing are often considered. For example, *multistage testing* begins with a set of routing items. Once these are given and scored, the computer branches to item groups that are explicitly targeted to appropriate difficulty levels, based on the evaluation of examinees' observed performance on the routing items. In general, the special requirements of adaptive testing necessitate some shift in the way in which items are developed and tried out. Although the fundamental principles of quality item development are no different, greater attention must be given to the interactions among content, format, and item difficulty to achieve item pools that are best suited to this testing approach.

Systems Supporting Item and Test Development

The increased reliance on technology and the need for speed and efficiency in the test development process require consideration of the systems supporting item and test development. Such systems can enhance good item and test development practice by facilitating item/task authoring and reviewing, providing item banking and automated tools to assist with test form development, and integrating item/task statistical information with item/task text and graphics. These systems can be developed to comply with interoperability and accessibility standards and frameworks that make it easier for test users to transition their testing programs from one test developer to another. Although the specifics of item databases and supporting systems are outside the scope of the *Standards*, the increased availability of such systems compels those responsible for developing such tests to consider applying technology to test design and development. Test developers should evaluate costs and benefits of different applications, considering issues such as speed of development, transportability across testing platforms, and security.

Item Development and Review

The test developer usually assembles an item pool that consists of more questions or tasks than are needed to populate the test form or forms to be built. This allows the test developer to select a set of items for one or more forms of the test that meet the test specifications. The quality of the items is usually ascertained through item review procedures and item tryouts, often referred to as *pretesting*. Items are reviewed for content quality, clarity, and construct-irrelevant aspects of content that influence test takers' responses. In most cases, sound practice dictates that items be reviewed for sensitivity and potential offensiveness that could introduce construct-irrelevant variance for individuals or groups of test takers. An attempt is generally made to avoid words and topics that may offend or otherwise disturb some test takers, if less offensive material is equally useful (see chap. 3). For constructed response questions and performance tasks, development includes item-specific scoring rubrics as well as prompts or task descriptions. Reviewers should be knowledgeable about test content and about the examinee groups covered by this review.

Often, new test items are administered to a group of test takers who are as representative as possible of the target population for the test, and where possible, who adequately represent individuals from intended subgroups. Item tryouts help determine some of the psychometric properties of the test items, such as an item's difficulty and ability to distinguish among test takers of different standing on the construct being assessed. Ongoing testing programs often pretest items by inserting them into existing operational tests (the tryout items do not contribute to the scores that test takers receive). Analyses of responses to these tryout items provide useful data for evaluating quality and appropriateness prior to operational use.

Statistical analyses of item tryout data commonly include studies of differential item functioning (see chap. 3, "Fairness in Testing"). Differential item functioning is said to exist when test takers from different groups (e.g., groups defined by gender, race/ethnicity, or age) who have approximately equal ability on the targeted construct or content domain differ in their responses to an item. In theory, the ultimate goal of such studies is to identify construct-irrelevant aspects of item content, item format, or scoring criteria that may differentially affect test scores of one or more

groups of test takers. When differential item functioning is detected, test developers try to identify plausible explanations for the differences, and they may then replace or revise items to promote sound score interpretations for all examinees. When items are dropped due to a differential item functioning index, the test developer must take care that any replacements or revisions do not compromise coverage of the specified test content.

Test developers sometimes use approaches involving structured interviews or think-aloud protocols with selected test takers. Such approaches, sometimes referred to as *cognitive labs,* are used to identify irrelevant barriers to responding correctly that might limit the accessibility of the test content. Cognitive labs are also used to provide evidence that the cognitive processes being followed by those taking the assessment are consistent with the construct to be measured.

Additional steps are involved in the evaluation of scoring rubrics for extended-response items or performance tasks. Test developers must identify responses that illustrate each scoring level, for use in training and checking scorers. Developers also identify responses at the borders between adjacent score levels for use in more detailed discussions during scorer training. Statistical analyses of scoring consistency and accuracy (agreement with scores assigned by experts) should be included in the analysis of tryout data.

Assembling and Evaluating Test Forms

The next step in test development is to assemble items into one or more test forms or to identify one or more pools of items for an adaptive or multistage test. The test developer is responsible for documenting that the items selected for the test meet the requirements of the test specifications. In particular, the set of items selected for a new test form or an item pool for an adaptive test must meet both content and psychometric specifications. In addition, editorial and content reviews are commonly conducted to replace items that are too similar to other items or that may provide clues to the answers to other items in the same test form or item pool. When multiple forms of a test are prepared, the test specifications govern each of the forms.

New test forms are sometimes tried out or field tested prior to operational use. The purpose of a field test is to determine whether items function as intended in the context of the new test form and to assess statistical properties, such as score precision or reliability, of the new form. When field tests are conducted, all relevant examinee groups should be included so that results and conclusions will generalize to the intended operational use of the new test forms and support further analyses of the fairness of the new forms.

Developing Procedures and Materials for Administration and Scoring

Many interested persons (e.g., practitioners, teachers) may be involved in developing items and scoring rubrics, and/or evaluating the subsequent performances. If a participatory approach is used, participants' knowledge about the domain being assessed and their ability to apply the scoring rubrics are of critical importance. Equally important for those involved in developing tests and evaluating performances is their familiarity with the nature of the population being tested. Relevant characteristics of the population being tested may include the typical range of expected skill levels, familiarity with the response modes required of them, typical ways in which knowledge and skills are displayed, and the primary language used.

Test development includes creation of a number of documents to support test administration as described in the test specifications. Instructions to test users are developed and tried out as part of pilot or field testing procedures. Instructions and training for test administrators must also be developed and tried out. A key consideration in developing test administration procedures and materials is that test administration should be fair to all examinees. This means that instructions for taking the test should be clear and that test administration conditions should be standardized for all examinees. It also means consideration must be given in advance to appropriate testing

accommodations for examinees who need them, as discussed in chapter 3.

For computer-administered tests, administration procedures must be consistent with hardware and software requirements included in the test specifications. Hardware requirements may cover processor speed and memory; keyboard, mouse, or other input devices; monitor size and display resolution; and connectivity to local servers or the Internet. Software requirements cover operating systems, browsers, or other common tools and provisions for blocking access to, or interference from, other software. Examinees taking computer-administered tests should be informed on how to respond to questions, how to navigate through the test, whether they can skip items, whether they can revisit previously answered items later in the testing period, whether they can suspend the testing session to a later time, and other exigencies that may occur during testing.

Test security procedures should also be implemented in conjunction with both administration and scoring of the tests. Such procedures often include tracking and storage of materials; encryption of electronic transmission of exam content and scores; nondisclosure agreements for test takers, scorers, and administrators; and procedures for monitoring examinees during the testing session. In addition, for testing programs that reuse test items or test forms, security procedures should include evaluation of changes in item statistics to assess the possibility of a security breach. Test developers or users might consider monitoring of websites for possible disclosure of test content.

Test Revisions

Tests and their supporting documents (e.g., test manuals, technical manuals, user guides) should be reviewed periodically to determine whether revisions are needed. Revisions or amendments are necessary when new research data, significant changes in the domain, or new conditions of test use and interpretation suggest that the test is no longer optimal or fully appropriate for some of its intended uses. As an example, tests are revised if the test content or language has become outdated and, therefore, may subsequently affect the validity of the test score interpretations. However, outdated norms may not have the same implications for revisions as an outdated test. For example, it may be necessary to update the norms for an achievement test after a period of rising or falling achievement in the norming population, or when there are changes in the test-taking population; but the test content itself may continue to be as relevant as it was when the test was developed. The timing of the need for review will vary as a function of test content and intended use(s). For example, tests of mastery of educational or training curricula should be reviewed whenever the corresponding curriculum is updated. Tests assessing psychological constructs should be reviewed when research suggests a revised conceptualization of the construct.

STANDARDS FOR TEST DESIGN AND DEVELOPMENT

The standards in this chapter begin with an overarching standard (numbered 4.0), which is designed to convey the central intent or primary focus of the chapter. The overarching standard may also be viewed as the guiding principle of the chapter, and is applicable to all tests and test users. All subsequent standards have been separated into four thematic clusters labeled as follows:

1. Standards for Test Specifications
2. Standards for Item Development and Review
3. Standards for Developing Test Administration and Scoring Procedures and Materials
4. Standards for Test Revision

Standard 4.0

Tests and testing programs should be designed and developed in a way that supports the validity of interpretations of the test scores for their intended uses. Test developers and publishers should document steps taken during the design and development process to provide evidence of fairness, reliability, and validity for intended uses for individuals in the intended examinee population.

Comment: Specific standards for designing and developing tests in a way that supports intended uses are described below. Initial specifications for a test, intended to guide the development process, may be modified or expanded as development proceeds and new information becomes available. Both initial and final documentation of test specifications and development procedures provide a basis on which external experts and test users can judge the extent to which intended uses have been or are likely to be supported, leading to valid interpretations of test results for all individuals. Initial test specifications may be modified as evidence is collected during development and implementation of the test.

Cluster 1. Standards for Test Specifications

Standard 4.1

Test specifications should describe the purpose(s) of the test, the definition of the construct or domain measured, the intended examinee population, and interpretations for intended uses. The specifications should include a rationale supporting the interpretations and uses of test results for the intended purpose(s).

Comment: The adequacy and usefulness of test interpretations depend on the rigor with which the purpose(s) of the test and the domain represented by the test have been defined and explicated. The domain definition should be sufficiently detailed and delimited to show clearly what dimensions of knowledge, skills, cognitive processes, attitudes, values, emotions, or behaviors are included and what dimensions are excluded. A clear description will enhance accurate judgments by reviewers and others about the degree of congruence between the defined domain and the test items. Clear specification of the intended examinee population and its characteristics can help to guard against construct-irrelevant characteristics of item content and format. Specifications should include plans for collecting evidence of the validity of the intended interpretations of the test scores for their intended uses. Test developers should also identify potential limitations on test use or possible inappropriate uses.

Standard 4.2

In addition to describing intended uses of the test, the test specifications should define the content of the test, the proposed test length, the item formats, the desired psychometric properties of the test items and the test, and the ordering of items and sections. Test specifications should also specify the amount of time allowed for

testing; directions for the test takers; procedures to be used for test administration, including permissible variations; any materials to be used; and scoring and reporting procedures. Specifications for computer-based tests should include a description of any hardware and software requirements.

Comment: Professional judgment plays a major role in developing the test specifications. The specific procedures used for developing the specifications depend on the purpose(s) of the test. For example, in developing licensure and certification tests, practice analyses or job analyses usually provide the basis for defining the test specifications; job analyses alone usually serve this function for employment tests. For achievement tests given at the end of a course, the test specifications should be based on an outline of course content and goals. For placement tests, developers will examine the required entry-level knowledge and skills for different courses. In developing psychological tests, descriptions and diagnostic criteria of behavioral, mental, and emotional deficits and psychopathology inform test specifications.

The types of items, the response formats, the scoring procedures, and the test administration procedures should be selected based on the purpose(s) of the test, the domain to be measured, and the intended test takers. To the extent possible, test content and administration procedures should be chosen so that intended inferences from test scores are equally valid for all test takers. Some details of the test specifications may be revised on the basis of initial pilot or field tests. For example, specifications of the test length or mix of item types might be modified based on initial data to achieve desired precision of measurement.

Standard 4.3

Test developers should document the rationale and supporting evidence for the administration, scoring, and reporting rules used in computer-adaptive, multistage-adaptive, or other tests delivered using computer algorithms to select items. This documentation should include procedures used in selecting items or sets of items for administration, in determining the starting point and termination conditions for the test, in scoring the test, and in controlling item exposure.

Comment: If a computerized adaptive test is intended to measure a number of different content subcategories, item selection procedures should ensure that the subcategories are adequately represented by the items presented to the test taker. Common rationales for computerized adaptive tests are that score precision is increased, particularly for high- and low-scoring examinees, or that comparable precision is achieved while testing time is reduced. Note that these tests are subject to the same requirements for documenting the validity of score interpretations for their intended use as other types of tests. Test specifications should include plans to collect evidence required for such documentation.

Standard 4.4

If test developers prepare different versions of a test with some change to the test specifications, they should document the content and psychometric specifications of each version. The documentation should describe the impact of differences among versions on the validity of score interpretations for intended uses and on the precision and comparability of scores.

Comment: Test developers may have a number of reasons for creating different versions of a test, such as allowing different amounts of time for test administration by reducing or increasing the number of items on the original test, or allowing administration to different populations by translating test questions into different languages. Test developers should document the extent to which the specifications differ from those of the original test, provide a rationale for the different versions, and describe the implications of such differences for interpreting the scores derived from the different versions. Test developers and users should monitor and document any psychometric differences among versions of the test based on evidence collected during development and implementation. Evidence of differences may involve judgments when the number of examinees receiving a particular version is small (e.g., a braille version). Note that these requirements are in addition to the normal requirements for demonstrating the equivalency of scores from different forms of the same test. When different languages are used in different test versions, the procedures used to develop and check translations into each language should be documented.

Standard 4.5

If the test developer indicates that the conditions of administration are permitted to vary from one test taker or group to another, permissible variation in conditions for administration should be identified. A rationale for permitting the different conditions and any requirements for permitting the different conditions should be documented.

Comment: Variation in conditions of administration may reflect administration constraints in different locations or, more commonly, may be designed as testing accommodations for specific examinees or groups of examinees. One example of a common variation is the use of computer administration of a test form in some locations and paper-and-pencil administration of the same form in other locations. Another example is small-group or one-on-one administration for test takers whose test performance might be limited by distractions in large group settings. Test accommodations, as discussed in chapter 3 ("Fairness in Testing"), are changes made in a test to increase fairness for individuals who otherwise would be disadvantaged by construct-irrelevant features of test items. Test developers should specify procedures for monitoring variations and for collecting evidence to show that the target construct is or is not altered by allowable variations. These procedures should be documented based on data collected during implementation.

Standard 4.6

When appropriate to documenting the validity of test score interpretations for intended uses, relevant experts external to the testing program should review the test specifications to evaluate their appropriateness for intended uses of the test scores and fairness for intended test takers. The purpose of the review, the process by which the review is conducted, and the results of the review should be documented. The qualifications, relevant experiences, and demographic characteristics of expert judges should also be documented.

Comment: A number of factors may be considered in deciding whether external review of test specifications is needed, including the extent of intended use, whether score interpretations may have important consequences, and the availability of external experts. Expert review of the test specifications may serve many useful purposes, such as helping to ensure content quality and representativeness. Use of experts external to the test development process supports objectivity in judgments of the quality of the test specifications. Review of the specifications prior to starting item development can avoid significant problems during subsequent test item reviews. The expert judges may include individuals representing defined populations of concern to the test specifications. For example, if the test is to be administered to different linguistic and cultural groups, the expert review typically includes members of these groups and experts on testing issues specific to these groups.

Cluster 2. Standards for Item Development and Review

Standard 4.7

The procedures used to develop, review, and try out items and to select items from the item pool should be documented.

Comment: The qualifications of individuals developing and reviewing items and the processes used to train and guide them in these activities are important aspects of test development documentation. Typically, several groups of individuals participate in the test development process, including item writers and individuals participating in reviews for item and test content, for sensitivity, or for other purposes.

Standard 4.8

The test review process should include empirical analyses and/or the use of expert judges to review items and scoring criteria. When expert judges are used, their qualifications, relevant experiences, and demographic characteristics should be documented, along with the instructions and training in the item review process that the judges receive.

Comment: When sample size permits, empirical analyses are needed to check the psychometric properties of test items and also to check whether test items function similarly for different groups. Expert judges may be asked to check item scoring and to identify material likely to be inappropriate, confusing, or offensive for groups in the test-taking population. For example, judges may be asked to identify whether lack of exposure to problem contexts in mathematics word problems may be of concern for some groups of students. Various groups of test takers can be defined by characteristics such as age, ethnicity, culture, gender, disability, or demographic region. When feasible, both empirical and judgmental evidence of the extent to which test items function similarly for different groups should be used in screening the items. (See chap. 3 for examples of appropriate types of evidence.)

Studies of the alignment of test forms to content specifications are sometimes conducted to support interpretations that test scores indicate mastery of targeted test content. Experts independent of the test developers judge the degree to which item content matches content categories in the test specifications and whether test forms provide balanced coverage of the targeted content.

Standard 4.9

When item or test form tryouts are conducted, the procedures used to select the sample(s) of test takers as well as the resulting characteristics of the sample(s) should be documented. The sample(s) should be as representative as possible of the population(s) for which the test is intended.

Comment: Conditions that may differentially affect performance on the test items by the tryout sample(s) as compared with the intended population(s) should be documented when appropriate. For example, test takers may be less motivated when they know their scores will not have an impact on them. Where possible, item and test characteristics should be examined and documented for relevant subgroups in the intended examinee population.

To the extent feasible, item and test form tryouts should include relevant examinee groups. Where sample size permits, test developers should determine whether item scores have different relationships to the construct being measured for different groups (differential item functioning). When testing accommodations are designed for specific examinee groups, information on item performance under accommodated conditions should also be collected. For relatively small groups, qualitative information may be useful. For example, test-taker interviews might be used to assess the effectiveness of accommodations in removing irrelevant variance.

Standard 4.10

When a test developer evaluates the psychometric properties of items, the model used for that purpose (e.g., classical test theory, item response theory, or another model) should be documented. The sample used for estimating item properties should be described and should be of adequate size and diversity for the procedure. The process by which items are screened and the data used for screening, such as item difficulty, item discrimination, or differential item functioning

(DIF) for major examinee groups, should also be documented. When model-based methods (e.g., IRT) are used to estimate item parameters in test development, the item response model, estimation procedures, and evidence of model fit should be documented.

Comment: Although overall sample size is relevant, there should also be an adequate number of cases in regions critical to the determination of the psychometric properties of items. If the test is to achieve greatest precision in a particular part of the score scale and this consideration affects item selection, the manner in which item statistics are used for item selection needs to be carefully described. When IRT is used as the basis of test development, it is important to document the adequacy of fit of the model to the data. This is accomplished by providing information about the extent to which IRT assumptions (e.g., unidimensionality, local item independence, or, for certain models, equality of slope parameters) are satisfied.

Statistics used for flagging items that function differently for different groups should be described, including specification of the groups to be analyzed, the criteria for flagging, and the procedures for reviewing and making final decisions about flagged items. Sample sizes for groups of concern should be adequate for detecting meaningful DIF.

Test developers should consider how any differences between the administration conditions of the field test and the final form might affect item performance. Conditions that can affect item statistics include motivation of the test takers, item position, time limits, length of test, mode of testing (e.g., paper-and-pencil versus computer administered), and use of calculators or other tools.

Standard 4.11

Test developers should conduct cross-validation studies when items or tests are selected primarily on the basis of empirical relationships rather than on the basis of content or theoretical considerations.

The extent to which the different studies show consistent results should be documented.

Comment: When data-based approaches to test development are used, items are selected primarily on the basis of their empirical relationships with an external criterion, their relationships with one another, or their power to discriminate among groups of individuals. Under these circumstances, it is likely that some items will be selected based on chance occurrences in the data used. Administering the test to a comparable sample of test takers or use of a separate validation sample provides independent verification of the relationships used in selecting items.

Statistical optimization techniques such as stepwise regression are sometimes used to develop test composites or to select tests for further use in a test battery. As with the empirical selection of items, capitalization on chance can occur. Cross-validation on an independent sample or the use of a formula that predicts the shrinkage of correlations in an independent sample may provide a less biased index of the predictive power of the tests or composite.

Standard 4.12

Test developers should document the extent to which the content domain of a test represents the domain defined in the test specifications.

Comment: Test developers should provide evidence of the extent to which the test items and scoring criteria yield scores that represent the defined domain. This affords a basis to help determine whether performance on the test can be generalized to the domain that is being assessed. This is especially important for tests that contain a small number of items, such as performance assessments. Such evidence may be provided by expert judges. In some situations, an independent study of the alignment of test questions to the content specifications is conducted to validate the developer's internal processing for ensuring appropriate content coverage.

Standard 4.13

When credible evidence indicates that irrelevant variance could affect scores from the test, then to the extent feasible, the test developer should investigate sources of irrelevant variance. Where possible, such sources of irrelevant variance should be removed or reduced by the test developer.

Comment: A variety of methods may be used to check for the influence of irrelevant factors, including analyses of correlations with measures of other relevant and irrelevant constructs and, in some cases, deeper cognitive analyses (e.g., use of follow-up probes to identify relevant and irrelevant reasons for correct and incorrect responses) of examinee standing on the targeted construct. A deeper understanding of irrelevant sources of variance may also lead to refinement of the description of the construct under examination.

Standard 4.14

For a test that has a time limit, test development research should examine the degree to which scores include a speed component and should evaluate the appropriateness of that component, given the domain the test is designed to measure.

Comment: At a minimum, test developers should examine the proportion of examinees who complete the entire test, as well as the proportion who fail to respond to (omit) individual test questions. Where speed is a meaningful part of the target construct, the distribution of the number of items answered should be analyzed to check for appropriate variability in the number of items attempted as well as the number of correct responses. When speed is not a meaningful part of the target construct, time limits should be determined so that examinees will have adequate time to demonstrate the targeted knowledge and skill.

Cluster 3. Standards for Developing Test Administration and Scoring Procedures and Materials

Standard 4.15

The directions for test administration should be presented with sufficient clarity so that it is possible for others to replicate the administration conditions under which the data on reliability, validity, and (where appropriate) norms were obtained. Allowable variations in administration procedures should be clearly described. The process for reviewing requests for additional testing variations should also be documented.

Comment: Because all people administering tests, including those in schools, industry, and clinics, need to follow test administration procedures carefully, it is essential that test administrators receive detailed instructions on test administration guidelines and procedures. Testing accommodations may be needed to allow accurate measurement of intended constructs for specific groups of test takers, such as individuals with disabilities and individuals whose native language is not English. (See chap. 3, "Fairness in Testing.")

Standard 4.16

The instructions presented to test takers should contain sufficient detail so that test takers can respond to a task in the manner that the test developer intended. When appropriate, sample materials, practice or sample questions, criteria for scoring, and a representative item identified with each item format or major area in the test's classification or domain should be provided to the test takers prior to the administration of the test, or should be included in the testing material as part of the standard administration instructions.

Comment: For example, in a personality inventory the intent may be that test takers give the first response that occurs to them. Such an expectation should be made clear in the inventory directions.

As another example, in directions for interest or occupational inventories, it may be important to specify whether test takers are to mark the activities they would prefer under ideal conditions or whether they are to consider both their opportunity and their ability realistically.

Instructions and any practice materials should be available in formats that can be accessed by all test takers. For example, if a braille version of the test is provided, the instructions and any practice materials should also be provided in a form that can be accessed by students who take the braille version.

The extent and nature of practice materials and directions depend on expected levels of knowledge among test takers. For example, in using a novel test format, it may be very important to provide the test taker with a practice opportunity as part of the test administration. In some testing situations, it may be important for the instructions to address such matters as time limits and the effects that guessing has on test scores. If expansion or elaboration of the test instructions is permitted, the conditions under which this may be done should be stated clearly in the form of general rules and by giving representative examples. If no expansion or elaboration is to be permitted, this should be stated explicitly. Test developers should include guidance for dealing with typical questions from test takers. Test administrators should be instructed on how to deal with questions that may arise during the testing period.

Standard 4.17

If a test or part of a test is intended for research use only and is not distributed for operational use, statements to that effect should be displayed prominently on all relevant test administration and interpretation materials that are provided to the test user.

Comment: This standard refers to tests that are intended for research use only. It does not refer to standard test development functions that occur prior to the operational use of a test (e.g., item and form tryouts). There may be legal requirements to inform participants of how the test developer will use the data generated from the test, including the user's personally identifiable information, how that information will be protected, and with whom it might be shared.

Standard 4.18

Procedures for scoring and, if relevant, scoring criteria, should be presented by the test developer with sufficient detail and clarity to maximize the accuracy of scoring. Instructions for using rating scales or for deriving scores obtained by coding, scaling, or classifying constructed responses should be clear. This is especially critical for extended-response items such as performance tasks, portfolios, and essays.

Comment: In scoring more complex responses, test developers must provide detailed rubrics and training in their use. Providing multiple examples of responses at each score level for use in training scorers and monitoring scoring consistency is also common practice, although these are typically added to scoring specifications during item development and tryouts. For monitoring scoring effectiveness, consistency criteria for qualifying scorers should be specified, as appropriate, along with procedures, such as double-scoring of some or all responses. As appropriate, test developers should specify selection criteria for scorers and procedures for training, qualifying, and monitoring scorers. If different groups of scorers are used with different administrations, procedures for checking the comparability of scores generated by the different groups should be specified and implemented.

Standard 4.19

When automated algorithms are to be used to score complex examinee responses, characteristics of responses at each score level should be documented along with the theoretical and empirical bases for the use of the algorithms.

Comment: Automated scoring algorithms should be supported by an articulation of the theoretical and methodological bases for their use that is sufficiently detailed to establish a rationale for linking the resulting test scores to the underlying construct of interest. In addition, the automated scoring algorithm should have empirical research support, such as agreement rates with human scorers, prior to operational use, as well as evidence that the scoring algorithms do not introduce systematic bias against some subgroups.

Because automated scoring algorithms are often considered proprietary, their developers are rarely willing to reveal scoring and weighting rules in public documentation. Also, in some cases, full disclosure of details of the scoring algorithm might result in coaching strategies that would increase scores without any real change in the construct(s) being assessed. In such cases, developers should describe the general characteristics of scoring algorithms. They may also have the algorithms reviewed by independent experts, under conditions of nondisclosure, and collect independent judgments of the extent to which the resulting scores will accurately implement intended scoring rubrics and be free from bias for intended examinee subpopulations.

Standard 4.20

The process for selecting, training, qualifying, and monitoring scorers should be specified by the test developer. The training materials, such as the scoring rubrics and examples of test takers' responses that illustrate the levels on the rubric score scale, and the procedures for training scorers should result in a degree of accuracy and agreement among scorers that allows the scores to be interpreted as originally intended by the test developer. Specifications should also describe processes for assessing scorer consistency and potential drift over time in raters' scoring.

Comment: To the extent possible, scoring processes and materials should anticipate issues that may arise during scoring. Training materials should address any common misconceptions about the rubrics used to describe score levels. When written text is being scored, it is common to include a set

of prescored responses for use in training and for judging scoring accuracy. The basis for determining scoring consistency (e.g., percentage of exact agreement, percentage within one score point, or some other index of agreement) should be indicated. Information on scoring consistency is essential to estimating the precision of resulting scores.

Standard 4.21

When test users are responsible for scoring and scoring requires scorer judgment, the test user is responsible for providing adequate training and instruction to the scorers and for examining scorer agreement and accuracy. The test developer should document the expected level of scorer agreement and accuracy and should provide as much technical guidance as possible to aid test users in satisfying this standard.

Comment: A common practice of test developers is to provide training materials (e.g., scoring rubrics, examples of test takers' responses at each score level) and procedures when scoring is done by test users and requires scorer judgment. Training provided to support local scoring should include standards for checking scorer accuracy during training and operational scoring. Training should also cover any special consideration for test-taker groups that might interact differently with the task to be scored.

Standard 4.22

Test developers should specify the procedures used to interpret test scores and, when appropriate, the normative or standardization samples or the criterion used.

Comment: Test specifications may indicate that the intended scores should be interpreted as indicating an absolute level of the construct being measured or as indicating standing on the construct relative to other examinees, or both. In absolute score interpretations, the score or average is assumed to reflect directly a level of competence or mastery in some defined criterion domain. In relative score interpretations the status of an individual (or group) is determined by comparing the score (or mean score) with the performance of others in one or more defined populations. Tests designed to facilitate one type of interpretation may function less effectively for the other type of interpretation. Given appropriate test design and adequate supporting data, however, scores arising from norm-referenced testing programs may provide reasonable absolute score interpretations, and scores arising from criterion-referenced programs may provide reasonable relative score interpretations.

Standard 4.23

When a test score is derived from the differential weighting of items or subscores, the test developer should document the rationale and process used to develop, review, and assign item weights. When the item weights are obtained based on empirical data, the sample used for obtaining item weights should be representative of the population for which the test is intended and large enough to provide accurate estimates of optimal weights. When the item weights are obtained based on expert judgment, the qualifications of the judges should be documented.

Comment: Changes in the population of test takers, along with other changes, for example in instructions, training, or job requirements, may affect the original derived item weights, necessitating subsequent studies. In many cases, content areas are weighted by specifying a different number of items from different areas. The rationale for weighting the different content areas should also be documented and periodically reviewed.

Cluster 4. Standards for Test Revision

Standard 4.24

Test specifications should be amended or revised when new research data, significant changes in the domain represented, or newly recommended conditions of test use may reduce the validity of test score interpretations. Although a test that remains useful need not be withdrawn or revised simply because of the passage of time, test developers and test publishers are responsible for monitoring changing conditions and for amending, revising, or withdrawing the test as indicated.

Comment: Test developers need to consider a number of factors that may warrant the revision of a test, including outdated test content and language, new evidence of relationships among measured or predicted constructs, or changes to test frameworks to reflect changes in curriculum, instruction, or job requirements. If an older version of a test is used when a newer version has been published or made available, test users are responsible for providing evidence that the older version is as appropriate as the new version for that particular test use.

Standard 4.25

When tests are revised, users should be informed of the changes to the specifications, of any adjustments made to the score scale, and of the degree of comparability of scores from the original and revised tests. Tests should be labeled as "revised" only when the test specifications have been updated in significant ways.

Comment: It is the test developer's responsibility to determine whether revisions to a test would influence test score interpretations. If test score interpretations would be affected by the revisions, it is appropriate to label the test "revised." When tests are revised, the nature of the revisions and their implications for test score interpretations should be documented. Examples of changes that require consideration include adding new areas of content, refining content descriptions, redistributing the emphasis across different content areas, and even just changing item format specifications. Note that creating a new test form using the same specifications is not considered a revision within the context of this standard.

5. SCORES, SCALES, NORMS, SCORE LINKING, AND CUT SCORES

BACKGROUND

Test scores are reported on scales designed to assist in score interpretation. Typically, scoring begins with responses to separate test items. These item scores are combined, sometimes by addition, to obtain a raw score when using classical test theory or to produce an IRT score when using *item response theory* (IRT) or other model-based techniques. Raw scores and IRT scores often are difficult to interpret in the absence of further information. Interpretation may be facilitated by converting raw scores or IRT scores to scale scores. Examples include various scale scores used on college admissions tests and those used to report results for intelligence tests or vocational interest and personality inventories. The process of developing a score scale is referred to as *scaling a test*. Scale scores may aid interpretation by indicating how a given score compares with those of other test takers, by enhancing the comparability of scores obtained through different forms of a test, and by helping to prevent confusion with other scores.

Another way of assisting score interpretation is to establish cut scores that distinguish different score ranges. In some cases, a single cut score defines the boundary between passing and failing. In other cases, a series of cut scores define distinct proficiency levels. Scale scores, proficiency levels, and cut scores can be central to the use and interpretation of test scores. For that reason, their defensibility is an important consideration in test score validation for the intended purposes.

Decisions about how many scale score points to use often are based on test score reliability concerns. If too few scale score points are used, then the reliability of scale scores is decreased as information is discarded. If too many scale-score points are used, then test users might attempt to interpret scale score differences that are small relative to the amount of measurement error in the scores.

In addition to facilitating interpretations of scores on a single test form, scale scores often are created to enhance comparability across *alternate forms*[2] of the same test, by using equating methods. *Score linking* is a general term for methods used to develop scales with similar scale properties. Score linking includes equating and other methods for transforming scores to enhance their comparability on tests designed to measure different constructs (e.g., related subtests in a battery). Linking methods are also used to relate scale scores on different measures of similar constructs (e.g., tests of a particular construct from different test developers) and to relate scale scores on tests that measure similar constructs given under different modes of administration (e.g., computer and paper-and-pencil administrations). *Vertical scaling methods* sometimes are used to place scores from different levels of an achievement test on a single scale to facilitate inferences about growth or development. The degree of score comparability that results from the application of a linking procedure varies along a continuum. Equating is intended to allow scores on alternate test forms to be used interchangeably, whereas comparability of scores associated with other types of linking may be more restricted.

Interpretations of Scores

An individual's raw scores or scale scores often are compared with the distribution of scores for one

---

[2]The term *alternate form* is used in this chapter to indicate test forms that have been built to the same content and statistical specifications and developed to measure the same construct. This term is not to be confused with the term *alternate assessment* as it is used in chapter 3, to indicate a test that has been modified or changed to increase access to the construct for subgroups of the population. The alternate assessment may or may not measure the same construct as the unaltered assessment.

or more comparison groups to draw useful inferences about the person's relative performance. Test score interpretations based on such comparisons are said to be *norm referenced*. Percentile rank norms, for example, indicate the standing of an individual or group within a defined population of individuals or groups. An example might be the percentile scores used in military enlistment testing, which compare each applicant's score with scores for the population of 18-to-23-year-old American youth. Percentiles, averages, or other statistics for such reference groups are called *norms*. By showing how the test score of a given examinee compares with those of others, norms assist in the classification or description of examinees.

Other test score interpretations make no direct reference to the performance of other examinees. These interpretations may take a variety of forms; most are collectively referred to as *criterion-referenced* interpretations. Scale scores supporting such interpretations may indicate the likely proportion of correct responses that would be obtained on some larger domain of similar items, or the probability that an examinee will answer particular sorts of items correctly. Other criterion-referenced interpretations may indicate the likelihood that some psychopathology is present. Still other criterion-referenced interpretations may indicate the probability that an examinee's level of tested knowledge or skill is adequate to perform successfully in some other setting. Scale scores to support such criterion-referenced score interpretations often are developed on the basis of statistical analyses of the relationships of test scores to other variables.

Some scale scores are developed primarily to support norm-referenced interpretations; others support criterion-referenced interpretations. In practice, however, there is not always a sharp distinction. Both criterion-referenced and norm-referenced scales may be developed and used with the same test scores if appropriate methods are used to validate each type of interpretation. Moreover, a norm-referenced score scale originally developed, for example, to indicate performance relative to some specific reference population might, over time, also come to support criterion-

referenced interpretations. This could happen as research and experience bring increased understanding of the capabilities implied by different scale score levels. Conversely, results of an educational assessment might be reported on a scale consisting of several ordered proficiency levels, defined by descriptions of the kinds of tasks students at each level are able to perform. That would be a criterion-referenced scale, but once the distribution of scores over levels is reported, say, for all eighth-grade students in a given state, individual students' scores will also convey information about their standing relative to that tested population.

Interpretations based on cut scores may likewise be either criterion referenced or norm referenced. If qualitatively different descriptions are attached to successive score ranges, a criterion-referenced interpretation is supported. For example, the descriptions of proficiency levels in some assessment task-scoring rubrics can enhance score interpretation by summarizing the capabilities that must be demonstrated to merit a given score. In other cases, criterion-referenced interpretations may be based on empirically determined relationships between test scores and other variables. But when tests are used for selection, it may be appropriate to rank-order examinees according to their test performance and establish a cut score so as to select a prespecified number or proportion of examinees from one end of the distribution, provided the selection use is sufficiently supported by relevant reliability and validity evidence to support rank ordering. In such cases, the cut score interpretation is norm referenced; the labels "reject" or "fail" versus "accept" or "pass" are determined primarily by an examinee's standing relative to others tested in the current selection process.

Criterion-referenced interpretations based on cut scores are sometimes criticized on the grounds that there is rarely a sharp distinction between those just below and those just above a cut score. A neuropsychological test may be helpful in diagnosing some particular impairment, for example, but the probability that the impairment is present is likely to increase continuously as a function of the test score rather than to change sharply at a particular score. Cut scores may aid in formulating rules for reaching decisions on the basis of test performance. It should be recognized, however, that the likelihood of misclassification will generally be relatively high for persons with scores close to the cut scores.

Norms

The validity of norm-referenced interpretations depends in part on the appropriateness of the reference group to which test scores are compared. Norms based on hospitalized patients, for example, might be inappropriate for some interpretations of nonhospitalized patients' scores. Thus, it is important that reference populations be carefully defined and clearly described. Validity of such interpretations also depends on the accuracy with which norms summarize the performance of the reference population. That population may be small enough that essentially the entire population can be tested (e.g., all test takers at a given grade level in a given district tested on the same occasion). Often, however, only a sample of examinees from the reference population is tested. It is then important that the norms be based on a technically sound, representative sample of test takers of sufficient size. Patients in a few hospitals in a small geographic region are unlikely to be representative of all patients in the United States, for example. Moreover, the usefulness of norms based on a given sample may diminish over time. Thus, for tests that have been in use for a number of years, periodic review is generally required to ensure the continued utility of their norms. Renorming may be required to maintain the validity of norm-referenced test score interpretations.

More than one reference population may be appropriate for the same test. For example, achievement test performance might be interpreted by reference to local norms based on sampling from a particular school district for use in making local instructional decisions, or to norms for a state or type of community for use in interpreting statewide testing results, or to national norms for use in making comparisons with national groups. For other tests, norms might be based on occupational or educational classifications. Descriptive statistics for all examinees who happen to be tested during a given period of time (sometimes called *user norms* or *program norms*) may be useful for some purposes, such as describing trends over time. But there must be a sound reason to regard that group of test takers as an appropriate basis for such inferences. When there is a suitable rationale for using such a group, the descriptive statistics should be clearly characterized as being based on a sample of persons routinely tested as part of an ongoing program.

Score Linking

Score linking is a general term that refers to relating scores from different tests or test forms. When different forms of a test are constructed to the same content and statistical specifications and administered under the same conditions, they are referred to as alternate forms or sometimes *parallel* or *equivalent* forms. The process of placing raw scores from such alternate forms on a common scale is referred to as *equating*. Equating involves small statistical adjustments to account for minor differences in the difficulty of the alternate forms. After equating, alternate forms of the same test yield scale scores that can be used interchangeably even though they are based on different sets of items. In many testing programs that administer tests multiple times, concerns with test security may be raised if the same form is used repeatedly. In other testing programs, the same test takers may be measured repeatedly, perhaps to measure change in levels of psychological dysfunction, attitudes, or educational achievement. In these cases, reusing the same test items may result in biased estimates of change. Score equating allows for the use of alternate forms, thereby avoiding these concerns.

Although alternate forms are built to the same content and statistical specifications, differences in test difficulty will occur, creating the need for equating. One approach to equating involves administering the forms to be equated to the same sample of examinees or to equivalent samples. Another approach involves administering a common set of items, referred to as *anchor items,* to the samples taking each form. Each approach has unique strengths, but also involves assumptions that could influence the equating results, and so these assumptions must be checked. Choosing among equating approaches may include the following considerations:

- Administering forms to the same sample allows for an estimate of the correlation between the scores on the two forms, as well as providing data needed to adjust for differences in difficulty. However, there could be order effects related to practice or fatigue that may affect the score distribution for the form administered second.

- Administering alternate forms to equivalent samples, usually through random assignment, avoids any order effects but does not provide a direct estimate of the correlation between the scores; other methods are needed to demonstrate that the two forms measure the same construct.

- Embedding a set of anchor items in each of the forms being equated provides a basis for adjusting for differences in the samples of examinees taking each form. The anchor items should cover the same content and difficulty range as each of the full forms being equated so that differences on the anchor items will accurately reflect differences on the full forms. Also, anchor item position and other context factors should be the same in both forms. It is important to check that the anchor items function similarly in the forms being equated. Anchor items are often dropped from the anchor if their relative difficulty is substantially different in the forms being equated.

- Sometimes an external anchor test is used in which the anchor items are administered in a separate section and do not contribute to the total score on the test. This approach eliminates some context factors as the presentation of the anchor items is identical for each examinee sample. Again, however, the anchor test must reflect the content and difficulty of the opera-

tional forms being equated. Both embedded and external anchor test designs involve strong statistical assumptions regarding the equivalence of the anchor and the forms being equated. These assumptions are particularly critical when the samples of examinees taking the different forms vary considerably on the construct being measured.

When claiming that scores on test forms are equated, it is important to document how the forms are built to the same content and statistical specifications and to demonstrate that scores on the alternate forms are measures of the same construct and have similar reliability. Equating should provide accurate score conversions for any set of persons drawn from the examinee population for which the test is designed; hence the stability of conversions across relevant subgroups should be documented. Whenever possible, the definitions of important examinee populations should include groups for which fairness may be a particular issue, such as examinees with disabilities or from diverse linguistic and cultural backgrounds. When sample sizes permit, it is important to examine the stability of equating conversions across these populations.

The increased use of tests delivered by computer raises special considerations for equating and linking because more flexible models for delivering tests become possible. These include adaptive testing as well as approaches where unique items or multiple intact sets of items are selected from a larger pool of available items. It has long been recognized that little is learned from examinees' responses to items that are much too easy or much too difficult for them. Consequently, some testing procedures use only a subset of the available items with each examinee. An adaptive test consists of a pool of items together with rules for selecting a subset of those items to be administered to an individual examinee and a procedure for placing different examinees' scores on a common scale. The selection of successive items is based in part on the examinees' responses to previous items. The item pool and item selection rules may be designed so that each examinee receives a representative set of items of appropriate difficulty. With some adaptive tests, it may happen that two examinees rarely if ever receive the same set of items. Moreover, two examinees taking the same adaptive test may be given sets of items that differ markedly in difficulty. Nevertheless, adaptive test scores can be reported on a common scale and function much like scores from a single alternate form of a test that is not adaptive.

Often, the adaptation of the test is done item by item. In other situations, such as in multistage testing, the exam process may branch from choosing among sets of items that are broadly representative of content and difficulty to choosing among sets of items that are targeted explicitly for a higher or lower level of the construct being measured, based on an interim evaluation of examinee performance.

In many situations, item pools for adaptive tests are updated by replacing some of the items in the pool with new items. In other cases, entire pools of items are replaced. In either case, statistical procedures are used to link item parameter estimates for the new items to the existing IRT scale so that scores from alternate pools can be used interchangeably, in much the same way that scores on alternate forms of tests are used when scores on the alternate forms are equated. To support comparability of scores on adaptive tests across pools, it is necessary to construct the pools to the same explicit content and statistical specifications and administer them under the same conditions. Most often, a common-item design is used in linking parameter estimates for the new items to the IRT scale used for adaptive testing. In such cases, stability checks should be made on the statistical characteristics of the common items, and the number of common items should be sufficient to yield stable results. The adequacy of the assumptions needed to link scores across pools should be checked.

Many other examples of linking exist that may not result in interchangeable scores, including the following:

- For the evaluation of examinee growth over time, it may be desirable to develop vertical scales that span a broad range of developmental or educational levels. The development of vertical scales typically requires linking of tests that are purposefully constructed to differ in difficulty.

- Test revision often brings a need to link scores obtained using newer and older test specifications.

- International comparative studies may require linking of scores on tests given in different languages.

- Scores may be linked on tests measuring different constructs, perhaps comparing an aptitude with a form of behavior, or linking measures of achievement in several content areas or across different test publishers.

- Sometimes linkings are made to compare performance of groups (e.g., school districts, states) on different measures of similar constructs, such as when linking scores on a state achievement test to scores on an international assessment.

- Results from linking studies are sometimes aligned or presented in a concordance table to aid users in estimating performance on one test from performance on another.

- In situations where complex item types are used, score linking is sometimes conducted through judgments about the comparability of item content from one test to another. For example, writing prompts built to be similar, where responses are scored using a common rubric, might be assumed to be equivalent in difficulty. When possible, these linkings should be checked empirically.

- In some situations, judgmental methods are used to link scores across tests. In these situations, the judgment processes and their reliability should be well documented and the rationale for their use should be clear.

Processes used to facilitate comparisons may be described with terms such as *linking, calibration, concordance, vertical scaling, projection,* or *moderation.*

These processes may be technically sound and may fully satisfy desired goals of comparability for one purpose or for one relevant subgroup of examinees, but they cannot be assumed to be stable over time or invariant across multiple subgroups of the examinee population, nor is there any assurance that scores obtained using different tests will be equally precise. Thus, their use for other purposes or with other populations than the originally intended population may require additional support. For example, a score conversion that was accurate for a group of native speakers might systematically overpredict or underpredict the scores of a group of nonnative speakers.

Cut Scores

A critical step in the development and use of some tests is to establish one or more cut scores dividing the score range to partition the distribution of scores into categories. These categories may be used just for descriptive purposes or may be used to distinguish among examinees for whom different programs are deemed desirable or different predictions are warranted. An employer may determine a cut score to screen potential employees or to promote current employees; proficiency levels of "basic," "proficient," and "advanced" may be established using standard-setting methods to set cut scores on a state test of mathematics achievement in fourth grade; educators may want to use test scores to identify students who are prepared to go on to college and take credit-bearing courses; or in granting a professional license, a state may specify a minimum passing score on a licensure test.

These examples differ in important respects, but all involve delineating categories of examinees on the basis of test scores. Such cut scores provide the basis for using and interpreting test results. Thus, in some situations, the validity of test score interpretations may hinge on the cut scores. There can be no single method for determining cut scores for all tests or for all purposes, nor can there be any single set of procedures for establishing their defensibility. In addition, although cut scores are helpful for informing selection, placement, and other classifications, it should be acknowledged that such categorical decisions are rarely made on the basis of test performance alone. The examples that follow serve only as illustrations.

The first example, that of an employer interviewing all those who earn scores above a given level on an employment test, is the most straightforward. Assuming that validity evidence has been provided for scores on the employment test for its intended use, average job performance typically would be expected to rise steadily, albeit slowly, with each increment in test score, at least for some range of scores surrounding the cut score. In such a case the designation of the particular value for the cut score may be largely determined by the number of persons to be interviewed or further screened.

In the second example, a state department of education establishes content standards for what fourth-grade students are to learn in mathematics and implements a test for assessing student achievement on these standards. Using a structured, judgmental standard-setting process, committees of subject matter experts develop or elaborate on *performance-level* descriptors (sometimes referred to as *achievement-level descriptors*) that indicate what students at achievement levels of "basic," "proficient," and "advanced" should know and be able to do in fourth-grade mathematics. In addition, committees examine test items and student performance to recommend cut scores that are used to assign students to each achievement level based on their test performance. The final decision about the cut scores is a policy decision typically made by a policy body such as the board of education for the state.

In the third example, educators wish to use test scores to identify students who are prepared to go on to college and take credit-bearing courses. Cut scores might initially be identified based on judgments about requirements for taking credit-bearing courses across a range of colleges. Alternatively, judgments about individual students might be collected and then used to find a score level that most effectively differentiates those judged to be prepared from those judged not to be. In such cases, judges must be familiar with both the college course requirements and the students themselves. Where possible, initial judgments could be followed up with longitudinal data indicating whether former examinees did or did not have to take remedial courses.

In the final example, that of a professional licensure examination, the cut score represents an informed judgment that those scoring below it are at risk of making serious errors because they lack the knowledge or skills tested. No test is perfect, of course, and regardless of the cut score chosen, some examinees with inadequate skills are likely to pass, and some with adequate skills are likely to fail. The relative probabilities of such false positive and false negative errors will vary depending on the cut score chosen. A given probability of exposing the public to potential harm by issuing a license to an incompetent individual (false positive) must be weighed against some corresponding probability of denying a license to, and thereby disenfranchising, a qualified examinee (false negative). Changing the cut score to reduce either probability will increase the other, although both kinds of errors can be minimized through sound test design that anticipates the role of the cut score in test use and interpretation. Determining cut scores in such situations cannot be a purely technical matter, although empirical studies and statistical models can be of great value in informing the process.

Cut scores embody value judgments as well as technical and empirical considerations. Where the results of the standard-setting process have highly significant consequences, those involved in the standard-setting process should be concerned that the process by which cut scores are determined be clearly documented and that it be defensible. When standard-setting involves judges or subject matter experts, their qualifications and the process by which they were selected are part of that documentation. Care must be taken to ensure that these persons understand what they are to do and that their judgments are as thoughtful and objective as possible. The process must be such that well-qualified participants can apply their knowledge and experience to reach meaningful and relevant judgments that accurately reflect their understandings and intentions. A sufficiently large and representative group of participants should be involved to provide reasonable assurance that the expert ratings across judges are sufficiently reliable and that the results of the judgments would not vary greatly if the process were replicated.

STANDARDS FOR SCORES, SCALES, NORMS, SCORE LINKING, AND CUT SCORES

The standards in this chapter begin with an overarching standard (numbered 5.0), which is designed to convey the central intent or primary focus of the chapter. The overarching standard may also be viewed as the guiding principle of the chapter, and is applicable to all tests and test users. All subsequent standards have been separated into four thematic clusters labeled as follows:

1. Interpretations of Scores
2. Norms
3. Score Linking
4. Cut Scores

Standard 5.0

Test scores should be derived in a way that supports the interpretations of test scores for the proposed uses of tests. Test developers and users should document evidence of fairness, reliability, and validity of test scores for their proposed use.

Comment: Specific standards for various uses and interpretations of test scores and score scales are described below. These include standards for norm-referenced and criterion-referenced interpretations, interpretations of cut scores, interchangeability of scores on alternate forms following equating, and score comparability following the use of other procedures for score linking. Documentation supporting such interpretations provides a basis for external experts and test users to judge the extent to which the interpretations are likely to be supported and can lead to valid interpretations of scores for all individuals in the intended examinee population.

Cluster 1. Interpretations of Scores

Standard 5.1

Test users should be provided with clear explanations of the characteristics, meaning, and intended interpretation of scale scores, as well as their limitations.

Comment: Illustrations of appropriate and inappropriate interpretations may be helpful, especially for types of scales or interpretations that are unfamiliar to most users. This standard pertains to score scales intended for criterion-referenced as well as norm-referenced interpretations. All scores (raw scores or scale scores) may be subject to misinterpretation. If the nature or intended uses of a scale are novel, it is especially important that its uses, interpretations, and limitations be clearly described.

Standard 5.2

The procedures for constructing scales used for reporting scores and the rationale for these procedures should be described clearly.

Comment: When scales, norms, or other interpretive systems are provided by the test developer, technical documentation should describe their rationale and enable users to judge the quality and precision of the resulting scale scores. For example, the test developer should describe any normative, content, or score precision information that is incorporated into the scale and provide a rationale for the number of score points that are used. This standard pertains to score scales intended for criterion-referenced as well as norm-referenced interpretations.

Standard 5.3

If there is sound reason to believe that specific misinterpretations of a score scale are likely, test users should be explicitly cautioned.

Comment: Test publishers and users can reduce misinterpretations of scale scores if they explicitly describe both appropriate uses and potential misuses. For example, a score scale point originally defined as the mean of some reference population should no longer be interpreted as representing average performance if the scale is held constant over time and the examinee population changes. Similarly, caution is needed if score meanings may vary for some test takers, such as the meaning of achievement scores for students who have not had adequate opportunity to learn the material covered by the test.

Standard 5.4

When raw scores are intended to be directly interpretable, their meanings, intended interpretations, and limitations should be described and justified in the same manner as is done for scale scores.

Comment: In some cases the items in a test are a representative sample of a well-defined domain of items with regard to both content and item difficulty. The proportion answered correctly on the test may then be interpreted as an estimate of the proportion of items in the domain that could be answered correctly. In other cases, different interpretations may be attached to scores above or below a particular cut score. Support should be offered for any such interpretations recommended by the test developer.

Standard 5.5

When raw scores or scale scores are designed for criterion-referenced interpretation, including the classification of examinees into separate categories, the rationale for recommended score interpretations should be explained clearly.

Comment: Criterion-referenced interpretations are score-based descriptions or inferences that do not take the form of comparisons of an examinee's test performance with the test performance of other examinees. Examples include statements that some psychopathology is likely present, that a prospective employee possesses specific skills required in a given position, or that a child scoring above a certain score point can successfully apply a given set of skills. Such interpretations may

refer to the absolute levels of test scores or to patterns of scores for an individual examinee. Whenever the test developer recommends such interpretations, the rationale and empirical basis should be presented clearly. Serious efforts should be made whenever possible to obtain independent evidence concerning the soundness of such score interpretations.

Standard 5.6

Testing programs that attempt to maintain a common scale over time should conduct periodic checks of the stability of the scale on which scores are reported.

Comment: The frequency of such checks depends on various characteristics of the testing program. In some testing programs, items are introduced into and retired from item pools on an ongoing basis. In other cases, the items in successive test forms may overlap very little, or not at all. In either case, if a fixed scale is used for reporting, it is important to ensure that the meaning of the scale scores does not change over time. When scales are based on the subsequent application of precalibrated item parameter estimates using item response theory, periodic analyses of item parameter stability should be routinely undertaken.

Standard 5.7

When standardized tests or testing procedures are changed for relevant subgroups of test takers, the individual or group making the change should provide evidence of the comparability of scores on the changed versions with scores obtained on the original versions of the tests. If evidence is lacking, documentation should be provided that cautions users that scores from the changed test or testing procedure may not be comparable with those from the original version.

Comment: Sometimes it becomes necessary to change original versions of a test or testing procedure when the test is given to relevant subgroups of the testing population, for example, individuals with disabilities or individuals with diverse linguistic and cultural backgrounds. A test may be translated into braille so that it is accessible to individuals who are blind, or the testing procedure may be changed to include extra time for certain groups of examinees. These changes may or may not have an effect on the underlying constructs that are measured by the test and, consequently, on the score conversions used with the test. If scores on the changed test will be compared with scores on the original test, the test developer should provide empirical evidence of the comparability of scores on the changed and original test whenever sample sizes are sufficiently large to provide this type of evidence.

Cluster 2. Norms

Standard 5.8

Norms, if used, should refer to clearly described populations. These populations should include individuals or groups with whom test users will ordinarily wish to compare their own examinees.

Comment: It is the responsibility of test developers to describe norms clearly and the responsibility of test users to use norms appropriately. Users need to know the applicability of a test to different groups. Differentiated norms or summary information about differences between gender, racial/ethnic, language, disability, grade, or age groups, for example, may be useful in some cases. The permissible uses of such differentiated norms and related information may be limited by law. Users also need to be alerted to situations in which norms are less appropriate for some groups or individuals than others. On an occupational interest inventory, for example, norms for persons actually engaged in an occupation may be inappropriate for interpreting the scores of persons not so engaged.

Standard 5.9

Reports of norming studies should include precise specification of the population that was sampled, sampling procedures and participation rates, any weighting of the sample, the dates of testing, and descriptive statistics. Technical documentation should indicate the precision of the norms themselves.

Comment: The information provided should be sufficient to enable users to judge the appropriateness of the norms for interpreting the scores of local examinees. The information should be presented so as to comply with applicable legal requirements and professional standards relating to privacy and data security.

Standard 5.10

When norms are used to characterize examinee groups, the statistics used to summarize each group's performance and the norms to which those statistics are referred should be defined clearly and should support the intended use or interpretation.

Comment: It is not possible to determine the percentile rank of a school's average test score if all that is known is the percentile rank of each of that school's students. It may sometimes be useful to develop special norms for group means, but when the sizes of the groups differ materially or when some groups are much more heterogeneous than others, the construction and interpretation of group norms is problematic. One common and acceptable procedure is to report the percentile rank of the median group member, for example, the median percentile rank of the pupils tested in a given school.

Standard 5.11

If a test publisher provides norms for use in test score interpretation, then as long as the test remains in print, it is the test publisher's responsibility to renorm the test with sufficient frequency to permit continued accurate and appropriate score interpretations.

Comment: Test publishers should ensure that up-to-date norms are readily available or provide evidence that older norms are still appropriate. However, it remains the test user's responsibility to avoid inappropriate use of norms that are out of date and to strive to ensure accurate and appropriate score interpretations.

Cluster 3. Score Linking

Standard 5.12

A clear rationale and supporting evidence should be provided for any claim that scale scores earned on alternate forms of a test may be used interchangeably.

Comment: For scores on alternate forms to be used interchangeably, the alternate forms must be built to common detailed content and statistical specifications. Adequate data should be collected and appropriate statistical methodology should be applied to conduct the equating of scores on alternate test forms. The quality of the equating should be evaluated to assess whether the resulting scale scores on the alternate forms can be used interchangeably.

Standard 5.13

When claims of form-to-form score equivalence are based on equating procedures, detailed technical information should be provided on the method by which equating functions were established and on the accuracy of the equating functions.

Comment: Evidence should be provided to show that equated scores on alternate forms measure essentially the same construct with very similar levels of reliability and conditional standard errors of measurement and that the results are appropriate for relevant subgroups. Technical information should include the design of the equating study, the statistical methods used, the size and relevant characteristics of examinee samples used in equating studies, and the characteristics of any anchor tests or anchor items. For tests for which equating is conducted prior to operational use (i.e., pre-equating), documentation of the item calibration process should be provided and the adequacy of the equating functions should be evaluated following

operational administration. When equivalent forms of computer-based tests are constructed dynamically, the algorithms used should be documented and the technical characteristics of alternate forms should be evaluated based on simulation and/or analysis of administration data. Standard errors of equating functions should be estimated and reported whenever possible. Sample sizes permitting, it may be informative to assess whether equating functions developed for relevant subgroups of examinees are similar. It may also be informative to use two or more anchor forms and to conduct the equating using each of the anchors. To be most useful, equating error should be presented in units of the reported score scale. For testing programs with cut scores, equating error near the cut score is of primary importance.

Standard 5.14

In equating studies that rely on the statistical equivalence of examinee groups receiving different forms, methods of establishing such equivalence should be described in detail.

Comment: Certain equating designs rely on the random equivalence of groups receiving different forms. Often, one way to ensure such equivalence is to mix systematically different test forms and then distribute them in a random fashion so that roughly equal numbers of examinees receive each form. Because administration designs intended to yield equivalent groups are not always adhered to in practice, the equivalence of groups should be evaluated statistically.

Standard 5.15

In equating studies that employ an anchor test design, the characteristics of the anchor test and its similarity to the forms being equated should be presented, including both content specifications and empirically determined relationships among test scores. If anchor items are used in the equating study, the representativeness and psychometric characteristics of the anchor items should be presented.

Comment: Scores on tests or test forms may be equated via common items embedded within each of them, or a common test administered together with each of them. These common items or tests are referred to as *linking items, common items, anchor items,* or *anchor tests.* Statistical procedures applied to anchor items make assumptions that substitute for the equivalence achieved with an equivalent groups design. Performances on these items are the only empirical evidence used to adjust for differences in ability between groups before making adjustments for test difficulty. With such approaches, the quality of the resulting equating depends strongly on the number of the anchor items used and how well the anchor items proportionally reflect the content and statistical characteristics of the test. The content of the anchor items should be exactly the same in each test form to be equated. The anchor items should be in similar positions to help reduce error in equating due to item context effects. In addition, checks should be made to ensure that, after controlling for examinee group differences, the anchor items have similar statistical characteristics on each test form.

Standard 5.16

When test scores are based on model-based psychometric procedures, such as those used in computerized adaptive or multistage testing, documentation should be provided to indicate that the scores have comparable meaning over alternate sets of test items.

Comment: When model-based psychometric procedures are used, technical documentation should be provided that supports the comparability of scores over alternate sets of items. Such documentation should include the assumptions and procedures that were used to establish comparability, including clear descriptions of model-based algorithms, software used, quality control procedures followed, and technical analyses conducted that justify the use of the psychometric models for the particular test scores that are intended to be comparable.

Standard 5.17

When scores on tests that cannot be equated are linked, direct evidence of score comparability should be provided, and the examinee population for which score comparability applies should be specified clearly. The specific rationale and the evidence required will depend in part on the intended uses for which score comparability is claimed.

Comment: Support should be provided for any assertion that linked scores obtained using tests built to different content or statistical specifications, tests that use different testing materials, or tests that are administered under different test administration conditions are comparable for the intended purpose. For these links, the examinee population for which score comparability is established should be specified clearly. This standard applies, for example, to tests that differ in length, tests administered in different formats (e.g., paper-and-pencil and computer-based tests), test forms designed for individual versus group administration, tests that are vertically scaled, computerized adaptive tests, tests that are revised substantially, tests given in different languages, tests administered under various accommodations, tests measuring different constructs, and tests from different publishers.

Standard 5.18

When linking procedures are used to relate scores on tests or test forms that are not closely parallel, the construction, intended interpretation, and limitations of those linkings should be described clearly.

Comment: Various linkings have been conducted relating scores on tests developed at different levels of difficulty, relating earlier to revised forms of published tests, creating concordances between different tests of similar or different constructs, or for other purposes. Such linkings often are useful, but they may also be subject to misinterpretation. The limitations of such linkings should be described clearly. Detailed technical information should be provided on the linking methodology and the quality of the linking. Technical information about the linking should include, as appropriate, the reliability of the sets of scores being linked, the correlation between test scores, an assessment of content similarity, the conditions of measurement for each test, the data collection design, the statistical methods used, the standard errors of the linking function, evaluations of sampling stability, and assessments of score comparability.

Standard 5.19

When tests are created by taking a subset of the items in an existing test or by rearranging items, evidence should be provided that there are no distortions of scale scores, cut scores, or norms for the different versions or for score linkings between them.

Comment: Some tests and test batteries are published in both a full-length version and a survey or short version. In other cases, multiple versions of a single test form may be created by rearranging its items. It should not be assumed that performance data derived from the administration of items as part of the initial version can be used to compute scale scores, compute linked scores, construct conversion tables, approximate norms, or approximate cut scores for alternative intact tests. Caution is required in cases where context effects are likely, including speeded tests, long tests where fatigue may be a factor, adaptive tests, and tests developed from calibrated item pools. Options for gathering evidence related to context effects might include examinations of model-data fit, operational recalibrations of item parameter estimates initially derived using pretest data, and comparisons of performance on original and revised test forms as administered to randomly equivalent groups.

Standard 5.20

If test specifications are changed from one version of a test to a subsequent version, such changes should be identified, and an indication should be given that converted scores for the two versions may not be strictly equivalent, even when statistical

procedures have been used to link scores from the different versions. When substantial changes in test specifications occur, scores should be reported on a new scale, or a clear statement should be provided to alert users that the scores are not directly comparable with those on earlier versions of the test.

Comment: Major shifts sometimes occur in the specifications of tests that are used for substantial periods of time. Often such changes take advantage of improvements in item types or shifts in content that have been shown to improve validity and therefore are highly desirable. It is important to recognize, however, that such shifts will result in scores that cannot be made strictly interchangeable with scores on an earlier form of the test, even when statistical linking procedures are used. To assess score comparability, it is advisable to evaluate the relationship between scores on the old and new versions.

Cluster 4. Cut Scores

Standard 5.21

When proposed score interpretations involve one or more cut scores, the rationale and procedures used for establishing cut scores should be documented clearly.

Comment: Cut scores may be established to select a specified number of examinees (e.g., to identify a fixed number of job applicants for further screening), in which case little further documentation may be needed concerning the specific question of how the cut scores are established, although attention should be paid to the rationale for using the test in selection and the precision of comparisons among examinees. In other cases, however, cut scores may be used to classify examinees into distinct categories (e.g., diagnostic categories, proficiency levels, or passing versus failing) for which there are no pre-established quotas. In these cases, the standard-setting method must be documented in more detail. Ideally, the role of cut scores in test use and interpretation is taken into account during test design. Adequate precision in regions of score scales where cut scores are established is prerequisite to reliable classification of examinees into categories. If standard setting employs data on the score distributions for criterion groups or on the relation of test scores to one or more criterion variables, those data should be summarized in technical documentation. If a judgmental standard-setting process is followed, the method employed should be described clearly, and the precise nature and reliability of the judgments called for should be presented, whether those are judgments of persons, of item or test performances, or of other criterion performances predicted by test scores. Documentation should also include the selection and qualifications of standard-setting panel participants, training provided, any feedback to participants concerning the implications of their provisional judgments, and any opportunities for participants to confer with one another. Where applicable, variability over participants should be reported. Whenever feasible, an estimate should be provided of the amount of variation in cut scores that might be expected if the standard-setting procedure were replicated with a comparable standard-setting panel.

Standard 5.22

When cut scores defining pass-fail or proficiency levels are based on direct judgments about the adequacy of item or test performances, the judgmental process should be designed so that the participants providing the judgments can bring their knowledge and experience to bear in a reasonable way.

Comment: Cut scores are sometimes based on judgments about the adequacy of item or test performances (e.g., essay responses to a writing prompt) or proficiency expectations (e.g., the scale score that would characterize a borderline examinee). The procedures used to elicit such judgments should result in reasonable, defensible proficiency standards that accurately reflect the standard-setting participants' values and intentions. Reaching such judgments may be most straight-

forward when participants are asked to consider kinds of performances with which they are familiar and for which they have formed clear conceptions of adequacy or quality. When the responses elicited by a test neither sample nor closely simulate the use of tested knowledge or skills in the actual criterion domain, participants are not likely to approach the task with such clear understandings of adequacy or quality. Special care must then be taken to ensure that participants have a sound basis for making the judgments requested. Thorough familiarity with descriptions of different proficiency levels, practice in judging task difficulty with feedback on accuracy, the experience of actually taking a form of the test, feedback on the pass rates entailed by provisional proficiency standards, and other forms of information may be beneficial in helping participants to reach sound and principled decisions.

Standard 5.23

When feasible and appropriate, cut scores defining categories with distinct substantive interpretations should be informed by sound empirical data concerning the relation of test performance to the relevant criteria.

Comment: In employment settings where it has been established that test scores are related to job performance, the precise relation of test and criterion may have little bearing on the choice of a cut score, if the choice is based on the need for a predetermined number of candidates. However, in contexts where distinct interpretations are applied to different score categories, the empirical relation of test to criterion assumes greater importance. For example, if a cut score is to be set on a high school mathematics test indicating readiness for college-level mathematics instruction, it may be desirable to collect empirical data establishing a relationship between test scores and grades obtained in relevant college courses. Cut scores used in interpreting diagnostic tests may be established on the basis of empirically determined score distributions for criterion groups. With many achievement or proficiency tests, such as those used in credentialing, suitable criterion groups (e.g., successful versus unsuccessful practitioners) are often unavailable. Nevertheless, when appropriate and feasible, the test developer should investigate and report the relation between test scores and performance in relevant practical settings. Professional judgment is required to determine an appropriate standard-setting approach (or combination of approaches) in any given situation. In general, one would not expect to find a sharp difference in levels of the criterion variable between those just below and those just above the cut score, but evidence should be provided, where feasible, of a relationship between test and criterion performance over a score interval that includes or approaches the cut score.

6. TEST ADMINISTRATION, SCORING, REPORTING, AND INTERPRETATION

BACKGROUND

The usefulness and interpretability of test scores require that a test be administered and scored according to the test developer's instructions. When directions, testing conditions, and scoring follow the same detailed procedures for all test takers, the test is said to be standardized. Without such standardization, the accuracy and comparability of score interpretations would be reduced. For tests designed to assess the test taker's knowledge, skills, abilities, or other personal characteristics, standardization helps to ensure that all test takers have the same opportunity to demonstrate their competencies. Maintaining test security also helps ensure that no one has an unfair advantage. The importance of adherence to appropriate standardization of administration procedures increases with the stakes of the test.

Sometimes, however, situations arise in which variations from standardized procedures may be advisable or legally mandated. For example, individuals with disabilities and persons of different linguistic backgrounds, ages, or familiarity with testing may need nonstandard modes of test administration or a more comprehensive orientation to the testing process, so that all test takers can have an unobstructed opportunity to demonstrate their standing on the construct(s) being measured. Different modes of presenting the test or its instructions, or of responding, may be suitable for specific individuals, such as persons with some kinds of disability, or persons with limited proficiency in the language of the test, in order to provide appropriate access to reduce construct-irrelevant variance (see chap. 3, "Fairness in Testing"). In clinical or neuropsychological testing situations, flexibility in administration may be required, depending on the individual's ability to comprehend and respond to test items or tasks and/or the construct required to be measured. Some situations and/or the construct (e.g., testing for memory impairment in a test taker with dementia who is in a hospital)

may require that the assessment be abbreviated or altered. Large-scale testing programs typically establish specific procedures for considering and granting accommodations and other variations from standardized procedures. Usually these accommodations themselves are somewhat standardized; occasionally, some alternative other than the accommodations foreseen and specified by the test developer may be indicated. Appropriate care should be taken to avoid unfair treatment and discrimination. Although variations may be made with the intent of maintaining score comparability, the extent to which that is possible often cannot be determined. Comparability of scores may be compromised, and the test may then not measure the same constructs for all test takers.

Tests and assessments differ in their degree of standardization. In many instances, different test takers are not given the same test form but receive equivalent forms that have been shown to yield comparable scores, or alternate test forms where scores are adjusted to make them comparable. Some assessments permit test takers to choose which tasks to perform or which pieces of their work are to be evaluated. Standardization can be maintained in these situations by specifying the conditions of the choice and the criteria for evaluation of the products. When an assessment permits a certain kind of collaboration between test takers or between test taker and test administrator, the limits of that collaboration should be specified. With some assessments, test administrators may be expected to tailor their instructions to help ensure that all test takers understand what is expected of them. In all such cases, the goal remains the same: to provide accurate, fair, and comparable measurement for everyone. The degree of standardization is dictated by that goal, and by the intended use of the test score.

Standardized directions help ensure that all test takers have a common understanding of the mechanics of test taking. Directions generally inform test takers on how to make their responses, what kind of help they may legitimately be given if they do not understand the question or task, how they can correct inadvertent responses, and the nature of any time constraints. General advice is sometimes given about omitting item responses. Many tests, including computer-administered tests, require special equipment or software. Instruction and practice exercises are often presented in such cases so that the test taker understands how to operate the equipment or software. The principle of standardization includes orienting test takers to materials and accommodations with which they may not be familiar. Some equipment may be provided at the testing site, such as shop tools or software systems. Opportunity for test takers to practice with the equipment will often be appropriate, unless ability to use the equipment is the construct being assessed.

Tests are sometimes administered via technology, with test responses entered by keyboard, computer mouse, voice input, or other devices. Increasingly, many test takers are accustomed to using computers. Those who are not may require training to reduce construct-irrelevant variance. Even those test takers who are familiar with computers may need some brief explanation and practice to manage test-specific details such as the test's interface. Special issues arise in managing the testing environment to reduce construct-irrelevant variance, such as avoiding light reflections on the computer screen that interfere with display legibility, or maintaining a quiet environment when test takers start or finish at different times from neighboring test takers. Those who administer computer-based tests should be trained so that they can deal with hardware, software, or test administration problems. Tests administered by computer in Web-based applications may require other supports to maintain standardized environments.

Standardized scoring procedures help to ensure consistent scoring and reporting, which are essential in all circumstances. When scoring is done by machine, the accuracy of the machine, including any scoring program or algorithm, should be established and monitored. When the scoring of complex responses is done by human scorers or automatic scoring engines, careful training is required. The training typically requires expert human raters to provide a sample of responses that span the range of possible score points or ratings. Within the score point ranges, trainers should also provide samples that exemplify the variety of responses that will yield the score point or rating. Regular monitoring can help ensure that every test performance is scored according to the same standardized criteria and that the test scorers do not apply the criteria differently as they progress through the submitted test responses.

Test scores, per se, are not readily interpreted without other information, such as norms or standards, indications of measurement error, and descriptions of test content. Just as a temperature of 50 degrees Fahrenheit in January is warm for Minnesota and cool for Florida, a test score of 50 is not meaningful without some context. Interpretive material should be provided that is readily understandable to those receiving the report. Often, the test user provides an interpretation of the results for the test taker, suggesting the limitations of the results and the relationship of any reported scores to other information. Scores on some tests are not designed to be released to test takers; only broad test interpretations, or dichotomous classifications, such as "pass/fail," are intended to be reported.

Interpretations of test results are sometimes prepared by computer systems. Such interpretations are generally based on a combination of empirical data, expert judgment, and experience and require validation. In some professional applications of individualized testing, the computer-prepared interpretations are communicated by a professional, who might modify the computer-based interpretation to fit special circumstances. Care should be taken so that test interpretations provided by nonalgorithmic approaches are appropriately consistent. Automatically generated reports are not a substitute for the clinical judgment of a professional evaluator who has worked directly with the test taker, or for the integration of other information, including but not limited to other test results, interviews, existing records, and behavioral observations.

In some large-scale assessments, the primary target of assessment is not the individual test taker but rather a larger unit, such as a school district or an industrial plant. Often, different test takers are given different sets of items, following a carefully balanced matrix sampling plan, to broaden the range of information that can be obtained in a reasonable time period. The results acquire meaning when aggregated over many individuals taking different samples of items. Such assessments may not furnish enough information to support even minimally valid or reliable scores for individuals, as each individual may take only an incomplete test, while in the aggregate, the assessment results may be valid and acceptably reliable for interpretations about performance of the larger unit.

Some further issues of administration and scoring are discussed in chapter 4, "Test Design and Development."

Test users and those who receive test materials, test scores, and ancillary information such as test takers' personally identifiable information are responsible for appropriately maintaining the security and confidentiality of that information.

STANDARDS FOR TEST ADMINISTRATION, SCORING, REPORTING, AND INTERPRETATION

The standards in this chapter begin with an overarching standard (numbered 6.0), which is designed to convey the central intent or primary focus of the chapter. The overarching standard may also be viewed as the guiding principle of the chapter, and is applicable to all tests and test users. All subsequent standards have been separated into three thematic clusters labeled as follows:

1. Test Administration
2. Test Scoring
3. Reporting and Interpretation

Standard 6.0

To support useful interpretations of score results, assessment instruments should have established procedures for test administration, scoring, reporting, and interpretation. Those responsible for administering, scoring, reporting, and interpreting should have sufficient training and supports to help them follow the established procedures. Adherence to the established procedures should be monitored, and any material errors should be documented and, if possible, corrected.

Comment: In order to support the validity of score interpretations, administration should follow any and all established procedures, and compliance with such procedures needs to be monitored.

Cluster 1. Test Administration

Standard 6.1

Test administrators should follow carefully the standardized procedures for administration and scoring specified by the test developer and any instructions from the test user.

Comment: Those responsible for testing programs should provide appropriate training, documentation, and oversight so that the individuals who administer

or score the test(s) are proficient in the appropriate test administration or scoring procedures and understand the importance of adhering to the directions provided by the test developer. Large-scale testing programs should specify accepted standardized procedures for determining accommodations and other acceptable variations in test administration. Training should enable test administrators to make appropriate adjustments if an accommodation or modification is required that is not covered by the standardized procedures.

Specifications regarding instructions to test takers, time limits, the form of item presentation or response, and test materials or equipment should be strictly observed. In general, the same procedures should be followed as were used when obtaining the data for scaling and norming the test scores. Some programs do not scale or establish norms, such as portfolio assessments and most alternate academic assessments for students with severe cognitive disabilities. However, these programs typically have specified standardized procedures for administration and scoring when they establish performance standards. A test taker with a disability may require variations to provide access without changing the construct that is measured. Other special circumstances may require some flexibility in administration, such as language support to provide access under certain conditions, or some clinical or neuropsychological evaluations, in addition to procedures related to accommodations. Judgments of the suitability of adjustments should be tempered by the consideration that departures from standard procedures may jeopardize the validity or complicate the comparability of the test score interpretations. These judgments should be made by qualified individuals and be consistent with the guidelines provided by the test user or test developer.

Policies regarding retesting should be established by the test developer or user. The test user and administrator should follow the established policy. Such retest policies should be clearly communicated by the test user as part of the conditions for standardized test administration. Retesting is intended to decrease the probability that a person will be incorrectly classified as not meeting some standard. For example, some testing programs specify that a person may retake the test; some offer multiple opportunities to take a test, for example when passing the test is required for high school graduation or credentialing.

Test developers should specify the standardized administration conditions that support intended uses of score interpretations. Test users should be aware of the implications of less controlled administration conditions. Test users are responsible for providing technical and other support to help ensure that test administrations meet these conditions to the extent possible. However, technology and the Internet have made it possible to administer tests in many settings, including settings in which the administration conditions may not be strictly controlled or monitored. Those who allow lack of standardization are responsible for providing evidence that the lack of standardization did not affect test-taker performance or the quality or comparability of the scores produced. Complete documentation would include reporting the extent to which standardized administration conditions were not met.

Characteristics such as time limits, choices about item types and response formats, complex interfaces, and instructions that potentially add construct-irrelevant variance should be scrutinized in terms of the test purpose and the constructs being measured. Appropriate usability and empirical research should be carried out, as feasible, to document and ideally minimize the impact of sources or conditions that contribute to construct-irrelevant variability.

Standard 6.2

When formal procedures have been established for requesting and receiving accommodations, test takers should be informed of these procedures in advance of testing.

Comment: When testing programs have established procedures and criteria for identifying and providing accommodations for test takers, the procedures and criteria should be carefully followed and documented. Ideally, these procedures include how to consider the instances when some alternative may be appropriate in addition to those accommodations foreseen and specified by the test developer. Test takers should be informed of any testing accommodations that may be available to them and the process and requirements, if any, for obtaining needed accommodations. Similarly, in educational settings, appropriate school personnel and parents/legal guardians should be informed of the requirements, if any, for obtaining needed accommodations for students being tested.

Standard 6.3

Changes or disruptions to standardized test administration procedures or scoring should be documented and reported to the test user.

Comment: Information about the nature of changes to standardized administration or scoring procedures should be maintained in secure data files so that research studies or case reviews based on test records can take it into account. This includes not only accommodations or modifications for particular test takers but also disruptions in the testing environment that may affect all test takers in the testing session. A researcher may wish to use only the records based on standardized administration. In other cases, research studies may depend on such information to form groups of test takers. Test users or test sponsors should establish policies specifying who secures the data files, who may have access to the files, and, if necessary, how to maintain confidentiality of respondents, for example by de-identifying respondents. Whether the information about deviations from standard procedures is reported to users of test data depends on considerations such as whether the users are admissions officers or users of individualized psychological reports in clinical settings. If such reports are made, it may be appropriate to include clear documentation of any deviation from standard administration procedures, discussion of how such administrative variations may have affected the results, and perhaps certain cautions. For example, test users may need to be informed about the comparability of scores when modifications are provided (see chap. 3, "Fairness in Testing," and chap. 9, "The Rights and Responsibilities of Test Users"). If a deviation or change to a standardized test administration procedure is judged significant enough to adversely affect the validity of score interpretation, then appropriate action should be taken, such as not reporting the scores, invalidating the scores, or providing opportunities for readministration under appropriate circumstances. Testing environments that are not monitored (e.g., in temporary conditions or on the Internet) should meet these standardized administration conditions; otherwise, the report on scores should note that standardized conditions were not guaranteed.

Standard 6.4

The testing environment should furnish reasonable comfort with minimal distractions to avoid construct-irrelevant variance.

Comment: Test developers should provide information regarding the intended test administration conditions and environment. Noise, disruption in the testing area, extremes of temperature, poor lighting, inadequate work space, illegible materials, and malfunctioning computers are among the conditions that should be avoided in testing situations, unless measuring the construct requires such conditions. The testing site should be readily accessible. Technology-based administrations should avoid distractions such as equipment or Internet-connectivity failures, or large variations in the time taken to present test items or score responses. Testing sessions should be monitored where appropriate to assist the test taker when a need arises and to maintain proper administrative procedures. In general, the testing conditions should be equivalent to those that prevailed when norms and other interpretative data were obtained.

Standard 6.5

Test takers should be provided appropriate instructions, practice, and other support necessary to reduce construct-irrelevant variance.

Comment: Instructions to test takers should clearly indicate how to make responses, except when doing so would obstruct measurement of the intended construct (e.g., when an individual's spontaneous approach to the test-taking situation is being assessed). Instructions should also be given in the use of any equipment or software likely to be unfamiliar to test takers, unless accommodating to unfamiliar tools is part of what is being assessed. The functions or interfaces of computer-administered tests may be unfamiliar to some test takers, who may need to be shown how to log on, navigate, or access tools. Practice opportunities should be given when equipment is involved, unless use of the equipment is being assessed. Some test takers may need practice responding with particular means required by the test, such as filling in a multiple-choice "bubble" or interacting with a multimedia simulation. Where possible, practice responses should be monitored to confirm that the test taker is making acceptable responses. If a test taker is unable to use the equipment or make the responses, it may be appropriate to consider alternative testing modes. In addition, test takers should be clearly informed on how their rate of work may affect scores, and how certain responses, such as not responding, guessing, or responding incorrectly, will be treated in scoring, unless such directions would undermine the construct being assessed.

Standard 6.6

Reasonable efforts should be made to ensure the integrity of test scores by eliminating opportunities for test takers to attain scores by fraudulent or deceptive means.

Comment: In testing programs where the results may be viewed as having important consequences, score integrity should be supported through active efforts to prevent, detect, and correct scores obtained by fraudulent or deceptive means. Such efforts may include, when appropriate and practicable, stipulating requirements for identification, constructing seating charts, assigning test takers to seats, requiring appropriate space between seats, and providing continuous monitoring of the testing process. Test developers should design test materials and procedures to minimize the possibility of cheating. A local change in the date or time of testing may offer an opportunity for cheating. Test administrators should be trained on how to take appropriate precautions against and detect opportunities to cheat, such as opportunities afforded by technology that would allow a test taker to communicate with an accomplice outside the testing area, or technology that would allow a test taker to copy test information for subsequent disclosure. Test administrators should follow established policies for dealing with any instances of testing irregularity. In general, steps should be taken to minimize the possibility of breaches in test security, and to detect any breaches. In any evaluation of work products (e.g., portfolios) steps should be taken to ensure that the product represents the test taker's own work, and that the amount and kind of assistance provided is consistent with the intent of the assessment. Ancillary documentation, such as the date when the work was done, may be useful. Testing programs may use technologies during scoring to detect possible irregularities, such as computer analyses of erasure patterns, similar answer patterns for multiple test takers, plagiarism from online sources, or unusual item parameter shifts. Users of such technologies are responsible for their accuracy and appropriate application. Test developers and test users may need to monitor for disclosure of test items on the Internet or from other sources. Testing programs with high-stakes consequences should have defined policies and procedures for detecting and processing potential testing irregularities—including a process by which a person charged with an irregularity can qualify for and/or present an appeal—and for invalidating test scores and providing opportunity for retesting.

Standard 6.7

Test users have the responsibility of protecting the security of test materials at all times.

Comment: Those who have test materials under their control should, with due consideration of ethical and legal requirements, take all steps necessary to ensure that only individuals with legitimate needs and qualifications for access to test materials are able to obtain such access before the test administration, and afterwards as well, if any part of the test will be reused at a later time. Concerns with inappropriate access to test materials include inappropriate disclosure of test content, tampering with test responses or results, and protection of test taker's privacy rights. Test users must balance test security with the rights of all test takers and test users. When sensitive test documents are at issue in court or in administrative agency challenges, it is important to identify security and privacy concerns and needed protections at the outset. Parties should ensure that the release or exposure of such documents (including specific sections of those documents that may warrant redaction) to third parties, experts, and the courts/agencies themselves are consistent with conditions (often reflected in protective orders) that do not result in inappropriate disclosure and that do not risk unwarranted release beyond the particular setting in which the challenge has occurred. Under certain circumstances, when sensitive test documents are challenged, it may be appropriate to employ an independent third party, using a closely supervised secure procedure to conduct a review of the relevant materials rather than placing tests, manuals, or a test taker's test responses in the public record. Those who have confidential information related to testing, such as registration information, scheduling, and payments, have similar responsibility for protecting that information. Those with test materials under their control should use and disclose such information only in accordance with any applicable privacy laws.

Cluster 2. Test Scoring

Standard 6.8

Those responsible for test scoring should establish scoring protocols. Test scoring that involves human judgment should include rubrics, procedures, and criteria for scoring. When scoring of complex responses is done by computer, the accuracy of the algorithm and processes should be documented.

Comment: A scoring protocol should be established, which may be as simple as an answer key for multiple-choice questions. For constructed responses, scorers—humans or machine programs—may be provided with scoring rubrics listing acceptable alternative responses, as well as general criteria. A common practice of test developers is to provide scoring training materials, scoring rubrics, and examples of test takers' responses at each score level. When tests or items are used over a period of time, scoring materials should be reviewed periodically.

Standard 6.9

Those responsible for test scoring should establish and document quality control processes and criteria. Adequate training should be provided. The quality of scoring should be monitored and documented. Any systematic source of scoring errors should be documented and corrected.

Comment: Criteria should be established for acceptable scoring quality. Procedures should be instituted to calibrate scorers (human or machine) prior to operational scoring, and to monitor how consistently scorers are scoring in accordance with those established standards during operational scoring. Where scoring is distributed across scorers, procedures to monitor raters' accuracy and reliability may also be useful as a quality control procedure. Consistency in applying scoring criteria is often checked by independently rescoring randomly selected test responses. Periodic checks of the statistical properties (e.g., means, standard deviations, percentage of agreement with scores previously determined to be accurate) of scores assigned by individual scorers during a scoring session can provide feedback for the scorers, helping them to maintain scoring standards. In addition, analyses might monitor possible effects on scoring accuracy of variables such as scorer, task, time or day of scoring, scoring trainer, scorer pairing, and so on, to inform appropriate corrective or preventative actions. When the same items are used in multiple administrations, programs should have procedures in place to monitor consistency of scoring across administrations (e.g., year-to-year comparability). One way to check for consistency over time is to rescore some responses from earlier administrations. Inaccurate or inconsistent scoring may call for retraining, rescoring, dismissing some scorers, and/or reexamining the scoring rubrics or programs. Systematic scoring errors should be corrected, which may involve rescoring responses previously scored, as well as correcting the source of the error. Clerical and mechanical errors should be examined. Scoring errors should be minimized and, when they are found, steps should be taken promptly to minimize their recurrence.

Typically, those responsible for scoring will document the procedures followed for scoring, procedures followed for quality assurance of that scoring, the results of the quality assurance, and any unusual circumstances. Depending on the test user, that documentation may be provided regularly or upon reasonable request. Computerized scoring applications of text, speech, or other constructed responses should provide similar documentation of accuracy and reliability, including comparisons with human scoring.

When scoring is done locally and requires scorer judgment, the test user is responsible for providing adequate training and instruction to the scorers and for examining scorer agreement and accuracy. The expected level of scorer agreement and accuracy should be documented, as feasible.

Cluster 3. Reporting and Interpretation

Standard 6.10

When test score information is released, those responsible for testing programs should provide interpretations appropriate to the audience. The interpretations should describe in simple language what the test covers, what scores represent, the precision/reliability of the scores, and how scores are intended to be used.

Comment: Test users should consult the interpretive material prepared by the test developer and should revise or supplement the material as necessary to present the local and individual results accurately and clearly to the intended audience, which may include clients, legal representatives, media, referral sources, test takers, parents, or teachers. Reports and feedback should be designed to support valid interpretations and use, and minimize potential negative consequences. Score precision might be depicted by error bands or likely score ranges, showing the standard error of measurement. Reports should include discussion of any administrative variations or behavioral observations in clinical settings that may affect results and interpretations. Test users should avoid misinterpretation and misuse of test score information. While test users are primarily responsible for avoiding misinterpretation and misuse, the interpretive materials prepared by the test developer or publisher may address common misuses or misinterpretations. To accomplish this, developers of reports and interpretive materials may conduct research to help verify that reports and materials can be interpreted as intended (e.g., focus groups with representative end-users of the reports). The test developer should inform test users of changes in the test over time that may affect test score interpretation, such as changes in norms, test content frameworks, or scale score meanings.

Standard 6.11

When automatically generated interpretations of test response protocols or test performance are reported, the sources, rationale, and empirical basis for these interpretations should be available, and their limitations should be described.

Comment: Interpretations of test results are sometimes automatically generated, either by a computer program in conjunction with computer scoring, or by manually prepared materials. Automatically generated interpretations may not be able to take into consideration the context of the individual's circumstances. Automatically generated interpretations should be used with care in diagnostic settings, because they may not take into account other relevant information about the individual test taker that provides context for test results, such as age, gender, education, prior employment, psychosocial situation, health, psychological history, and symptomatology. Similarly, test developers and test users of automatically generated interpretations of academic performance and accompanying prescriptions for instructional follow-up should report the bases and limitations of the interpretations. Test interpretations should not imply that empirical evidence exists for a relationship among particular test results, prescribed interventions, and desired outcomes, unless empirical evidence is available for populations similar to those representative of the test taker.

Standard 6.12

When group-level information is obtained by aggregating the results of partial tests taken by individuals, evidence of validity and reliability/precision should be reported for the level of aggregation at which results are reported. Scores should not be reported for individuals without appropriate evidence to support the interpretations for intended uses.

Comment: Large-scale assessments often achieve efficiency by "matrix sampling" the content domain by asking different test takers different questions.

The testing then requires less time from each test taker, while the aggregation of individual results provides for domain coverage that can be adequate for meaningful group- or program-level interpretations, such as for schools or grade levels within a locality or particular subject areas. However, because the individual is administered only an incomplete test, an individual score would have limited meaning, if any.

Standard 6.13

When a material error is found in test scores or other important information issued by a testing organization or other institution, this information and a corrected score report should be distributed as soon as practicable to all known recipients who might otherwise use the erroneous scores as a basis for decision making. The corrected report should be labeled as such. What was done to correct the reports should be documented. The reason for the corrected score report should be made clear to the recipients of the report.

Comment: A material error is one that could change the interpretation of the test score and make a difference in a significant way. An example is an erroneous test score (e.g., incorrectly computed or fraudulently obtained) that would affect an important decision about the test taker, such as a credentialing decision or the awarding of a high school diploma. Innocuous typographical errors would be excluded. Timeliness is essential for decisions that will be made soon after the test scores are received. Where test results have been used to inform high-stakes decisions, corrective actions by test users may be necessary to rectify circumstances affected by erroneous scores, in addition to issuing corrected reports. The reporting or corrective actions may not be possible or practicable in certain work or other settings. Test users should develop a policy of how to handle material errors in test scores and should document what was done in the case of suspected or actual material errors.

Standard 6.14

Organizations that maintain individually identifiable test score information should develop a clear set of policy guidelines on the duration of retention of an individual's records and on the availability and use over time of such data for research or other purposes. The policy should be documented and available to the test taker. Test users should maintain appropriate data security, which should include administrative, technical, and physical protections.

Comment: In some instances, test scores become obsolete over time, no longer reflecting the current state of the test taker. Outdated scores should generally not be used or made available, except for research purposes. In other cases, test scores obtained in past years can be useful, as in longitudinal assessment or the tracking of deterioration of function or cognition. The key issue is the valid use of the information. Organizations and individuals who maintain individually identifiable test score information should be aware of and comply with legal and professional requirements. Organizations and individuals who maintain test scores on individuals may be requested to provide data to researchers or other third-party users. Where data release is deemed appropriate and is not prohibited by statutes or regulations, the test user should protect the confidentiality of the test takers through appropriate policies, such as de-identifying test data or requiring nondisclosure and confidentiality of the data. Organizations and individuals who maintain or use confidential information about test takers or their scores should have and implement an appropriate policy for maintaining security and integrity of the data, including protecting from accidental or deliberate modification as well as preventing loss or unauthorized destruction. In some cases, organizations may need to obtain test takers' consent to use or disclose records. Adequate security and appropriate protocols should be established when confidential test data are made part of a larger record (e.g., an electronic medical record) or merged into a data warehouse. If records are to be released for clinical and/or forensic evaluations, care should be taken to release them to appropriately licensed individuals, with appropriate signed release authorization by the test taker or appropriate legal authority.

Standard 6.15

When individual test data are retained, both the test protocol and any written report should also be preserved in some form.

Comment: The protocol may be needed to respond to a possible challenge from a test taker or to facilitate interpretation at a subsequent time. The protocol would ordinarily be accompanied by testing materials and test scores. Retention of more detailed records of responses would depend on circumstances and should be covered in a retention policy. Record keeping may be subject to legal and professional requirements. Policy for the release of any test information for other than research purposes is discussed in chapter 9, "The Rights and Responsibilities of Test Users."

Standard 6.16

Transmission of individually identified test scores to authorized individuals or institutions should be done in a manner that protects the confidential nature of the scores and pertinent ancillary information.

Comment: Care is always needed when communicating the scores of identified test takers, regardless of the form of communication. Similar care may be needed to protect the confidentiality of ancillary information, such as personally identifiable information on disability status for students or clinical test scores shared between practitioners. Appropriate caution with respect to confidential information should be exercised in communicating face to face, as well as by telephone, fax, and other forms of written communication. Similarly, transmission of test data through electronic media and transmission and storage on computer networks—including wireless transmission and storage or processing on the Internet—require caution to maintain appropriate confidentiality and security. Data integrity must also be maintained by preventing inappropriate modification of results during such transmissions. Test users are responsible for understanding and adhering to applicable legal obligations in their data management, transmission, use, and retention practices, including collection, handling, storage, and disposition. Test users should set and follow appropriate security policies regarding confidential test data and other assessment information. Release of clinical raw data, tests, or protocols to third parties should follow laws, regulations, and guidelines provided by professional organizations and should take into account the impact of availability of tests in public domains (e.g., court proceedings) and the potential for violation of intellectual property rights.

7. SUPPORTING DOCUMENTATION FOR TESTS

BACKGROUND

This chapter provides general standards for the preparation and publication of test documentation by test developers, publishers, and other providers of tests. Other chapters contain specific standards that should be useful in the preparation of materials to be included in a test's documentation. In addition, test users may have their own documentation requirements. The rights and responsibilities of test users are discussed in chapter 9.

The supporting documents for tests are the primary means by which test developers, publishers, and other providers of tests communicate with test users. These documents are evaluated on the basis of their completeness, accuracy, currency, and clarity and should be available to qualified individuals as appropriate. A test's documentation typically specifies the nature of the test; the use(s) for which it was developed; the processes involved in the test's development; technical information related to scoring, interpretation, and evidence of validity, fairness, and reliability/precision; scaling, norming, and standard-setting information if appropriate to the instrument; and guidelines for test administration, reporting, and interpretation. The objective of the documentation is to provide test users with the information needed to help them assess the nature and quality of the test, the resulting scores, and the interpretations based on the test scores. The information may be reported in documents such as test manuals, technical manuals, user's guides, research reports, specimen sets, examination kits, directions for test administrators and scorers, or preview materials for test takers.

Regardless of who develops a test (e.g., test publisher, certification or licensure board, employer, or educational institution) or how many users exist, the development process should include thorough, timely, and useful documentation. Although proper documentation of the evidence supporting the interpretation of test scores for proposed uses of a test is important, failure to formally document such evidence in advance does not automatically render the corresponding test use or interpretation invalid. For example, consider an unpublished employment selection test developed by a psychologist solely for internal use within a single organization, where there is an immediate need to fill vacancies. The test may properly be put to operational use after needed validity evidence is collected but before formal documentation of the evidence is completed. Similarly, a test used for certification may need to be revised frequently, in which case technical reports describing the test's development as well as information concerning item, exam, and candidate performance should be produced periodically, but not necessarily prior to every exam.

Test documentation is effective if it communicates information to user groups in a manner that is appropriate for the particular audience. To accommodate the breadth of training of those who use tests, separate documents or sections of documents may be written for identifiable categories of users such as practitioners, consultants, administrators, researchers, educators, and sometimes examinees. For example, the test user who administers the tests and interprets the results needs guidelines for doing so. Those who are responsible for selecting tests need to be able to judge the technical adequacy of the tests and therefore need some combination of technical manuals, user's guides, test manuals, test supplements, examination kits, and specimen sets. Ordinarily, these supporting documents are provided to potential test users or test reviewers with sufficient information to enable them to evaluate the appropriateness and technical adequacy of a test. The types of information presented in these documents typically include a description of the intended test-taking population, stated purpose of the test, test specifications, item formats, administration and scoring procedures, test security protocols, cut scores or other standards, and a description of the test development process. Also typically provided are summaries of technical data such as psychometric indices of the items; reliability/precision and validity evidence; normative data; and cut scores or rules for combining scores, including those for computer-generated interpretations of test scores.

An essential feature of the documentation for every test is a discussion of the common appropriate and inappropriate uses and interpretations of the test scores and a summary of the evidence supporting these conclusions. The inclusion of examples of score interpretations consistent with the test developer's intended applications helps users make accurate inferences on the basis of the test scores. When possible, examples of improper test uses and inappropriate test score interpretations can help guard against the misuse of the test or its scores. When feasible, common negative unintended consequences of test use (including missed opportunities) should be described and suggestions given for avoiding such consequences.

Test documents need to include enough information to allow test users and reviewers to determine the appropriateness of the test for its intended uses. Other materials that provide more details about research by the publisher or independent investigators (e.g., the samples on which the research is based and summative data) should be cited and should be readily obtainable by the

test user or reviewer. This supplemental material can be provided in any of a variety of published or unpublished forms and in either paper or electronic formats.

In addition to technical documentation, descriptive materials are needed in some settings to inform examinees and other interested parties about the nature and content of a test. The amount and type of information provided will depend on the particular test and application. For example, in situations requiring informed consent, information should be sufficient for test takers (or their representatives) to make a sound judgment about the test. Such information should be phrased in nontechnical language and should contain information that is consistent with the use of the test scores and is sufficient to help the user make an informed decision. The materials may include a general description and rationale for the test; intended uses of the test results; sample items or complete sample tests; and information about conditions of test administration, confidentiality, and retention of test results. For some applications, however, the true nature and purpose of the test are purposely hidden or disguised to prevent faking or response bias. In these instances, examinees may be motivated to reveal more or less of a characteristic intended to be assessed. Hiding or disguising the true nature or purpose of a test is acceptable provided that the actions involved are consistent with legal principles and ethical standards.

STANDARDS FOR SUPPORTING DOCUMENTATION FOR TESTS

The standards in this chapter begin with an over-arching standard (numbered 7.0), which is designed to convey the central intent or primary focus of the chapter. The overarching standard may also be viewed as the guiding principle of the chapter, and is applicable to all tests and test users. All subsequent standards have been separated into four thematic clusters labeled as follows:

1. Content of Test Documents: Appropriate Use
2. Content of Test Documents: Test Development
3. Content of Test Documents: Test Administration and Scoring
4. Timeliness of Delivery of Test Documents

Standard 7.0

Information relating to tests should be clearly documented so that those who use tests can make informed decisions regarding which test to use for a specific purpose, how to administer the chosen test, and how to interpret test scores.

Comment: Test developers and publishers should provide general information to help test users and researchers determine the appropriateness of an intended test use in a specific context. When test developers and publishers become aware of a particular test use that cannot be justified, they should indicate this fact clearly. General information also should be provided for test takers and legal guardians who must provide consent prior to a test's administration. (See Standard 8.4 regarding informed consent.) Administrators and even the general public may also need general information about the test and its results so that they can correctly interpret the results.

Test documents should be complete, accurate, and clearly written so that the intended audience can readily understand the content. Test documentation should be provided in a format that is accessible to the population for which it is intended. For tests used for educational accountability purposes, documentation should be made publicly available in a format and language that are accessible to potential users, including appropriate school personnel, parents, students from all relevant subgroups of intended test takers, and the members of the community (e.g., via the Internet). Test documentation in educational settings might also include guidance on how users could use test materials and results to improve instruction.

Test documents should provide sufficient detail to permit reviewers and researchers to evaluate important analyses published in the test manual or technical report. For example, reporting correlation matrices in the test document may allow the test user to judge the data on which decisions and conclusions were based. Similarly, describing in detail the sample and the nature of factor analyses that were conducted may allow the test user to replicate reported studies.

Test documentation will also help those who are affected by the score interpretations to decide whether to participate in the testing program or how to participate if participation is not optional.

Cluster 1. Content of Test Documents: Appropriate Use

Standard 7.1

The rationale for a test, recommended uses of the test, support for such uses, and information that assists in score interpretation should be documented. When particular misuses of a test can be reasonably anticipated, cautions against such misuses should be specified.

Comment: Test publishers should make every effort to caution test users against known misuses of tests. However, test publishers cannot anticipate all possible misuses of a test. If publishers do know of persistent test misuse by a test user, additional educational efforts, including providing information regarding potential harm to the individual, organization, or society, may be appropriate.

Standard 7.2

The population for whom a test is intended and specifications for the test should be documented. If normative data are provided, the procedures used to gather the data should be explained; the norming population should be described in terms of relevant demographic variables; and the year(s) in which the data were collected should be reported.

Comment: Known limitations of a test for certain populations should be clearly delineated in the test documents. For example, a test used to assess educational progress may not be appropriate for employee selection in business and industry.

Other documentation can assist the user in identifying the appropriate normative information to use to interpret test scores appropriately. For example, the time of year in which the normative data were collected may be relevant in some educational settings. In organizational settings, information on the context in which normative data were gathered (e.g., in concurrent or predictive studies; for development or selection purposes) may also have implications for which norms are appropriate for operational use.

Standard 7.3

When the information is available and appropriately shared, test documents should cite a representative set of the studies pertaining to general and specific uses of the test.

Comment: If a study cited by the test publisher is not published, summaries should be made available on request to test users and researchers by the publisher.

Cluster 2. Content of Test Documents: Test Development

Standard 7.4

Test documentation should summarize test development procedures, including descriptions and

the results of the statistical analyses that were used in the development of the test, evidence of the reliability/precision of scores and the validity of their recommended interpretations, and the methods for establishing performance cut scores.

Comment: When applicable, test documents should include descriptions of the procedures used to develop items and create the item pool, to create tests or forms of tests, to establish scales for reported scores, and to set standards and rules for cut scores or combining scores. Test documents should also provide information that allows the user to evaluate bias or fairness for all relevant groups of intended test takers when it is meaningful and feasible for such studies to be conducted. In addition, other statistical data should be provided as appropriate, such as item-level information, information on the effects of various cut scores (e.g., number of candidates passing at potential cut scores, level of adverse impact at potential cut scores), information about raw scores and reported scores, normative data, the standard errors of measurement, and a description of the procedures used to equate multiple forms. (See chaps. 3 and 4 for more information on the evaluation of fairness and on procedures and statistics commonly used in test development.)

Standard 7.5

Test documents should record the relevant characteristics of the individuals or groups of individuals who participated in data collection efforts associated with test development or validation (e.g., demographic information, job status, grade level); the nature of the data that were contributed (e.g., predictor data, criterion data); the nature of judgments made by subject matter experts (e.g., content validation linkages); the instructions that were provided to participants in data collection efforts for their specific tasks; and the conditions under which the test data were collected in the validity study.

Comment: Test developers should describe the relevant characteristics of those who participated in various steps of the test development process and what tasks each person or group performed. For example, the participants who set the test cut scores and their relevant expertise should be documented. Depending on the use of the test results, relevant characteristics of the participants may include race/ethnicity, gender, age, employment status, education, disability status, and primary language. Descriptions of the tasks and the specific instructions provided to the participants may help future test users select and subsequently use the test appropriately. Testing conditions, such as the extent of proctoring in the validity study, may have implications for the generalizability of the results and should be documented. Any changes to the standardized testing conditions, such as accommodations or modifications made to the test or test administration, should also be documented. Test developers and users should take care to comply with applicable legal requirements and professional standards relating to privacy and data security when providing the documentation required by this standard.

Standard 7.6

When a test is available in more than one language, the test documentation should provide information on the procedures that were employed to translate and adapt the test. Information should also be provided regarding the reliability/precision and validity evidence for the adapted form when feasible.

Comment: In addition to providing information on translation and adaptation procedures, the test documents should include the demographics of translators and samples of test takers used in the adaptation process, as well as information on any score interpretation issues for each language into which the test has been translated and adapted. Evidence of reliability/precision, validity, and comparability of translated and adapted scores should be provided in test documentation when feasible. (See Standard 3.14, in chap. 3, for further discussion of translations.)

Cluster 3. Content of Test Documents: Test Administration and Scoring

Standard 7.7

Test documents should specify user qualifications that are required to administer and score a test, as well as the user qualifications needed to interpret the test scores accurately.

Comment: Statements of user qualifications should specify the training, certification, competencies, and experience needed to allow access to a test or scores obtained with it. When user qualifications are expressed in terms of the knowledge, skills, abilities, and other characteristics required to administer, score, and interpret a test, the test documentation should clearly define the requirements so the user can properly evaluate the competence of administrators.

Standard 7.8

Test documentation should include detailed instructions on how a test is to be administered and scored.

Comment: Regardless of whether a test is to be administered in paper-and-pencil format, computer format, or orally, or whether the test is performance based, instructions for administration should be included in the test documentation. As appropriate, these instructions should include all factors related to test administration, including qualifications, competencies, and training of test administrators; equipment needed; protocols for test administrators; timing instructions; and procedures for implementation of test accommodations. When available, test documentation should also include estimates of the time required to administer the test to clinical, disabled, or other special populations for whom the test is intended to be used, based on data obtained from these groups during the norming of the test. In addition, test users need instructions on how to score a test and what cut scores to use (or whether to use cut scores) in interpreting scores. If the test user does not score the test, instructions should be given on how to have a test scored. Finally, test administration documentation should include instructions for dealing with irregularities in test administration and guidance on how they should be documented.

If a test is designed so that more than one method can be used for administration or for recording responses—such as marking responses in a test booklet, on a separate answer sheet, or via computer—then the manual should clearly document the extent to which scores arising from application of these methods are interchangeable. If the scores are not interchangeable, this fact should be reported, and guidance should be given on the comparability of scores obtained under the various conditions or methods of administration.

Standard 7.9

If test security is critical to the interpretation of test scores, the documentation should explain the steps necessary to protect test materials and to prevent inappropriate exchange of information during the test administration session.

Comment: When the proper interpretation of test scores assumes that the test taker has not been exposed to the test content or received illicit assistance, the instructions should include procedures for ensuring the security of the testing process and of all test materials at all times. Security procedures may include guidance for storing and distributing test materials as well as instructions for maintaining a secure testing process, such as identifying test takers and seating test takers to prevent exchange of information. Test users should be aware that federal and state laws, regulations, and policies may affect security procedures.

In many situations, test scores should also be maintained securely. For example, in promotional testing in some employment settings, only the candidate and the staffing personnel are authorized to see the scores, and the candidate's current supervisor is specifically prohibited from viewing them. Documentation may include information on how test scores are stored and who is authorized to see the scores.

Standard 7.10

Tests that are designed to be scored and interpreted by test takers should be accompanied by scoring instructions and interpretive materials that are written in language the test takers can understand and that assist them in understanding the test scores.

Comment: If a test is designed to be scored by test takers or its scores interpreted by test takers, the publisher and test developer should develop procedures that facilitate accurate scoring and interpretation. Interpretive material may include information such as the construct that was measured, the test taker's results, and the comparison group. The appropriate language for the scoring procedures and interpretive materials is one that meets the particular language needs of the test taker. Thus, the scoring and interpretive materials may need to be offered in the native language of the test taker to be understood.

Standard 7.11

Interpretive materials for tests that include case studies should provide examples illustrating the diversity of prospective test takers.

Comment: When case studies can assist the user in the interpretation of the test scores and profiles, the case studies should be included in the test documentation and represent members of the subgroups for which the test is relevant. To illustrate the diversity of prospective test takers, case studies might cite examples involving women and men of different ages, individuals differing in sexual orientation, persons representing various racial/ethnic or cultural groups, and individuals with disabilities. Test developers may wish to inform users that the inclusion of such examples is intended to illustrate the diversity of prospective test takers and not to promote interpretation of test scores in a manner that conflicts with legal requirements such as race or gender norming in employment contexts.

Standard 7.12

When test scores are used to make predictions about future behavior, the evidence supporting those predictions should be provided to the test user.

Comment: The test user should be informed of any cut scores or rules for combining raw or reported scores that are necessary for understanding score interpretations. A description of both the group of judges used in establishing the cut scores and the methods used to derive the cut scores should be provided. When security or proprietary reasons necessitate the withholding of cut scores or rules for combining scores, the owners of the intellectual property are responsible for documenting evidence in support of the validity of interpretations for intended uses. Such evidence might be provided, for example, by reporting the finding of an independent review of the algorithms by qualified professionals. When any interpretations of test scores, including computer-generated interpretations, are provided, a summary of the evidence supporting the interpretations should be given, as well as the rules and guidelines used in making the interpretations.

Cluster 4. Timeliness of Delivery of Test Documents

Standard 7.13

Supporting documents (e.g., test manuals, technical manuals, user's guides, and supplemental material) should be made available to the appropriate people in a timely manner.

Comment: Supporting documents should be supplied in a timely manner. Some documents (e.g., administration instructions, user's guides, sample tests or items) must be made available prior to the first administration of the test. Other documents (e.g., technical manuals containing information based on data from the first administration) cannot be supplied prior to that administration; however, such documents should be created promptly.

The test developer or publisher should judge carefully which information should be included in first editions of the test manual, technical manual, or user's guide and which information can be provided in supplements. For low-volume, unpublished tests, the documentation may be relatively brief. When the developer is also the user, documentation and summaries are still necessary.

Standard 7.14

When substantial changes are made to a test, the test's documentation should be amended, supplemented, or revised to keep information for users current and to provide useful additional information or cautions.

Comment: Supporting documents should clearly note the date of their publication as well as the name or version of the test for which the documentation is relevant. When substantial changes are made to items and scoring, information on the extent to which the old scores and new scores are interchangeable should be included in the test documentation.

Sometimes it is necessary to change a test or testing procedure to remove construct-irrelevant variance that may arise due to the characteristics of an individual that are unrelated to the construct being measured (e.g., when testing individuals with disabilities). When a test or testing procedures are altered, the documentation for the test should include a discussion of how the alteration may affect the validity and comparability of the test scores, and evidence should be provided to demonstrate the effect of the alteration on the scores obtained from the altered test or testing procedures, if sample size permits.

8. THE RIGHTS AND RESPONSIBILITIES OF TEST TAKERS

BACKGROUND

This chapter addresses issues of fairness from the point of view of the individual test taker. Most aspects of fairness affect the validity of interpretations of test scores for their intended uses. The standards in this chapter address test takers' rights and responsibilities with regard to test security, their access to test results, and their rights when irregularities in their testing process are claimed. Other issues of fairness are addressed in chapter 3 ("Fairness in Testing"). General considerations concerning reports of test results are covered in chapter 6 ("Test Administration, Scoring, Reporting, and Interpretation"). Issues related to test takers' rights and responsibilities in clinical or individual settings are also discussed in chapter 10 ("Psychological Testing and Assessment").

The standards in this chapter are directed to test providers, not to test takers. It is the shared responsibility of the test developer, test administrator, test proctor (if any), and test user to provide test takers with information about their rights and their own responsibilities. The responsibility to inform the test taker should be apportioned according to particular circumstances.

Test takers have the right to be assessed with tests that meet current professional standards, including standards of technical quality, consistent treatment, fairness, conditions for test administration, and reporting of results. The chapters in Part I, "Foundations," and Part II, "Operations," deal specifically with fair and appropriate test design, development, administration, scoring, and reporting. In addition, test takers have a right to basic information about the test and how the test results will be used. In most situations, fair and equitable treatment of test takers involves providing information about the general nature of the test, the intended use of test scores, and the confidentiality of the results in advance of testing. When full disclosure of this information is not appropriate (as is the case with some psychological or em-

ployment tests), the information that is provided should be consistent across test takers. Test takers, or their legal representatives when appropriate, need enough information about the test and the intended use of test results to reach an informed decision about their participation.

In some instances, the laws or standards of professional practice, such as those governing research on human subjects, require formal informed consent for testing. In other instances (e.g., employment testing), informed consent is implied by other actions (e.g., submission of an employment application), and formal consent is not required. The greater the consequences to the test taker, the greater the importance of ensuring that the test taker is fully informed about the test and voluntarily consents to participate, except when testing without consent is permitted by law (e.g., when participating in testing is legally required or mandated by a court order). If a test is optional, the test taker has the right to know the consequences of taking or not taking the test. Under most circumstances, the test taker has the right to ask questions or express concerns and should receive a timely response to legitimate inquiries.

When consistent with the purposes and nature of the assessment, general information is usually provided about the test's content and purposes. Some programs, in the interest of fairness, provide all test takers with helpful materials, such as study guides, sample questions, or complete sample tests, when such information does not jeopardize the validity of the interpretations of results from future test administrations. Practice materials should have the same appearance and format as the actual test. A practice test for a Web-based assessment, for example, should be available via computer. Employee selection programs may legitimately provide more training to certain classes of test takers (e.g., internal applicants) and not to others (e.g., external applicants). For example, an organization may train current employees on skills that are measured on employment tests in the context of an employee development program but not offer that training to external applicants. Advice may also be provided about test-taking strategies, including time management and the advisability of omitting a response to an item (when omitting a response is permitted). Information on various testing policies, for example about making accommodations available and determining for which individuals the accommodations are appropriate, is also provided to the test taker. In addition, communications to test takers should include policies on retesting when major disruptions of the test administration occur, when the test taker feels that the present performance does not appropriately reflect his or her true capabilities, or when the test taker improves on his or her underlying knowledge, skills, abilities, or other personal characteristics.

As participants in the assessment, test takers have responsibilities as well as rights. Their responsibilities include being prepared to take the test, following the directions of the test administrator, representing themselves honestly on the test, and protecting the security of the test materials. Requests for accommodations or modifications are the responsibility of the test taker, or in the case of minors, the test taker's guardian. In group testing situations, test takers should not interfere with the performance of other test takers. In some testing programs, test takers are also expected to inform the appropriate persons in a timely manner if they believe there are reasons that their test results will not reflect their true capabilities.

The validity of score interpretations rests on the assumption that a test taker has earned fairly a particular score or categorical decision, such as "pass" or "fail." Many forms of cheating or other malfeasant behaviors can reduce the validity of the interpretations of test scores and cause harm to other test takers, particularly in competitive situations in which test takers' scores are compared. There are many forms of behavior that affect test scores, such as using prohibited aids or arranging for someone to take the test in the test taker's place. Similarly, there are many forms of behavior that jeopardize the security of test materials, including communicating the specific content of the test to other test takers in advance. The test taker is obligated to respect the copyrights in test materials and may not reproduce the materials without authorization or disseminate in any form material that is similar in nature to the test. Test takers, as well as test administrators, have the responsibility to protect test security by refusing to divulge any details of the test content to others, unless the particular test is designed to be openly available in advance. Failure to honor these responsibilities may compromise the validity of test score interpretations for the test taker and for others. Outside groups that develop items for test preparation should base those items on publicly disclosed information and not on information that has been inappropriately shared by test takers.

Sometimes, testing programs use special scores, statistical indicators, and other indirect information about irregularities in testing to examine whether the test scores have been obtained fairly. Unusual patterns of responses, large changes in test scores upon retesting, response speed, and similar indicators may trigger careful scrutiny of certain testing protocols and test scores. The details of the procedures for detecting problems are generally kept secure to avoid compromising their use. However, test takers should be informed that in special circumstances, such as response or test score anomalies, their test responses may receive special scrutiny. Test takers should be informed that their score may be canceled or other action taken if evidence of impropriety or fraud is discovered.

STANDARDS FOR TEST TAKERS' RIGHTS AND RESPONSIBILITIES

The standards in this chapter begin with an overarching standard (numbered 8.0), which is designed to convey the central intent or primary focus of the chapter. The overarching standard may also be viewed as the guiding principle of the chapter, and is applicable to all tests and test users. All subsequent standards have been separated into four thematic clusters labeled as follows:

1. Test Takers' Rights to Information Prior to Testing
2. Test Takers' Rights to Access Their Test Results and to Be Protected From Unauthorized Use of Test Results
3. Test Takers' Rights to Fair and Accurate Score Reports
4. Test Takers' Responsibilities for Behavior Throughout the Test Administration Process

Standard 8.0

Test takers have the right to adequate information to help them properly prepare for a test so that the test results accurately reflect their standing on the construct being assessed and lead to fair and accurate score interpretations. They also have the right to protection of their personally identifiable score results from unauthorized access, use, or disclosure. Further, test takers have the responsibility to represent themselves accurately in the testing process and to respect copyright in test materials.

Comment: Specific standards for test takers' rights and responsibilities are described below. These include standards for the kinds of information that should be provided to test takers prior to testing so they can properly prepare to take the test and so that their results accurately reflect their standing on the construct being assessed. Standards also cover test takers' access to their test results; protection of the results from unauthorized access, use, or disclosure by others; and test takers' rights to fair and accurate score reports. In addition, standards

in this chapter address the responsibility of test takers to represent themselves fairly and accurately during the testing process and to respect the confidentiality of copyright in all test materials.

Cluster 1. Test Takers' Rights to Information Prior to Testing

Standard 8.1

Information about test content and purposes that is available to any test taker prior to testing should be available to all test takers. Shared information should be available free of charge and in accessible formats.

Comment: The intent of this standard is equitable treatment for all test takers with respect to access to basic information about a testing event, such as when and where the test will be given, what materials should be brought, what the purpose of the test is, and how the results will be used. When applicable, such offerings should be made to all test takers and, to the degree possible, should be in formats accessible to all test takers. Accessibility of formats also applies to information that may be provided on a public website. For example, depending on the format of the information, conversions can be made so that individuals with visual disabilities can access textual or graphical material. For test takers with disabilities, providing these materials in accessible formats may be required by law.

It merits noting that while general information about test content and purpose should be made available to all test takers, some organizations may supplement this information with additional training or coaching. For example, some employers may teach basic skills to workers to help them qualify for higher level positions. Similarly, one teacher in a school may choose to drill students on a topic that will be tested while other teachers focus on other topics.

Standard 8.2

Test takers should be provided in advance with as much information about the test, the testing process, the intended test use, test scoring criteria, testing policy, availability of accommodations, and confidentiality protection as is consistent with obtaining valid responses and making appropriate interpretations of test scores.

Comment: When appropriate, test takers should be informed in advance about test content, including subject area, topics covered, and item formats. General advice should be given about test-taking strategies. For example, test takers should usually be informed about the advisability of omitting responses and made aware of any imposed time limits, so that they can manage their time appropriately. For computer administrations, test takers should be shown samples of the interface they will be expected to use during the test and be provided an opportunity to practice with those tools and master their use before the test begins. In addition, they should be told about possibilities for revisiting items they have previously answered or omitted.

In most testing situations, test takers should be informed about the intended use of test scores and the extent of the confidentiality of test results, and should be told whether and when they will have access to their results. Exceptions occur when knowledge of the purposes or intended score uses would violate the integrity of the interpretations of the scores, such as when the test is intended to detect malingering. If a record of the testing session is kept in written, video, audio, or any other form, or if other records associated with the testing event, such as scoring information, are kept, test takers are entitled to know what testing information will be released and to whom and for what purposes the results will be used. In some cases, legal standards apply to information about the use and confidentiality of, and test-taker access to, test scores. Policies concerning retesting should also be communicated. Test takers should be warned against improper behavior and made cognizant of the consequences of misconduct, such

as cheating, that could result in their being prohibited from completing the test or receiving test scores, or could make them subject to other sanctions. Test takers should be informed, at least in a general way, if there will be special scrutiny of testing protocols or score patterns to detect breaches of security, cheating, or other improper behavior.

Standard 8.3

When the test taker is offered a choice of test format, information about the characteristics of each format should be provided.

Comment: Test takers sometimes may choose between paper-and-pencil administration of a test and computer administration. Some tests are offered in different languages. Sometimes, an alternative assessment is offered. Test takers need to know the characteristics of each alternative that is available to them so that they can make an informed choice.

Standard 8.4

Informed consent should be obtained from test takers, or from their legal representatives when appropriate, before testing begins, except (a) when testing without consent is mandated by law or governmental regulation, (b) when testing is conducted as a regular part of school activities, or (c) when consent is clearly implied, such as in employment settings. Informed consent may be required by applicable law and professional standards.

Comment: Informed consent implies that the test takers or their representatives are made aware, in language that they can understand, of the reasons for testing, the types of tests to be used, the intended uses of test takers' test results or other information, and the range of material consequences of the intended use. It is generally recommended that persons be asked directly to give their formal consent rather than being asked only to indicate if they are withholding their consent.

Consent is not required when testing is legally mandated, as in the case of a court-ordered psychological assessment, although there may be legal requirements for providing information about the testing session outcomes to the test taker. Nor is consent typically required in educational settings for tests administered to all pupils. When testing is required for employment, credentialing, or educational admissions, applicants, by applying, have implicitly given consent to the testing. When feasible, the person explaining the reason for a test should be experienced in communicating with individuals within the intended population for the test (e.g., individuals with disabilities or from different linguistic backgrounds).

Cluster 2. Test Takers' Rights to Access Their Test Results and to Be Protected From Unauthorized Use of Test Results

Standard 8.5

Policies for the release of test scores with identifying information should be carefully considered and clearly communicated to those who have access to the scores. Policies should make sure that test results containing the names of individual test takers or other personal identifying information are released only to those who have a legitimate, professional interest in the test takers and are permitted to access such information under applicable privacy laws, who are covered by the test takers' informed consent documents, or who are otherwise permitted by law to access the results.

Comment: Test results of individuals identified by name, or by some other information by means of which a person can be readily identified, or readily identified when the information is combined with other information, should be kept confidential. In some situations, information may be provided on a confidential basis to other practitioners with a legitimate interest in the particular case, consistent with legal and ethical

considerations, including, as applicable, privacy laws. Information may be provided to researchers if several conditions are all met: (a) each test taker's confidentiality is maintained, (b) the intended use is consistent with accepted research practice, (c) the use is in compliance with current legal and institutional requirements for subjects' rights and with applicable privacy laws, and (d) the use is consistent with the test taker's informed consent documents that are on file or with the conditions of implied consent that are appropriate in some settings.

Standard 8.6

Test data maintained or transmitted in data files, including all personally identifiable information (not just results), should be adequately protected from improper access, use, or disclosure, including by reasonable physical, technical, and administrative protections as appropriate to the particular data set and its risks, and in compliance with applicable legal requirements. Use of facsimile transmission, computer networks, data banks, or other electronic data-processing or transmittal systems should be restricted to situations in which confidentiality can be reasonably assured. Users should develop and/or follow policies, consistent with any legal requirements, for whether and how test takers may review and correct personal information.

Comment: Risk of compromise is reduced by avoiding identification numbers or codes that are linked to individuals and used for other purposes (e.g., Social Security numbers or employee IDs). If facsimile or computer communication is used to transmit test responses to another site for scoring or if scores are similarly transmitted, reasonable provisions should be made to keep the information confidential, such as encrypting the information. In some circumstances, applicable data security laws may require that specific measures be taken to protect the data. In most cases, these policies will be developed by the owner of the data.

Cluster 3. Test Takers' Rights to Fair and Accurate Score Reports

Standard 8.7

When score reporting assigns scores of individual test takers into categories, the labels assigned to the categories should be chosen to reflect intended inferences and should be described precisely.

Comment: When labels are associated with test results, care should be taken to avoid labels with unnecessarily stigmatizing implications. For example, descriptive labels such as "basic," "proficient," and "advanced" would carry less stigmatizing interpretations than terms such as "poor" or "unsatisfactory." In addition, information should be provided regarding the accuracy of score classifications (e.g., decision accuracy and decision consistency).

Standard 8.8

When test scores are used to make decisions about a test taker or to make recommendations to a test taker or a third party, the test taker should have timely access to a copy of any report of test scores and test interpretation, unless that right has been waived explicitly in the test taker's informed consent document or implicitly through the application procedure in education, credentialing, or employment testing or is prohibited by law or court order.

Comment: In some cases, a test taker may be adequately informed when the test report is given to an appropriate third party (e.g., treating psychologist or psychiatrist) who can interpret the findings for the test taker. When the test taker is given a copy of the test report and there is a credible reason to believe that test scores might be incorrectly interpreted, the examiner or a knowledgeable third party should be available to interpret them, even if the score report is clearly written, as the test taker may misunderstand or raise questions not specifically answered in the report. In employment testing situations, when test results are used solely for the purpose of aiding selection decisions, waivers of access are often a condition of employment applications, although access to test information may often be appropriately required in other circumstances.

Cluster 4. Test Takers' Responsibilities for Behavior Throughout the Test Administration Process

Standard 8.9

Test takers should be made aware that having someone else take the test for them, disclosing confidential test material, or engaging in any other form of cheating is unacceptable and that such behavior may result in sanctions.

Comment: Although the *Standards* cannot regulate test takers' behavior, test takers should be made aware of their personal and legal responsibilities. Arranging for someone else to impersonate the test taker constitutes fraud. In tests designed to measure a test taker's independent thinking, providing responses that make use of the work of others without attribution or that were prepared by someone other than the test taker constitutes plagiarism. Disclosure of confidential testing material for the purpose of giving other test takers advance knowledge interferes with the validity of test score interpretations; and circulation of test items in print or electronic form may constitute copyright infringement. In licensure and certification tests, such actions may compromise public health and safety. In general, the validity of test score interpretations is compromised by inappropriate test disclosure.

Standard 8.10

In educational and credentialing testing programs, when an individual score report is expected to be significantly delayed beyond a brief investigative period because of possible irregularities such as suspected misconduct, the test taker should be notified and given the reason for the investigation.

Reasonable efforts should be made to expedite the review and to protect the interests of the test taker. The test taker should be notified of the disposition when the investigation is closed.

Standard 8.11

In educational and credentialing testing programs, when it is deemed necessary to cancel or withhold a test taker's score because of possible testing irregularities, including suspected misconduct, the type of evidence and the general procedures to be used to investigate the irregularity should be explained to all test takers whose scores are directly affected by the decision. Test takers should be given a timely opportunity to provide evidence that the score should not be canceled or withheld. Evidence considered in deciding on the final action should be made available to the test taker on request.

Comment: Any form of cheating or behavior that reduces the validity and fairness of the interpretations of test results should be investigated promptly, with appropriate action taken. A test score may be withheld or canceled because of suspected misconduct by the test taker or because of some anomaly involving others, such as theft or administrative mishap. An avenue of appeal should be available and made known to candidates whose scores may be amended or withheld. Some testing organizations offer the option of a prompt and free retest or arbitration of disputes. The information provided to the test takers should be specific enough for them to understand the evidence that is being used to support the contention of a testing irregularity but not specific enough to divulge trade secrets or to facilitate cheating.

Standard 8.12

In educational and credentialing testing programs, a test taker is entitled to fair treatment and a reasonable resolution process, appropriate to the particular circumstances, regarding charges associated with testing irregularities, or challenges issued by the test taker regarding accuracies of the scoring or scoring key. Test takers are entitled to be informed of any available means of recourse.

Comment: When a test taker's score is questioned and invalidated, or when a test taker seeks a review or revision of his or her score or of some other aspect of the testing, scoring, or reporting process, the test taker is entitled to some orderly process for effective input into or review of the decision making of the test administrator or test user. Depending on the magnitude of the consequences associated with the test, this process can range from an internal review of all relevant data by a test administrator, to an informal conversation with an examinee, to a full administrative hearing. The greater the consequences, the greater the extent of procedural protections that should be made available. Test takers should also be made aware of procedures for recourse, possible fees associated with recourse procedures, expected time for resolution, and any other significant related issues, including consequences for the test taker. Some testing programs advise that the test taker may be represented by an attorney, although possibly at the test taker's expense. Depending on the circumstances and context, principles of due process under law may be relevant to the process afforded to test takers.

9. THE RIGHTS AND RESPONSIBILITIES OF TEST USERS

BACKGROUND

The previous chapters have dealt primarily with the responsibilities of those who develop, promote, evaluate, or mandate the administration of tests and with the rights and responsibilities of test takers. The present chapter centers attention on the responsibilities of those who may be considered the users of tests. Test users are professionals who select the specific instruments or supervise test administration—on their own authority or at the behest of others—as well as all other professionals who actively participate in the interpretation and use of test results. They include psychologists, educators, employers, test developers, test publishers, and other professionals. Given the reliance on test results in many settings, pressure has typically been placed on test users to explain test-based decisions and testing practices; in many circumstances, test users have legal obligations to document the validity and fairness of those decisions and practices. The standards in this chapter provide guidance with regard to test administration procedures and decision making in which tests play a part. Thus, the present chapter includes standards of a general nature that apply in almost all testing contexts.

These *Standards* presume that a legitimate educational, psychological, credentialing, or employment purpose justifies the time and expense of test administration. In most settings, the user communicates this purpose to those who have a legitimate interest in the measurement process and subsequently conveys the implications of examinee performance to those entitled to receive the information. Depending on the measurement setting, this group may include individual test takers, parents and guardians, educators, employers, policy makers, the courts, or the general public.

Validity and reliability are critical considerations in test selection and use, and test users should consider evidence of (a) the validity of the interpretation for intended uses of the scores, (b) the reliability/precision of the scores, (c) the applicability of the normative data available in the test manual, and (d) the potential positive and negative consequences of use. The accumulated research literature should also be considered, as well as, where appropriate, demographic characteristics (e.g., race/ethnicity; gender; age; income; socioeconomic, cultural, and linguistic background; education; and other socioeconomic variables) of the group for which the test was originally constructed and for which normative data are available. Test users can also consult with measurement professionals. The name of the test alone never provides adequate information for deciding whether to select it.

In some cases, the selection of tests and inventories is individualized for a particular client. In other settings, a predetermined battery of tests is taken by all participants. In both cases, test users should be well versed in proper administrative procedures and are responsible for understanding the validity and reliability evidence and articulating that evidence if the need arises. Test users who oversee testing and assessment are responsible for ensuring that the test administrators who administer and score tests have received the appropriate education and training needed to perform these tasks. A higher level of competence is required of the test user who interprets the scores and integrates the inferences derived from the scores and other relevant information.

Test scores ideally are interpreted in light of the available data, the psychometric properties of the scores, indicators of effort, and the effects of moderator variables and demographic characteristics on test results. Because items or tasks contained in a test that was designed for a particular group may introduce construct-irrelevant variance when used with other groups, selecting a test with demographically appropriate reference groups is important to the generalizability of the inference that the test user seeks to make. When a test developed and normed for one group is applied to other groups, score interpretations should be qualified and presented as hypotheses rather than conclusions. Further, statistical analyses conducted on only one group should be evaluated for appropriateness when generalized to other examinee populations. The test user should rely on any available extant research evidence for the test to draw appropriate inferences and should be aware of requirements restricting certain practices (e.g., norming by race or gender in certain contexts).

Moreover, where applicable, an interpretation of test takers' scores needs to consider not only the demonstrated relationship between the scores and the criteria, but also the appropriateness of the latter. The criteria need to be subjected to an examination similar to the examination of the predictors if one is to understand the degree to which the underlying constructs are congruent with the inferences under consideration. It is important that data which are not supportive of the inferences should be acknowledged and either reconciled or noted as limits to the confidence that can be placed in the inferences. The education and experience necessary to interpret group tests are generally less stringent than the qualifications necessary to interpret individually administered tests.

Test users should follow the standardized test administration procedures outlined by the test developers. Computer administration of tests should also follow standardized procedures, and sufficient oversight should be provided to ensure the integrity of test results. When nonstandard procedures are needed, they should be described and justified. Test users are also responsible for providing appropriate testing conditions. For example, the test user may need to determine whether a test taker is capable of reading at the level required and whether a test taker with vision, hearing, or neurological disabilities is adequately accommodated. Chapter 3 ("Fairness in Testing") addresses equal access considerations and standards in detail.

Where administration of tests or use of test data is mandated for a specific population by governmental authorities, educational institutions, licensing boards, or employers, the developer and user of an instrument may be essentially the same.

In such settings, there is often no clear separation in terms of professional responsibilities between those who develop the instrument and those who administer it and interpret the results. Instruments produced by independent publishers, on the other hand, present a somewhat different picture. Typically, these will be used by different test users with a variety of populations and for diverse purposes.

The conscientious developer of a standardized test attempts to control who has access to the test and to educate potential users. Furthermore, most publishers and test sponsors work to prevent the misuse of standardized measures and the misinterpretation of individual scores and group averages. Test manuals often illustrate sound and unsound interpretations and applications. Some identify specific practices that are not appropriate and should be discouraged. Despite the best efforts of test developers, however, appropriate test use and sound interpretation of test scores are likely to remain primarily the responsibility of the test user.

Test takers, parents and guardians, legislators, policy makers, the media, the courts, and the public at large often prefer unambiguous interpretations of test data. In particular, they often tend to attribute positive or negative results, including group differences, to a single factor or to the conditions that prevail in one social institution—most often, the home or the school. These consumers of test data frequently press for score-based rationales for decisions that are based only in part on test scores. The wise test user helps all interested parties understand that sound decisions regarding test use and score interpretation involve an element of professional judgment. It is not always obvious to the consumers that the choice of various information-gathering procedures involves experience that is not easily quantified or verbalized. The user can help consumers appreciate the fact that the weighting of quantitative data, educational and occupational information, behavioral observations, anecdotal reports, and other relevant data often cannot be specified precisely. Nonetheless, test users should provide reports and interpretations of test data that are clear and understandable.

Because test results are frequently reported as numbers, they often appear to be precise, and test data are sometimes allowed to override other sources of evidence about test takers. There are circumstances in which selection based exclusively on test scores may be appropriate (e.g., in pre-employment screening). However, in educational, psychological, forensic, and some employment settings, test users are well advised, and may be legally required, to consider other relevant sources of information on test takers, not just test scores. In such situations, psychologists, educators, or other professionals familiar with the local setting and with local test takers are often best qualified to integrate this diverse information effectively.

It is not appropriate for these standards to dictate minimal levels of test-criterion correlation, classification accuracy, or reliability/precision for any given purpose. Such levels depend on factors such as the nature of the measured construct, the age of the tested individuals, and whether decisions must be made immediately on the strength of the best available evidence, however weak, or whether they can be delayed until better evidence becomes available. But it is appropriate to expect the user to ascertain what the alternatives are, what the quality and consequences of these alternatives are, and whether a delay in decision making would be beneficial. Cost-benefit compromises become necessary in test use, as they often are in test development. However, in some contexts, legal requirements may place limits on the extent to which such compromises can be made. As with standards for the various phases of test development, when relevant standards are not met in test use, the reasons should be persuasive. The greater the potential impact on test takers, for good or ill, the greater the need to identify and satisfy the relevant standards.

In selecting a test and interpreting a test score, the test user is expected to have a clear understanding of the purposes of the testing and its probable consequences. The knowledgeable user has definite ideas on how to achieve these purposes and how to avoid unfairness and undesirable consequences. In subscribing to the *Standards,* test publishers

and agencies mandating test use agree to provide information on the strengths and weaknesses of their instruments. They accept the responsibility to warn against likely misinterpretations by unsophisticated interpreters of individual scores or aggregated data. However, the ultimate responsibility for appropriate test use and interpretation lies predominantly with the test user. In assuming this responsibility, the user must become knowledgeable about a test's appropriate uses and the populations for which it is suitable. The test user should be prepared to develop a logical analysis that supports the various facets of the assessment and the inferences made from the assessment results. Test users in all settings (e.g., clinical, counseling, credentialing, educational, employment, forensic, psychological) must also become adept in communicating the implications of test results to those entitled to receive them.

In some instances, users may be obligated to collect additional evidence about a test's technical quality. For example, if performance assessments are locally scored, evidence of the degree of interscorer agreement may be required. Users should also be alert to the probable local consequences of test use, particularly in the case of large-scale testing programs. If the same test material is used in successive years, users should actively monitor the program to determine if reuse has compromised the integrity of the results.

Some of the standards that follow reiterate ideas contained in other chapters, principally chapter 3 ("Fairness in Testing"), chapter 6 ("Test Administration, Scoring, Reporting, and Interpretation"), chapter 8 ("The Rights and Responsibilities of Test Takers"), chapter 10 ("Psychological Testing and Assessment"), chapter 11 ("Workplace Testing and Credentialing"), and chapter 12 ("Educational Testing and Assessment"). This repetition is intentional. It permits an enumeration in one chapter of the major obligations that must be assumed largely by the test administrator and user, although these responsibilities may refer to topics that are covered more fully in other chapters.

STANDARDS FOR TEST USERS' RIGHTS AND RESPONSIBILITIES

The standards in this chapter begin with an over-arching standard (numbered 9.0), which is designed to convey the central intent or primary focus of the chapter. The overarching standard may also be viewed as the guiding principle of the chapter, and is applicable to all tests and test users. All subsequent standards have been separated into three thematic clusters labeled as follows:

1. Validity of Interpretations
2. Dissemination of Information
3. Test Security and Protection of Copyrights

Standard 9.0

Test users are responsible for knowing the validity evidence in support of the intended interpretations of scores on tests that they use, from test selection through the use of scores, as well as common positive and negative consequences of test use. Test users also have a legal and ethical responsibility to protect the security of test content and the privacy of test takers and should provide pertinent and timely information to test takers and other test users with whom they share test scores.

Comment: Test users are professionals who fall into several categories, including those who administer tests and those who interpret and use the results of tests. Test users who interpret and use the results of tests are responsible for ascertaining that there is appropriate validity evidence supporting their interpretations and uses of test results. In some circumstances, test users are also legally responsible for ascertaining the effect of their testing practices on relevant subgroups and for considering appropriate measures if negative consequences exist. In addition, although test users are often required to share the results of tests with test takers and other groups of test users, they must also remember that test content has to be protected to maintain the integrity of test scores, and that test takers have reasonable expectations of privacy, which may be specified in certain federal or state laws and regulations.

Cluster 1. Validity of Interpretations

Standard 9.1

Responsibility for test use should be assumed by or delegated to only those individuals who have the training, professional credentials, and/or experience necessary to handle this responsibility. All special qualifications for test administration or interpretation specified in the test manual should be met.

Comment: Test users should only interpret the scores of test takers whose special needs or characteristics are within the range of the test users' qualifications. This standard has special significance in areas such as clinical testing, forensic testing, personality testing, testing in special education, testing of people with disabilities or limited exposure to the dominant culture, testing of English language learners, and in other such situations where the potential impact is great. When the situation or test-taker group falls outside the user's experience, assistance should be obtained. A number of professional organizations have codes of ethics that specify the qualifications required of those who administer tests and interpret scores within the organizations' scope of practice. Ultimately, the professional is responsible for ensuring that the clinical training requirements, ethical codes, and legal standards for administering and interpreting tests are met.

Standard 9.2

Prior to the adoption and use of a published test, the test user should study and evaluate the materials provided by the test developer. Of particular importance are materials that summarize the test's purposes, specify the procedures for test administration, define the intended population(s) of test takers, and discuss the score interpretations for which validity and reliability/precision data are available.

Comment: A prerequisite to sound test use is knowledge of the materials accompanying the instrument. At a minimum, these include manuals provided by the test developer. Ideally, the user should be conversant with relevant studies reported in the professional literature, and should be able to discriminate between appropriate and inappropriate tests for the intended use with the intended population. The level of score reliability/precision and the types of validity evidence required for sound score interpretations depend on the test's role in the assessment process and the potential impact of the process on the people involved. The test user should be aware of legal restrictions that may constrain the use of the test. On occasion, professional judgment may lead to the use of instruments for which there is little evidence of validity of the score interpretations for the chosen use. In these situations, the user should not imply that the scores, decisions, or inferences are based on well-documented evidence with respect to reliability or validity.

Standard 9.3

The test user should have a clear rationale for the intended uses of a test or evaluation procedure in terms of the validity of interpretations based on the scores and the contribution the scores make to the assessment and decision-making process.

Comment: The test user should be clear about the reasons that a test is being given. In other words, justification for the role of each instrument in selection, diagnosis, classification, and decision making should be arrived at before test administration, not afterwards. In some cases, the reasons for the referrals provide the rationale for the choice of the tests, inventories, and diagnostic procedures to be used, and the rationale may also be supported in printed materials prepared by the test publisher. The rationale may come from other sources as well, such as the empirical literature.

Standard 9.4

When a test is to be used for a purpose for which little or no validity evidence is available, the user is responsible for documenting the rationale for the selection of the test and obtaining evidence of the reliability/precision of the test scores and the validity of the interpretations supporting the use of the scores for this purpose.

Comment: The individual who uses test scores for purposes that are not specifically recommended by the test developer is responsible for collecting the necessary validity evidence. Support for such uses may sometimes be found in the professional literature. If previous evidence is not sufficient, then additional data should be collected over time as the test is being used. The provisions of this standard should not be construed as prohibiting the generation of hypotheses from test data. However, these hypotheses should be clearly labeled as tentative. Interested parties should be made aware of the potential limitations of the test scores in such situations.

Standard 9.5

Test users should be alert to the possibility of scoring errors and should take appropriate action when errors are suspected.

Comment: The costs of scoring errors are great, particularly in high-stakes testing programs. In some cases, rescoring may be requested by the test taker. If such a test-taker right is recognized in published materials, it should be respected. However, test users should not depend entirely on test takers to alert them to the possibility of scoring errors. Monitoring scoring accuracy should be a routine responsibility of testing program administrators wherever feasible, and rescoring should be done when mistakes are suspected.

Standard 9.6

Test users should be alert to potential misinterpretations of test scores; they should take steps

143

to minimize or avoid foreseeable misinterpretations and inappropriate uses of test scores.

Comment: Untrained audiences may adopt simplistic interpretations of test results or may attribute high or low scores or averages to a single causal factor. Test users can sometimes anticipate such misinterpretations and should try to prevent them. Obviously, not every unintended interpretation can be anticipated, and unforeseen negative consequences can occur. What is required is a reasonable effort to encourage sound interpretations and uses and to address any negative consequences that occur.

Standard 9.7

Test users should verify periodically that their interpretations of test data continue to be appropriate, given any significant changes in the population of test takers, the mode(s) of test administration, or the purposes in testing.

Comment: Over time, a gradual change in the characteristics of an examinee population may significantly affect the accuracy of inferences drawn from group averages. Modifications in test administration in response to unforeseen circumstances also may affect interpretations.

Standard 9.8

When test results are released to the public or to policy makers, those responsible for the release should provide and explain any supplemental information that will minimize possible misinterpretations of the data.

Comment: Test users have a responsibility to report results in ways that facilitate the intended interpretations for the proposed use(s) of the scores, and this responsibility extends beyond the individual test taker to any individuals or groups who are provided with test scores. Test users in group testing situations are responsible for ensuring that the individuals who use the test results are trained to interpret the scores properly. Preliminary briefings prior to the release of test results can give reporters, policy makers, or members of the public an opportunity to assimilate relevant data. Misinterpretation often can be the result of inadequate presentation of information that bears on test score interpretation.

Standard 9.9

When a test user contemplates an alteration in test format, mode of administration, instructions, or the language used in administering a test, the user should have a sound rationale and empirical evidence, when possible, for concluding that the reliability/precision of scores and the validity of interpretations based on the scores will not be compromised.

Comment: In some instances, minor changes in format or mode of administration may be reasonably expected, without evidence, to have little or no effect on test scores, classification decisions, and/or appropriateness of norms. In other instances, however, changes in the format or administrative procedures could have significant effects on the validity of interpretations of the scores—that is, these changes modify or change the construct being assessed. If a given modification becomes widespread, evidence for validity should be gathered; if appropriate, norms should also be developed under the modified conditions.

Standard 9.10

Test users should not rely solely on computer-generated interpretations of test results.

Comment: The user of automatically generated scoring and reporting services has the obligation to be familiar with the principles on which such interpretations were derived. All users who are making inferences and decisions on the basis of these reports should have the ability to evaluate a computer-based score interpretation in the light of other relevant evidence on each test taker. Automated narrative reports can be misleading, if used in isolation, and are not a substitute for sound professional judgment.

Standard 9.11

When circumstances require that a test be administered in the same language to all examinees in a linguistically diverse population, the test user should investigate the validity of the score interpretations for test takers with limited proficiency in the language of the test.

Comment: The achievement, abilities, and traits of examinees who do not speak the language of the test as their primary language may be mismeasured by the test, even if administering an alternative test is legally unacceptable. Sound practice requires ongoing evaluation of data to provide evidence supporting the use of the test with all linguistic groups or evidence to challenge the use of the test when language proficiency is not relevant.

Standard 9.12

When a major purpose of testing is to describe the status of a local, regional, or particular examinee population, the criteria for inclusion or exclusion of individuals should be adhered to strictly.

Comment: Biased results can arise from the exclusion of particular subgroups of examinees. Thus, decisions to exclude or include examinees should be based on appropriately representing the population.

Standard 9.13

In educational, clinical, and counseling settings, a test taker's score should not be interpreted in isolation; other relevant information that may lead to alternative explanations for the examinee's test performance should be considered.

Comment: It is neither necessary nor feasible to make an intensive review of every test taker's score. In some settings, there may be little or no collateral information of value. In counseling, clinical, and educational settings, however, con-

siderable relevant information is sometimes available. Obvious alternative explanations of low scores include low motivation, limited fluency in the language of the test, limited opportunity to learn, unfamiliarity with cultural concepts on which test items are based, and perceptual or motor impairments. The test user corroborates results from testing with additional information from a variety of sources, such as interviews and results from other tests (e.g., to address the concept of reliability of performance across time and/or tests). When an inference is based on a single study or based on studies with samples that are not representative of the test takers, the test user should be more cautious about the inference that is made. In clinical and counseling settings, the test user should not ignore how well the test taker is functioning in daily life. If tests are being administered by computers and other electronic devices or via the Internet, test users still have a responsibility to provide support for the interpretation of test scores, including considerations of alternative explanations, when appropriate.

Standard 9.14

Test users should inform individuals who may need accommodations in test administration (e.g., older adults, test takers with disabilities, or English language learners) about the availability of accommodations and, when required, should see that these accommodations are appropriately made available.

Comment: Appropriate accommodations depend on the nature of the test and the needs of the test takers, and should be in keeping with the documentation provided with the test. Test users should inform test takers of the availability of accommodations, and the onus may then fall on the test takers or their guardians to request accommodations and provide documentation in support of their requests. Test users should be able to indicate the information or evidence (e.g., test manual, research study) used to choose an appropriate accommodation.

Cluster 2. Dissemination of Information

Standard 9.15

Those who have a legitimate interest in an assessment should be informed about the purposes of testing, how tests will be administered, the factors considered in scoring examinee responses, how the scores will be used, how long the records will be retained, and to whom and under what conditions the records may be released.

Comment: Individuals with a legitimate interest in assessment results include, but may not be limited to, test takers, parents or guardians of test takers, educators, and courts. This standard has greater relevance and application to educational and clinical testing than to employment testing. In most uses of tests for screening job applicants and applicants to educational programs, for licensing professionals and awarding credentials, or for measuring achievement, the purposes of testing and the uses to be made of the test scores are obvious to the test takers. Nevertheless, it is wise to communicate this information at least briefly even in these settings. In some situations, however, the rationale for the testing may be clear to relatively few test takers. In such settings, a more detailed and explicit discussion may be warranted. Retention of records, security requirements, and privacy of records are often governed by legal requirements or institutional practices, even in situations where release of records would clearly benefit the examinees. Prior to testing, where appropriate, the test user should tell the test taker who will have access to the test results and the written report, how the test results will be shared with the test taker, and whether and under what conditions the test results will be shared with a third party or the public (e.g., in court proceedings).

Standard 9.16

Unless circumstances clearly require that test results be withheld, a test user is obligated to provide a timely report of the results to the test taker and others entitled to receive this information.

Comment: The nature of score reports is often dictated by practical considerations. In some cases (e.g., with some certification or employment tests), only a brief printed report may be feasible. In other cases, it may be desirable to provide both an oral and a written report. The interpretation should vary according to the level of sophistication of the recipient. When the examinee is a young child, an explanation of the test results is typically provided to parents or guardians. Feedback in the form of a score report or interpretation is not always provided when tests are administered for personnel selection or promotion, or in certain other circumstances. In some cases, federal or state privacy laws may govern the scope of information disclosed and to whom it may be disclosed.

Standard 9.17

If a test taker or test user is concerned about the integrity of the test taker's scores, the test user should inform the test taker of his or her relevant rights, including the possibility of appeal and representation by counsel.

Comment: Proctors in entrance or licensure testing programs may report irregularities in the test administration process that result in challenges from test takers (e.g., fire alarm in building or temporary failure of Internet access). Other challenges may be raised by test users (e.g., university admissions officers) when test scores are grossly inconsistent with other applicant information. Test takers should be apprised of their rights, if any, in such situations.

Standard 9.18

Test users should explain to test takers their opportunities, if any, to retake an examination; users should also indicate whether any earlier as well as later scores will be reported to those entitled to receive the score reports.

Comment: Some testing programs permit test takers to retake an examination several times, to cancel scores, or to have scores withheld from potential recipients. Test takers and other score recipients should be informed of such privileges, if any, and the conditions under which they apply.

Standard 9.19

Test users are obligated to protect the privacy of examinees and institutions that are involved in a testing program, unless a disclosure of private information is agreed upon or is specifically authorized by law.

Comment: Protection of the privacy of individual examinees is a well-established principle in psychological and educational measurement. Storage and transmission of this type of information should meet existing professional and legal standards, and care should be taken to protect the confidentiality of scores and ancillary information (e.g., disability status). In certain circumstances, test users and testing agencies may adopt more stringent restrictions on the communication and sharing of test results than relevant law dictates. Privacy laws may apply to certain types of information, and similar or more rigorous standards sometimes arise through the codes of ethics adopted by relevant professional organizations. In some testing programs the conditions for disclosure are stated to the examinee prior to testing, and taking the test can constitute agreement to the disclosure of test score information as specified. In other programs, the test taker or his or her parents or guardians must formally agree to any disclosure of test information to individuals or agencies other than those specified in the test administrator's published literature. Applicable privacy laws, if any, may govern and allow (as in the case of school districts for accountability purposes) or prohibit (as in clinical settings) the disclosure of test information. It should be noted that the right of the public and the media to examine the aggregate test results of public school systems is often guaranteed by law. This may often include test scores disaggregated by demographic subgroups when the numbers are sufficient to yield statistically sound results and to prevent the identification of individual test takers.

Standard 9.20

In situations where test results are shared with the public, test users should formulate and share the established policy regarding the release of the results (e.g., timeliness, amount of detail) and apply that policy consistently over time.

Comment: Test developers and test users should consider the practices of the communities they serve and facilitate the creation of common policies regarding the release of test results. For example, in many states, the release of data from large-scale educational tests is often required by law. However, even when the release of data is not required but is routinely done, test users should have clear policies governing the release procedures. Different policies without appropriate rationales can confuse the public and lead to unnecessary controversy.

Cluster 3. Test Security and Protection of Copyrights

Standard 9.21

Test users have the responsibility to protect the security of tests, including that of previous editions.

Comment: When tests are used for purposes of selection, credentialing, educational accountability, or for clinical diagnosis, treatment, and monitoring, the rigorous protection of test security is essential, for reasons related to validity of inferences drawn, protection of intellectual property rights, and the costs associated with developing tests. Test developers, test publishers, and individuals who hold the copyrights on tests provide specific guidelines about test security and disposal of test materials. The test user is responsible for helping to ensure the security of test materials according to the professional guidelines established for that test as well as any applicable legal standards. Resale of copyrighted materials in open forums is a violation of this standard, and audio and video recordings for training purposes must also be handled in such a way that they are not released to the public. These prohibitions also apply to outdated and previous editions of tests; test users should help to ensure that test materials are securely disposed of when no longer in use (e.g., upon retirement or after purchase of a new edition). Consistency and clarity in the definition of acceptable and unacceptable practices is critical in such situations. When tests are involved in litigation, inspection of the instruments should be restricted—to the extent permitted by law—to those who are obligated legally or by professional ethics to safeguard test security.

Standard 9.22

Test users have the responsibility to respect test copyrights, including copyrights of tests that are administered via electronic devices.

Comment: Legally and ethically, test users may not reproduce or create electronic versions of copyrighted materials for routine test use without consent of the copyright holder. These materials—in both paper and electronic form—include test items, test protocols, ancillary forms such as

answer sheets or profile forms, scoring templates, conversion tables of raw scores to reported scores, and tables of norms. Storage and transmission of test information should satisfy existing legal and professional standards.

Standard 9.23

Test users should remind all test takers, including those taking electronically administered tests, and others who have access to test materials that copyright policies and regulations may prohibit the disclosure of test items without specific authorization.

Comment: In some cases, information on copyrights and prohibitions on the disclosure of test items are provided in written form or verbally as part of the procedure prior to beginning the test or as part of the administration procedures. However, even in cases where this information is not a formal part of the test administration, if materials are copyrighted, test users should inform test takers of their responsibilities in this area.

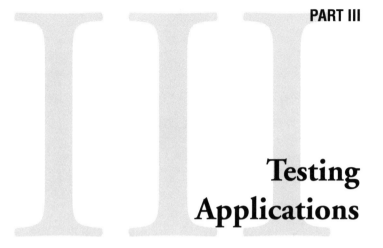

PART III

Testing
Applications

10. PSYCHOLOGICAL TESTING AND ASSESSMENT

BACKGROUND

This chapter addresses issues important to professionals who use psychological tests to assess individuals. Topics covered in this chapter include test selection and administration, test score interpretation, use of collateral information in psychological testing, types of tests, and purposes of psychological testing. The types of psychological tests reviewed in this chapter include cognitive and neuropsychological, problem behavior, family and couples, social and adaptive behavior, personality, and vocational. In addition, the chapter includes an overview of five common uses of psychological tests: for diagnosis; neuropsychological evaluation; intervention planning and outcome evaluation; judicial and governmental decisions; and personal awareness, social identity, and psychological health, growth, and action. The standards in this chapter are applicable to settings where in-depth assessment of people, individually or in groups, is conducted. Psychological tests are used in several other contexts as well, most notably in employment and educational settings. Tests designed to measure specific job-related characteristics across multiple candidates for selection purposes are treated in the text and standards of chapter 11; tests used in educational settings are addressed in depth in chapter 12.

It is critical that professionals who use tests to conduct assessments of individuals have knowledge of educational, linguistic, national, and cultural factors as well as physical capabilities that influence (a) a test taker's development, (b) the methods for obtaining and conveying information, and (c) the planning and implementation of interventions. Therefore, readers are encouraged to review chapter 3, which discusses fairness in testing; chapter 8, which focuses on rights of test takers; and chapter 9, which focuses on rights and responsibilities of test users. In chapters 1, 2, 4, 5, 6, and 7, readers will find important additional detail on validity; on reliability and precision; on test development;

on scaling and equating; on test administration, scoring, reporting, and interpretation; and on supporting documentation.

The use of psychological tests provides one approach to collecting information within the larger framework of a psychological assessment of an individual. Typically, psychological assessments involve an interaction between a professional, who is trained and experienced in testing, the test taker, and a client who may be the test taker or another party. The test taker may be a child, an adolescent, or an adult. The client usually is the person or agency that arranges for the assessment. Clients may be patients, counselees, parents, children, employees, employers, attorneys, students, government agencies, or other responsible parties. The settings in which psychological tests or inventories are used include (but are not limited to) preschools; elementary, middle, and secondary schools; colleges and universities; pre-employment settings; hospitals; prisons; mental health and health clinics; and other professionals' offices.

The tasks involved in a psychological assessment—collecting, evaluating, integrating, and reporting salient information relevant to the aspects of a test taker's functioning that are under examination—comprise a complex and sophisticated set of professional activities. A psychological assessment is conducted to answer specific questions about a test taker's psychological functioning or behavior during a particular time interval or to predict an aspect of a test taker's psychological functioning or behavior in the future. Because test scores characteristically are interpreted in the context of other information about the test taker, an individual psychological assessment usually also includes interviewing the test taker; observing the test taker's behavior in the appropriate setting; reviewing educational, health, psychological, and other relevant records; and integrating these findings with other information that may be provided by third parties. The results from tests and inventories used in psychological assessments may help the professional to understand test takers more fully and to develop more informed and accurate hypotheses, inferences, and decisions about aspects of the test taker's psychological functioning or appropriate interventions.

The interpretation of test and inventory scores can be a valuable part of the assessment process and, if used appropriately, can provide useful information to test takers as well as to other users of the test interpretation. For example, the results of tests and inventories may be used to assess the psychological functioning of an individual; to assign diagnostic classification; to detect and characterize neuropsychological impairment, developmental delays, and learning disabilities; to determine the validity of a symptom; to assess cognitive and personality strengths or mental health and emotional behavior problems; to assess vocational interests and values; to determine developmental stages; to assist in health decision making; or to evaluate treatment outcomes. Test results also may provide information used to make decisions that have a powerful and lasting impact on people's lives (e.g., vocational and educational decisions; diagnoses; treatment plans, including plans for psychopharmacological intervention; intervention and outcome evaluations; health decisions; disability determinations; decisions on parole sentencing, civil commitment, child custody, and competency to stand trial; personal injury litigation; and death penalty decisions).

Test Selection and Administration

The selection and administration of psychological tests and inventories often is individualized for each participant. However, in some settings predetermined tests may be taken by all participants, and interpretations of results may be provided in a group setting.

The assessment process begins by clarifying, as much as possible, the reasons why a test taker will be assessed. Guided by these reasons or other relevant concerns, the tests, inventories, and diagnostic procedures to be used are selected, and

other sources of information needed to evaluate the test taker are identified. Preliminary findings may lead to the selection of additional tests. The professional is responsible for being familiar with the evidence of validity for the intended uses of scores from the tests and inventories selected, including computer-administered or online tests. Evidence of the reliability/precision of scores, and the availability of applicable normative data in the test's accumulated research literature also should be considered during test selection. In the case of tests that have been revised, editions currently supported by the publisher usually should be selected. On occasion, use of an earlier edition of an instrument is appropriate (e.g., when longitudinal research is conducted, or when an earlier edition contains relevant subtests not included in a later edition). In addition, professionals are responsible for guarding against reliance on test scores that are outdated; in such cases, retesting is appropriate. In international applications, it is especially important to verify that the construct being assessed has equivalent meaning across international borders and cultural contexts.

Validity and reliability/precision considerations are paramount, but the demographic characteristics of the group(s) for which the test originally was constructed and for which initial and subsequent normative data are available also are important test selection considerations. Selecting a test with demographically and clinically appropriate normative groups relevant for the test taker and for the purpose of the assessment is important for the generalizability of the inferences that the professional seeks to make. Applying a test constructed for one group to other groups may not be appropriate, and score interpretations, if the test is used, should be qualified and presented as hypotheses rather than conclusions.

Tests and inventories that meet high technical standards of quality are a necessary but not a sufficient condition for the responsible administration and scoring of tests and interpretation and use of test scores. A professional conducting a psychological assessment must complete the appropriate education and training, acquire appropriate credentials, adhere to professional ethical guidelines, and possesses a high degree of professional judgment and scientific knowledge.

Professionals who oversee testing and assessment should be thoroughly versed in proper test administration procedures. They are responsible for ensuring that all persons who administer and score tests have received the appropriate education and training needed to perform their assigned tasks. Test administrators should administer tests in the manner that the test manuals indicate and should adhere to ethical and professional standards. The education and experience necessary to administer group tests and/or to proctor computer-administered tests generally are less extensive than the qualifications necessary to administer and interpret scores from individually administered tests that require interactions between the test taker and the test administrator. In many situations where complex behavioral observations are required, the use of a nonprofessional to administer or score tests may be inappropriate. Prior to beginning the assessment process, the test taker or a responsible party acting on the test taker's behalf (e.g., parent, legal guardian) should understand who will have access to the test results and the written report, how test results will be shared with the test taker, and whether and when decisions based on the test results will be shared with the test taker and/or a third party or the public (e.g., in court proceedings).

Test administrators must be aware of any personal limitations that affect their ability to administer and score the test fairly and accurately. These limitations may include physical, perceptual, and cognitive factors. Some tests place considerable demands on the test administrator (e.g., recording responses rapidly, manipulating equipment, or performing complex item scoring during administration). Test administrators who cannot comfortably meet these demands should not administer such tests. For tests that require oral instructions prior to or during administration, test administrators should be sure that there are no barriers to being clearly understood by test takers.

When using a battery of tests, the professional should determine the appropriate order of tests to be administered. For example, when administering cognitive and neuropsychological tests,

some professionals first administer tests to assess basic domains (e.g., attention) and end with tests to assess more complex domains (e.g., executive functions). Professionals also are responsible for establishing testing conditions that are appropriate to the test taker's needs and abilities. For example, the examiner may need to determine if the test taker is capable of reading at the level required and if vision, hearing, psychomotor, or clinical impairments or neurological deficits are adequately accommodated. Chapter 3 addresses access considerations and standards in detail.

Standardized administration is not required for all tests but is important for the interpretation of test scores for many tests and purposes. In those situations, standardized test administration procedures should be followed. When nonstandard administration procedures are needed or allowed, they should be described and justified. The interpreter of the test results should be informed if the test was unproctored or if it was administered under nonstandardized procedures. In some circumstances, test administration may provide the opportunity for skilled examiners to carefully observe the performance of test takers under standardized conditions. For example, the test administrators' observations may allow them to record behaviors being assessed, to understand the manner in which test takers arrived at their answers, to identify test-taker strengths and weaknesses, and to make modifications in the testing process. If tests are administered by computer or other technological devices or online, the professional is responsible for determining if the purpose of the assessment and the capabilities of the test taker require the presence of a proctor or support staff (e.g., to assist with the use of the computer equipment or software). Also, some computer-administered tests may require giving the test taker the opportunity to receive instructions and to practice prior to the test administration. Chapters 4 and 6 provide additional detail on technologically administered tests.

Inappropriate effort on the part of the person being assessed may affect the results of psychological assessment and may introduce error into the measurement of the construct in question. Therefore, in some cases, the importance of expending appropriate effort when taking the test should be explained to the test taker. For many tests, measures of effort can be derived from stand-alone tests or from responses embedded within a standard assessment procedure (e.g., increased numbers of errors, inconsistent responding, and unusual responses relevant to symptom patterns), and effort may be measured throughout the assessment process. When low levels of effort and motivation are evident during the test administration, continuing an evaluation may result in inappropriate score interpretations.

Professionals are responsible for protecting the confidentiality and security of the test results and the testing materials. Storage and transmission of this type of information should satisfy relevant professional and legal standards.

Test Score Interpretation

Test scores used in psychological assessment ideally are interpreted in light of a number of factors, including the available normative data appropriate to the characteristics of the test taker, the psychometric properties of the test, indicators of effort, the circumstances of the test taker at the time the test is given, the temporal stability of the constructs being measured, and the effects of moderator variables and demographic characteristics on test results. The professional rarely has the resources available to personally conduct the research or to assemble representative norms that, in some types of assessment, might be needed to make accurate inferences about each individual test taker's past, current, and future functioning. Therefore, the professional may need to rely on the research and the body of scientific knowledge available for the test that support appropriate inferences. Presentation of validity and reliability/precision evidence often is not needed in the written report summarizing the findings of the assessment, but the professional should strive to understand, and be prepared to articulate, such evidence as the need arises.

When making inferences about a test taker's past, present, and future behaviors and other characteristics from test scores, the professional should consider other available data that support or challenge the inferences. For example, the professional should review the test taker's history and information about past behaviors, as well as the relevant literature, to develop familiarity with supporting evidence. At times, the professional also should corroborate results from one testing session with results from other tests and testing sessions to address reliability/precision and validity of the inferences made about the test taker's performance across time and/or tests. Triangulation of multiple sources of information—including stylistic and test-taking behaviors inferred from observation during the test administration—may strengthen confidence in the inference. Importantly, data that are not supportive of the inferences should be acknowledged and either reconciled with other information or noted as a limitation to the confidence placed in the inference. When there is strong evidence for the reliability/precision and validity of the scores for the intended uses of a test and strong evidence for the appropriateness of the test for the test taker being assessed, then the professional's ability to draw appropriate inferences increases. When an inference is based on a single study or based on several studies whose samples are of limited generalizability to the test taker, then the professional should be more cautious about the inference and note in the report limitations regarding conclusions drawn from the inference.

Threats to the interpretability of obtained scores are minimized by clearly defining how particular psychological tests are to be used. These threats occur as a result of construct-irrelevant variance (i.e., aspects of the test and the testing process that are not relevant to the purpose of the test scores) and construct underrepresentation (i.e., failure of the test to account for important facets relevant to the purpose of the testing). Response bias and faking are examples of construct-irrelevant components that may significantly skew the obtained scores, possibly resulting in inaccurate or misleading interpretations. In situations where response bias or faking is anticipated, professionals may choose a test that has scales (e.g., percentage of "yes" answers, percentage of "no" answers; "faking good," "faking bad") that clarify the threats to validity. In so doing, the professionals may be able to assess the degree to which test takers are acquiescing to the perceived demands of the test administrator or attempting to portray themselves as impaired by "faking bad," or as well functioning by "faking good."

For some purposes, including career counseling and neuropsychological assessment, batteries of tests are frequently used. For example, career counseling batteries may include tests of abilities, values, interests, and personality. Neuropsychological batteries may include measures of orientation, attention, communication skills, executive function, fluency, visual-motor and visual-spatial skills, problem solving, organization, memory, intelligence, academic achievement, and/or personality, along with tests of effort. When psychological test batteries incorporate multiple methods and scores, patterns of test results frequently are interpreted as reflecting a construct or even an interaction among constructs underlying test performance. Interactions among the constructs underlying configurations of test outcomes may be postulated on the basis of test score patterns. The literature reporting evidence of reliability/precision and validity of configurations of scores that supports the proposed interpretations should be identified when possible. However, it is understood that little, if any, literature exists that describes the validity of interpretations of scores from highly customized or flexible batteries of tests. The professional should recognize that variability in scores on different tests within a battery commonly occurs in the general population, and should use base rate data, when available, to determine whether the observed variability is exceptional. If the literature is incomplete, the resulting inferences may be presented with the qualification that they are hypotheses for future verification rather than probabilistic statements regarding the likelihood of some behavior that imply some known validity evidence.

Collateral Information Used in Psychological Testing and Assessment

Test scores that are used as part of a psychological assessment are best interpreted in the context of the test taker's personal history and other relevant traits and personal characteristics. The quality of interpretations made from psychological tests and assessments often can be enhanced by obtaining credible collateral information from various third-party sources, such as significant others, teachers, health professionals, and school, legal, military, and employment records. The quality of collateral information is enhanced by using various methods to acquire it. Structured behavioral observations, checklists, ratings, and interviews are a few of the methods that may be used, along with objective test scores to minimize the need for the scorer to rely on individual judgment. For example, an evaluation of career goals may be enhanced by obtaining a history of employment as well as by administering tests to assess academic aptitude and achievement, vocational interests, work values, personality, and temperament. The availability of information on multiple traits or attributes, when acquired from various sources and through the use of various methods, enables professionals to assess more accurately an individual's psychosocial functioning and facilitates more effective decision making. When using collateral data, the professional should take steps to ascertain their accuracy and reliability, especially when the data come from third parties who may have a vested interest in the outcome of the assessment.

Types of Psychological Testing and Assessment

For purposes of this chapter, the types of psychological tests have been divided into six categories: cognitive and neuropsychological tests; problem behavior tests; family and couples tests; social and adaptive behavior tests; personality tests; and vocational tests.

Cognitive and Neuropsychological Testing and Assessment

Tests often are used to assess various classes of cognitive and neuropsychological functioning, including intelligence, broad ability domains, and more focused domains (e.g., abstract reasoning and categorical thinking; academic achievement; attention; cognitive ability; executive function;

language; learning and memory; motor and sensorimotor functions and lateral preferences; and perception and perceptual organization/integration). Overlap may occur in the constructs that are assessed by tests of differing functions or domains. In common with other types of tests, cognitive and neuropsychological tests require a minimally sufficient level of test-taker capacity to maintain attention as well as appropriate effort. For example, when administering cognitive and neuropsychological tests, some professionals first administer tests to assess basic domains (e.g., attention) and end with administration of tests to assess more complex domains (e.g., executive function).

Abstract reasoning and categorical thinking. Tests of reasoning and thinking measure a broad array of skills and abilities, including the examinee's ability to infer relationships, to form new concepts or strategies, to respond to changing environmental circumstances, and to act in goal-oriented situations, as well as the ability to understand a problem or a concept, to develop a strategy to solve that problem, and, as necessary, to alter such concepts or strategies as situations vary.

Academic achievement. Academic achievement tests are measures of knowledge and skills that a person has acquired in formal and informal learning situations. Two major types of academic achievement tests include general achievement batteries and diagnostic achievement tests. General achievement batteries are designed to assess a person's level of learning in multiple areas (e.g., reading, mathematics, and spelling). In contrast, diagnostic achievement tests typically focus on one subject area (e.g., reading) and assess an academic skill in greater detail. Test results are used to determine the test taker's strengths and may also help identify sources of academic difficulties or deficiencies. Chapter 12 provides additional detail on academic achievement testing in educational settings.

Attention. Attention refers to a domain that encompasses the constructs of arousal, establishment of sets, strategic deployment of attention, sustained attention, divided attention, focused attention, selective attention, and vigilance. Tests may measure (a) levels of alertness, orientation, and localization; (b) the ability to focus, shift, and maintain attention and to track one or more stimuli under various conditions; (c) span of attention; and (d) short-term information storage functioning. Scores for each aspect of attention that have been examined should be reported individually so that the nature of an attention disorder can be clarified.

Cognitive ability. Measures designed to quantify cognitive abilities are among the most widely administered tests. The interpretation of results from a cognitive ability test is guided by the theoretical constructs used to develop the test. Some cognitive ability assessments are based on results from multidimensional test batteries that are designed to assess a broad range of skills and abilities. Test results are used to draw inferences about a person's overall level of intellectual functioning and about strengths and weaknesses in various cognitive abilities, and to diagnose cognitive disorders.

Executive function. This class of functions is involved in the organized performances (e.g., cognitive flexibility, inhibitory control, multitasking) that are necessary for the independent, purposive, and effective attainment of goals in various cognitive-processing, problem-solving, and social situations. Some tests emphasize (a) reasoned plans of action that anticipate consequences of alternative solutions, (b) motor performance in problem-solving situations that require goal-oriented intentions, and/or (c) regulation of performance for achieving a desired outcome.

Language. Language deficiencies typically are identified with assessments that focus on phonology, morphology, syntax, semantics, supralinguistics, and pragmatics. Various functions may be assessed, including listening, reading, and spoken and written language skills and abilities. Language disorder assessments focus on functional speech and verbal comprehension measured through oral, written, or gestural modes; lexical access and elaboration; repetition of spoken language; and associative verbal fluency. If a multilingual person is assessed for a possible language disorder, the degree to which the disorder may be due more directly to developmental language issues (e.g., phonological, morphological, syntactic, semantic, or pragmatic delays; intellectual disabilities; peripheral, sensory, or central neurological impairment; psychological conditions; or sensory disorders) than to lack of proficiency in a given language must be addressed.

Learning and memory. This class of functions involves the acquisition, retention, and retrieval of information beyond the requirements of immediate or short-term information processing and storage. These tests may measure acquisition of new information through various sensory channels and by means of assorted test formats (e.g., word lists, prose passages, geometric figures, formboards, digits, and musical melodies). Memory tests also may require retention and recall of old information (e.g., personal data as well as commonly learned facts and skills). In addition, testing of recognition of stored information may be used in understanding memory deficits.

Motor functions, sensorimotor functions, and lateral preferences. Motor functions (e.g., finger tapping) and sensory functions (e.g., tactile stimulation) are often measured as part of a comprehensive neuropsychological evaluation. Motor tests assess various aspects of movement such as speed, dexterity, coordination, and purposeful movement. Sensory tests evaluate function in the areas of vision, hearing, touch, and sometimes smell. Testing also is done to examine the integration of perceptual and motor functions.

Perception and perceptual organization/integration. This class of functioning involves reasoning and judgment as they relate to the processing and elaboration of complex sensory combinations and inputs. Tests of perception may emphasize immediate perceptual processing but also may require conceptualizations that involve some reasoning and judgmental processes. Some tests have motor components ranging from making simple movements to building complex constructions. These tests assess activities ranging from perceptual speed to choice reaction time, to complex information processing and visual-spatial reasoning.

Problem Behavior Testing and Assessment

Problem behaviors include behavioral adjustment difficulties that interfere with a person's effective functioning in daily life situations. Tests are used to assess the individual's behavior and self-perceptions for differential diagnosis and educational classification for a variety of emotional and behavioral disorders and to aid in the development of treatment plans. In some cases (e.g., death penalty evaluations), retrospective analysis is required and multiple sources of information help provide the most comprehensive assessment possible. Observing a person in her or his environment often is helpful for understanding fully the specific demands of the environment, not only to offer a more comprehensive assessment but to provide more useful recommendations.

Family and Couples Testing and Assessment

Family testing addresses the issues of family dynamics, cohesion, and interpersonal relations among family members, including partners, parents, children, and extended family members. Tests developed to assess families and couples are distinguished by whether they measure the interaction patterns of partial or whole families, in both cases requiring simultaneous focus on two or more family members in terms of their transactions. Testing with couples may address factors such as issues of intimacy, compatibility, shared interests, trust, and spiritual beliefs.

Social and Adaptive Behavior Testing and Assessment

Measures of social and adaptive behaviors assess motivation and ability to care for oneself and relate to others. Social and adaptive behaviors are based on a repertoire of knowledge, skills, and abilities that enable a person to meet the daily demands and expectations of the environment, such as eating, dressing, working, participating in leisure activities, using transportation, interacting with peers, communicating with others, making purchases, managing money, maintaining a schedule, living independently, being socially responsive, and engaging in healthy behaviors.

Personality Testing and Assessment

The assessment of personality requires a synthesis of aspects of an individual's functioning that contribute to the formulation and expression of thoughts, attitudes, emotions, and behaviors. Some of these aspects are stable over time; others change with age or are situation specific. Cognitive and emotional functioning may be considered separately in assessing an individual, but their influences are interrelated. For example, a person whose perceptions are highly accurate, or who is relatively stable emotionally, may be able to control suspiciousness better than a person whose perceptions are inaccurate or distorted or who is emotionally unstable.

Scores or personality descriptors derived from a personality test may be regarded as reflecting the underlying theoretical constructs or empirically derived scales or factors that guided the test's construction. The stimulus-and-response formats of personality tests vary widely. Some include a series of questions (e.g., self-report inventories) to which the test taker is required to respond by choosing from multiple well-defined options; others involve being placed in a novel situation in which the test taker's response is not completely structured (e.g., responding to visual stimuli, telling stories, discussing pictures, or responding to other projective stimuli). Results may consist of themes, patterns, or diagnostic indicators, as well as scores. The responses are scored and combined into either logically or statistically derived dimensions established by previous research.

Personality tests may be designed to assess normal or abnormal attitudes, feelings, traits, and related characteristics. Tests intended to measure normal personality characteristics are constructed to yield scores reflecting the degree to which a person manifests personality dimensions empirically identified and hypothesized to be present in the behavior of most individuals. A person's configuration of scores on these dimensions is then used to infer how the person behaves presently and

how she or he may behave in new situations. Test scores outside the expected range may be considered strong expressions of normal traits or may be indicative of psychopathology. Such scores also may reflect normal functioning of the person within a culture different from that of the population on which the norms are based.

Other personality tests are designed specifically to measure constructs underlying abnormal functioning and psychopathology. Developers of some of these tests use previously diagnosed individuals to construct their scales and base their interpretations on the association between the test's scale scores, within a given range, and the behavioral correlates of persons who scored within that range, as compared with clinical samples. If interpretations made from scores go beyond the theory that guided the test's construction, then evidence of the validity of the interpretations should be collected and analyzed from additional relevant data.

Vocational Testing and Assessment

Vocational testing generally includes the measurement of interests, work needs, and values, as well as consideration and assessment of related elements of career development, maturity, and indecision. Academic achievement and cognitive abilities, discussed earlier in the section on cognitive ability, also are important components in vocational testing and assessment. Results from these tests often are used to enhance personal growth and understanding and for career counseling, outplacement counseling, and vocational decision making. These interventions frequently take place in the context of educational and vocational rehabilitation. However, vocational testing may also be used in the workplace as part of corporate programs for career planning.

Interest inventories. The measurement of interests is designed to identify a person's preferences for various activities. Self-report interest inventories are widely used to assess personal preferences, including likes and dislikes for various work and leisure activities, school subjects, occupations, or types of people. The resulting scores may provide insight into types and patterns of interests in educational curricula (e.g., college majors), in various fields of work (e.g., specific occupations), or in more general or basic areas of interests related to specific activities (e.g., sales, office practices, or mechanical activities).

Work values inventories. The measurement of work values identifies a person's preferences for the various reinforcements one may obtain from work activities. Sometimes these values are identified as needs that persons seek to satisfy. Work values or needs may be categorized as intrinsic and important for the pleasure gained from the activity (e.g., being independent, using one's abilities) or as extrinsic and important for the rewards they bring (e.g., pay, promotion). The format of work values tests usually involves a self-rating of the importance of the value associated with qualities described by the items.

Measures of career development, maturity, and indecision. Additional areas of vocational assessment include measures of career development and maturity and measures of career indecision. Inventories that measure career development and maturity typically elicit self-descriptions in response to items that inquire about individuals' knowledge of the world of work; self-appraisal of their decision-making skills; attitudes toward careers and career choices; and the degree to which the individuals already have engaged in career planning. Measures of career indecision usually are constructed and standardized to assess both the level of career indecision of a test taker and the reasons for, or antecedents of, this indecision. Results from tests such as these are often used with individuals and groups to guide the design and delivery of career services and to evaluate the effectiveness of career interventions.

Purposes of Psychological Testing and Assessment

For purposes of this chapter, psychological test uses have been divided into five categories: testing for diagnosis; testing for neuropsychological eval-

uations; testing for intervention planning and outcome evaluation; testing for judicial and governmental decisions; and testing for personal awareness, social identity, and psychological health, growth, and action. However, these categories are not always mutually exclusive.

Testing for Diagnosis

Diagnosis refers to a process that includes the collection and integration of test results with prior and current information about a person, together with relevant contextual conditions, to identify characteristics of healthy psychological functioning as well as psychological disorders. Disorders may manifest themselves in information obtained during the testing of an individual's cognitive, emotional, adaptive, behavioral, personality, neuropsychological, physical, or social attributes.

Psychological tests are helpful to professionals involved in the diagnosis of an individual's psychological health. Testing may be performed to confirm a hypothesized diagnosis or to rule out alternative diagnoses. Diagnosis is complicated by the prevalence of comorbidity between diagnostic categories. For example, an individual diagnosed with dementia may simultaneously be diagnosed as depressed. Or a child diagnosed as having a learning disability also may be diagnosed as suffering from an attention deficit/hyperactivity disorder. The goal of diagnosis is to provide a brief description of the test taker's psychological dysfunction and to assist each test taker in receiving the appropriate interventions for the psychological or behavioral dysfunctions that the client, or a third party, views as impairing the client's expected functioning and/or enjoyment of life. When the intent of assessment is differential diagnosis, the professional should use tests for which there is evidence that the scores distinguish between two or more diagnostic groups. Group mean differences do not provide sufficient evidence for the accuracy of differential diagnosis; additional information, such as effect sizes or data indicating the degree of overlap between criterion groups, also should be provided by the test developers. In developing treatment plans, professionals often use noncategorical diagnostic descriptions of client functioning along treatment-relevant dimensions (e.g., functional capacity, degree of anxiety, amount of suspiciousness, openness to interpretations, amount of insight into behaviors, and level of intellectual functioning).

Diagnostic criteria may vary from one nomenclature system to another. Noting which nomenclature system is being used is an important initial step because different diagnostic systems may use the same diagnostic term to describe different symptoms. Even within one diagnostic system, the symptoms described by the same term may differ between editions of the manual. Similarly, a test that uses a diagnostic term in its title may differ significantly from another test using a similar title or from a subscale using the same term. For example, some diagnostic systems may define *depression* by behavioral symptomatology (e.g., psychomotor retardation, disturbance in appetite or sleep), by affective symptomatology (e.g., dysphoric feeling, emotional flatness), or by cognitive symptomatology (e.g., thoughts of hopelessness, morbidity). Further, rarely are the symptoms of diagnostic categories mutually exclusive. Hence, it can be expected that a given symptom may be shared by several diagnostic categories. More knowledgeable and precisely drawn inferences relating to a diagnosis may be obtained from test scores if appropriate weight is given to the symptoms included in the diagnostic category and to the suitability of each test for assessing the symptoms. Therefore, the first step in evaluating a test's suitability for yielding scores or information indicative of a particular diagnostic syndrome is to compare the construct that the test is intended to measure with the symptomatology described in the diagnostic criteria.

Different methods may be used to assess particular diagnostic categories. Some methods rely primarily on structured interviews using a "yes"/"no" or "true"/"false" format, in which the professional is interested in the presence or absence of diagnosis-specific symptomatology. Other methods often rely principally on tests of personality or cognitive functioning and use configurations of obtained scores. These configurations of scores indicate the degree to which a test taker's responses are similar to those of individuals who have been determined by prior research to belong to a specific diagnostic group.

Diagnoses made with the help of test scores typically are based on empirically demonstrated relationships between the test score and the diagnostic category. Validity studies that demonstrate relationships between test scores and diagnostic categories currently are available for some, but not all, diagnostic categories. Many more studies demonstrate evidence of validity for the relations between test scores and various subsets of symptoms that contribute to a diagnostic category. Although it often is not feasible for individual professionals to personally conduct research into relationships between obtained scores and diagnostic categories, familiarity with the research literature that examines these relationships is important.

The professional often can enhance the diagnostic interpretations derived from test scores by integrating the test results with inferences made from other sources of information regarding the test taker's functioning, such as self-reported history, information provided by significant others, or systematic observations in the natural environment or in the testing setting. In arriving at a diagnosis, a professional also looks for information that does not corroborate the diagnosis, and in those instances, places appropriate limits on the degree of confidence placed in the diagnosis. When relevant to a referral decision, the professional should acknowledge alternative diagnoses that may require consideration. Particular attention should be paid to all relevant available data before concluding that a test taker falls into a diagnostic category. Cultural competency is paramount in the effort to avoid misdiagnosing or overpathologizing culturally appropriate behavior, affect, or cognition. Tests also are used to assess the appropriateness of continuing the initial diagnosis, especially after a course of treatment or if the client's psychological functioning has changed over time.

Testing for Neuropsychological Evaluations

Neuropsychological testing analyzes the test taker's current psychological and behavioral status, including manifestations of neurological, neuropathological, and neurochemical changes that may arise during development or from psychopathology, bodily and/or brain injury, or illness. The purposes of neuropsychological testing typically include, but are not limited to, the following: differential diagnosis associated with the sources of cognitive, perceptual, and personality dysfunction; differential diagnosis between two or more suspected etiologies of cerebral dysfunction; evaluation of impaired functioning secondary to a cortical or subcortical event; establishment of neuropsychological baseline measurements for monitoring progressive cerebral disease or recovery effects; comparison of test results before and after pharmacologic, surgical, behavioral, or psychological interventions; identification of patterns of higher cortical functions and dysfunctions for the formulation of rehabilitation strategies and for the design of remedial procedures; and characterization of brain behavior functions to assist in criminal and civil legal actions.

Testing for Intervention Planning and Outcome Evaluation

Professionals often rely on test results for assistance in planning, executing, and evaluating interventions. Therefore, their awareness of validity information that supports or does not support the relationships among test results, prescribed interventions, and desired outcomes is important. Interventions may be used to prevent the onset of one or more symptoms, to remediate deficits, and to provide for a person's basic physical, psychological, and social needs to enhance quality of life. Intervention planning typically occurs following an evaluation of the nature, evolution, and severity of a disorder and a review of personal and contextual conditions that may affect its resolution. Subsequent evaluations that require the repeated administration of the same test may occur in an effort to further diagnose the nature and severity of the disorder, to review the effects of interventions, to revise the interventions as needed, and to meet ethical and legal standards.

Testing for Judicial and Governmental Decisions

Clients may voluntarily seek psychological assessment to assist in matters before a court of law or other government agency. Conversely, courts or other government agencies sometimes require a person to submit involuntarily to a psychological assessment that may involve a wide range of psychological tests. The goal of these psychological assessments is to provide important information to a third party (e.g., test taker's attorney, opposing attorney, judge, or administrative board) about the psychological functioning of the test taker that has bearing on the legal issues in question. Informed consent generally should be obtained; informed consent for children or mentally incompetent individuals (e.g., individuals with dementia) should be obtained from legal guardians. At the outset of the evaluation for judicial and government decisions, the professional should explain the intended purposes of the evaluation and identify who is expected to have access to the test results and the report. Often, the professional and the test taker are not fully aware of legal issues or parameters that impinge on the evaluation, and if the test taker declines to proceed after being notified of the nature and purpose of the examination, the professional, as appropriate, may attempt to administer the assessment, postpone the assessment, advise the test taker to contact her or his attorney, or notify the individual or agency requesting the assessment about the test taker's unwillingness to proceed.

Assessments for legal reasons may occur as part of a civil proceeding (e.g., involuntary commitment, testamentary capacity, competence to stand trial, ruling of child custody, personal injury, law suit), a criminal proceeding (e.g., competence to stand trial, ruling of not guilty by reason of insanity, mitigating circumstances in sentencing), determination of reasonable accommodations for employees with disabilities, or an administrative proceeding or decision (e.g., license revocation, parole, worker's compensation). The professional is responsible for explaining test scores and the interpretations made from them in terms of the legal criteria by which the jury, judge, or administrative board will decide the legal issue. In instances involving legal issues, it is important to assess the examinee's test-taking orientation, including response bias, to ensure that the legal proceedings have not affected the responses given. For example, persons seeking to obtain the greatest possible monetary award for a personal injury may be motivated to exaggerate cognitive and emotional symptoms, whereas persons attempting to forestall the loss of a professional license may attempt to portray themselves in the best possible light by minimizing symptoms or deficits. In forming an assessment opinion, it is necessary to interpret the test scores with informed knowledge relating to the available validity and reliability evidence. When forming such opinions, it also is necessary to integrate a test taker's test scores with all other sources of information that bear on the test taker's current status, including psychological, health, educational, occupational, legal, sociocultural, and other relevant collateral records.

Some tests are intended to provide information about a client's functioning that helps clarify a given legal issue (e.g., parental functioning in a child custody case or a defendant's ability to understand charges in hearings on competency to stand trial). The manuals of some tests also provide demographic and actuarial data for normative groups that are representative of persons involved in the legal system. However, many tests measure constructs that are generally relevant to the legal issues even though norms specific to the judicial or governmental context may not be available. Professionals are expected to make every effort to be aware of evidence of validity and reliability/precision that supports or does not support their interpretations and to place appropriate limits on the opinions rendered. Test users who practice in judicial and governmental settings are expected to be aware of conflicts of interest that may lead to bias in the interpretation of test results.

Protecting the confidentiality of a test taker's test results and of the test instrument itself poses particular challenges for professionals involved with attorneys, judges, jurors, and other legal decision makers. The test taker has the right to expect that test results will be communicated only to persons who are legally authorized to receive them and that other information from the testing session that is not relevant to the evaluation will not be reported. The professional should be apprised of possible threats to confidentiality and

test security (e.g., releasing the test questions, the examinee's responses, or raw or standardized scores on tests to another qualified professional) and should seek, if necessary, appropriate legal and professional remedies.

Testing for Personal Awareness, Social Identity, and Psychological Health, Growth, and Action

Tests and inventories frequently are used to provide information to help individuals understand themselves, identify their own strengths and weaknesses, and clarify issues important to their own development. For example, test results from personality inventories may help test takers better understand themselves and their interactions with others. Measures of ethnic identity and acculturation—two components of social identity—that assess the cognitive, affective, and behavioral facets of the ways in which people identify with their cultural backgrounds, also may be informative.

Psychological tests are used sometimes to assess an individual's ability to understand and adapt to health conditions. In these instances, observations and checklists, as well as tests, are used to measure the understanding that an individual with a health condition (e.g., diabetes) has about the disease process and about behavioral and cognitive techniques applicable to the amelioration or control of the symptoms of the disease state.

Results from interest inventories and tests of ability may be useful to individuals who are making educational and career decisions. Appropriate cognitive and neuropsychological tests that have been normed and standardized for children may facilitate the monitoring of development and growth during the formative years, when relevant interventions may be more efficacious for recognizing and preventing potentially disabling learning difficulties. Test scores for young adults or children on these types of measures may change in later years; therefore, test users should be cautious about overreliance on results that may be outdated.

Test results may be used in several ways for self-exploration, growth, and decision making. First, the results can provide individuals with new information that allows them to compare themselves with others or to evaluate themselves by focusing on self-descriptions and self-characterizations. Test results may also serve to stimulate discussions between test taker and professional, to facilitate test-taker insights, to provide directions for future treatment considerations, to help individuals identify strengths and weaknesses, and to provide the professional with a general framework for organizing and integrating information about an individual. Testing for personal growth may take place in training and development programs, within an educational curriculum, during psychotherapy, in rehabilitation programs as part of an educational or career-planning process, or in other situations.

Summary

The responsible use of tests in psychological practice requires a commitment by the professional to develop and maintain the necessary knowledge and competence to select, administer, and interpret tests and inventories as crucial elements of the psychological testing and assessment process (see chap. 9). The standards in this chapter provide a framework for guiding the professional toward achieving relevance and effectiveness in the use of psychological tests within the boundaries or limits defined by the professional's educational, experiential, and ethical foundations. Earlier chapters and standards that are relevant to psychological testing and assessment describe general aspects of test quality (chaps. 1 and 2), fairness (chap. 3), test design and development (chap. 4), and test administration (chap. 6). Chapter 11 discusses test uses for the workplace, including credentialing, and the importance of collecting data that provide evidence of a test's accuracy for predicting job performance; chapter 12 discusses educational applications; and chapter 13 discusses test use in program evaluation and public policy.

STANDARDS FOR PSYCHOLOGICAL TESTING AND ASSESSMENT

The standards in this chapter have been separated into five thematic clusters labeled as follows:

1. Test User Qualifications
2. Test Selection
3. Test Administration
4. Test Interpretation
5. Test Security

Cluster 1. Test User Qualifications

Standard 10.1

Those who use psychological tests should confine their testing and related assessment activities to their areas of competence, as demonstrated through education, training, experience, and appropriate credentials.

Comment: Responsible use and interpretation of test scores require appropriate levels of experience, sound professional judgment, and understanding of the empirical and theoretical foundations of tests. For many assessments, competency also requires sufficient familiarity with the population of which the test taker is a member to facilitate test selection, test administration, and test score interpretation. For example, when personality tests and neuropsychological tests are administered as part of a psychological assessment of an individual, the test scores must be understood in the context of the individual's physical and psychological state; cultural and linguistic development; and educational, gender, health, and occupational background. Scoring also must take into account other evidence relevant to the tests used. Test score interpretation requires professionally responsible judgment that is exercised within the boundaries of knowledge and skill afforded by the professional's education, training, and supervised experience, as well as the context in which the assessment is being performed.

Standard 10.2

Those who select tests and draw inferences from test scores should be familiar with the relevant evidence of validity and reliability/precision for the intended uses of the test scores and assessments, and should be prepared to articulate a logical analysis that supports all facets of the assessment and the inferences made from the assessment.

Comment: A presentation and analysis of validity and reliability/precision evidence generally is not needed in a report that is provided for the test taker or a third party, because it is too cumbersome and of little interest to most report readers. However, in situations in which the selection of tests may be problematic (e.g., oral subtests with deaf test takers), a brief description of the rationale for using or not using particular measures is advisable.

When potential inferences derived from psychological test scores are not supported by current data yet may hold promise for future validation, they may be described by the test developer and test user as hypotheses for further validation in test score interpretation. Those receiving interpretations of such results should be cautioned that such inferences do not yet have adequately demonstrated evidence of validity and should not be the basis for a diagnostic decision or prognostic formulation.

Standard 10.3

Professionals should verify that persons under their supervision have appropriate knowledge and skills to administer and score tests.

Comment: Individuals administering tests but not involved in their selection or interpretation should be supervised by a professional. They should have knowledge of, as well as experience with, the test takers' presenting problems (e.g., brain injury) and the test settings (e.g., clinical, forensic).

Cluster 2. Test Selection

Standard 10.4

Tests that are combined to form a battery of tests should be appropriate for the purposes of the assessment.

Comment: For example, in a neuropsychological assessment for evidence of an injury to an area of the brain, it is necessary to select a combination of tests with known diagnostic sensitivity and specificity to impairments arising from trauma to specific regions of the brain.

Standard 10.5

Tests selected for use in psychological testing should be suitable for the characteristics and background of the test taker.

Comment: When tests are part of a psychological assessment, the professional generally should take into account characteristics of the individual test taker, including age and developmental level, race/ethnicity, gender, and linguistic and/or physical characteristics that may affect the ability of the test taker to meet the requirements of the test. The professional should also take into account the availability of norms and evidence of validity for a population representative of the test taker. If no normative or validity studies are available for a relevant population, test interpretations should be qualified and presented as hypotheses rather than conclusions.

Standard 10.6

When differential diagnosis is needed, the professional should choose, if possible, a test or tests for which there is credible evidence that the scores of the test(s) distinguish between the two or more diagnostic groups of concern rather than merely distinguishing abnormal cases from the general population.

Comment: Professionals will find it particularly helpful if evidence of validity is in a form that enables them to determine how much confidence can be placed in interpretations for an individual. Differences between group means and their statistical significance provide inadequate information regarding validity for individual diagnostic purposes. Additional information that might be considered includes effect sizes or a table showing the degree of overlap of predictor distributions among different criterion groups.

Cluster 3. Test Administration

Standard 10.7

Prior to testing, professionals and test administrators should provide the test taker, or appropriate others as applicable, with introductory information in a manner understandable to the test taker.

Comment: The goal of optimal test administration is to reduce error in the measurement of the construct. For example, the test taker should understand parameters surrounding the test, such as testing time limits, feedback or lack thereof, and opportunities to take breaks. In addition, the test taker should have an understanding of the limits of confidentiality, who will have access to the test results, whether and when test results or decisions based on the scores will be shared with the test taker, whether the test taker will have an opportunity to retest, and under what circumstances retesting could occur.

Standard 10.8

Professionals and test administrators should follow administration instructions, including calibration of technical equipment and verification of scoring accuracy and replicability, and should provide settings for testing that facilitate the performance of test takers.

Comment: Because the normative data against which a test taker's performance will be evaluated were collected under the reported standard procedures, the professional needs to be aware of and take into account the effect that any nonstandard procedures may have on the test taker's obtained score and the interpretation of that score. When using tests that employ an unstructured response format, such as some projective tests, the professional should follow the administration instructions provided and apply objective scoring criteria when available and appropriate.

In some cases, testing may be conducted in a realistic setting to determine how a test taker responds in these settings. For example, an assessment for an attention disorder may be conducted in a noisy or distracting environment rather than in an environment that typically protects the test taker from such external threats to performance efficiency.

Standard 10.9

Professionals should take into account the purpose of the assessment, the construct being measured, and the capabilities of the test taker when deciding whether technology-based administration of tests should be used.

Comment: Quality control should be integral to the administration of computerized or technology-based tests. Some technology-based tests may require that test takers have an opportunity to receive instruction and to practice prior to the test administration, unless assessing ability to use the equipment is the purpose of the test. The professional is responsible for determining whether the technology-based administration of the test should be proctored, or whether technical support staff are necessary to assist with the use of the test equipment and software. The interpreter of the test scores should be informed if the test was unproctored or if no support staff were available.

Cluster 4. Test Interpretation

Standard 10.10

Those who select tests and interpret test results should not allow individuals or groups with vested interests in the outcomes of an assessment

to have an inappropriate influence on the interpretation of the assessment results.

Comment: Individuals or groups with a vested interest in the significance or meaning of the findings from psychological testing may include but are not limited to employers, health professionals, legal representatives, school personnel, third-party payers, and family members. In some instances, legal requirements may limit a professional's ability to prevent inappropriate interpretations of assessments from affecting decisions, but professionals have an obligation to document any disagreement in such circumstances.

Standard 10.11

Professionals should share test scores and interpretations with the test taker when appropriate or required by law. Such information should be expressed in language that the test taker or, when appropriate, the test taker's legal representative, can understand.

Comment: Test scores and interpretations should be expressed in terms that can be understood readily by the test taker or others entitled to the results. In most instances, a report should be generated and made available to the referral source. That report should adhere to standards required by the profession and/or the referral source, and the information should be documented in a manner that is understandable to the referral source. In some clinical situations, providing feedback to the test taker may actually cause harm. Care should be taken to minimize unintended consequences of test feedback. Any disclosure of test results to an individual or any decision not to release such results should be consistent with applicable legal standards, such as privacy laws.

Standard 10.12

In psychological assessment, the interpretation of test scores or patterns of test battery results should consider other factors that may influence a particular testing outcome. Where appropriate,

a description of such factors and an analysis of the alternative hypotheses or explanations regarding what may have contributed to the pattern of results should be included in the report.

Comment: Many factors (e.g., culture, gender, race/ethnicity, educational level, effort, employment status, left- or right-handedness, current mental state, health status, linguistic preference, and testing situation) may influence individual test results and the overall outcome of the psychological assessment. When preparing test score interpretations and reports drawn from an assessment, professionals should consider the extent to which these factors may introduce construct-irrelevant variance into the test results. The interpretation of test results in the assessment process also should be informed, when possible or appropriate, by an analysis of stylistic and other qualitative features of test-taking behavior that may be obtained from observations, interviews, and historical information. Inclusion of qualitative information may assist in understanding the outcome of tests and evaluations. In addition, tests of faking or effort often are used to determine the possibility of deception or malingering.

Standard 10.13

When the validity of a diagnosis is appraised by evaluating the level of agreement between interpretations of the test scores and the diagnosis, the diagnostic terms or categories employed should be carefully defined or identified.

Comment: Two diagnostic systems typically used are psychiatric (i.e., based on the *Diagnostic and Statistical Manual of Mental Disorders*) and health related (i.e., based on the *International Classification of Disease*). As applicable, the system used to diagnose the test taker should be noted. Some syndromes (e.g., Mild Cognitive Impairment, Social Learning Disability) do not appear in either system; for these, a description of the deficits should be used, with the closest diagnosis possible.

Standard 10.14

Criterion-related evidence of validity should be available when recommendations or decisions are presented by the professional as having an actuarial basis.

Comment: Test score interpretations should not imply that empirical evidence exists for a relationship among particular test results, prescribed interventions, and desired outcomes, unless such evidence is available for populations similar to those representative of the examinee.

Standard 10.15

The interpretation of test or test battery results for diagnostic purposes should be based on multiple sources of test and collateral information and on an understanding of the normative, empirical, and theoretical foundations, as well as the limitations, of such tests and data.

Comment: A given pattern of test performances represents a cross-sectional view of the individual being assessed within a particular context. The interpretation of findings derived from a complex battery of tests in such contexts requires appropriate education about, supervised experience with, and knowledge of procedural, theoretical, and empirical limitations of the tests and the evaluation procedure.

Standard 10.16

If a publisher suggests that tests are to be used in combination with one another, the professional should review the recommended procedures and evidence for combining tests and determine whether the rationale provided by the publisher is appropriate for the specific combination of tests and their intended uses.

Comment: For example, if measures of intelligence are packaged with measures of memory, or if measures of interests and personality styles are packaged together, then supporting reliability/precision and validity data for such combinations of the test scores and interpretations should be available.

Standard 10.17

Those who use computer-generated interpretations of test data should verify that the quality of the evidence of validity is sufficient for the interpretations.

Comment: Efforts to reduce a complex set of data into computer-generated interpretations of a given construct may yield misleading or oversimplified analyses of the meanings of test scores, which in turn may lead to faulty diagnostic and prognostic decisions. Norms on which the interpretations are based should be reviewed for their relevance and appropriateness.

Cluster 5. Test Security

Standard 10.18

Professionals and others who have access to test materials and test results should maintain the confidentiality of the test results and testing materials consistent with scientific, professional, legal, and ethical requirements. Tests (including obsolete versions) should not be made available to the public or resold to unqualified test users.

Comment: Professionals should be knowledgeable about and should conform to record-keeping and confidentiality guidelines required by applicable federal law and within the jurisdictions where they practice, as well as guidelines of the professional organizations to which they belong. The test publisher, the test user, the test taker, and third parties (e.g., school, court, employer) may have different levels of understanding or recognition of the need for confidentiality of test materials. To the extent possible, the professional who uses tests is responsible for managing the confidentiality of test information across all parties. It is important for the professional to be aware of possible threats to confidentiality and the legal and professional remedies available. Professionals also are responsible for maintaining the security of testing materials and respecting the copyrights of all tests. Distribution, display, or resale of test materials (including obsolete editions) to unauthorized recipients infringes the copyright of the materials and compromises test security. When it is necessary to reveal test content in the process of explaining results or in a court proceeding, this should happen in a controlled environment. When possible, copies of the content should not be distributed, or should be distributed in a manner that protects test security to the extent possible.

11. WORKPLACE TESTING AND CREDENTIALING

BACKGROUND

Organizations use employment testing for many purposes, including employee selection, placement, and promotion. *Selection* generally refers to decisions about which individuals will enter the organization; *placement* refers to decisions about how to assign individuals to positions within the organization; and *promotion* refers to decisions about which individuals within the organization will advance. What all three have in common is a focus on the prediction of future job behaviors, with the goal of influencing organizational outcomes such as efficiency, growth, productivity, and employee motivation and satisfaction.

Testing used in the processes of licensure and certification, which will here be generically called *credentialing*, focuses on an applicant's current skill or competence in a specified domain. In many occupations, individual practitioners must be licensed by governmental agencies. In other occupations, it is professional societies, employers, or other organizations that assume responsibility for credentialing. Although licensure typically involves provision of a credential for entry into an occupation, credentialing programs may exist at various levels, from novice to expert in a given field. Certification is usually sought voluntarily, although occupations differ in the degree to which obtaining certification influences employability or advancement. The credentialing process may include testing and other requirements, such as education or supervised experiences. The *Standards* applies to the use of tests as a component of the broader credentialing process.

Testing is also conducted in workplaces for a variety of purposes other than staffing decisions and credentialing. Testing as a tool for personal growth can be part of training and development programs, in which instruments measuring personality characteristics, interests, values, preferences, and work styles are commonly used with the goal of providing self-insight to employees. Testing can also take place in the context of program evaluation, as in the case of an experimental study of the effectiveness of a training program, where tests may be administered as pre- and post-measures. Some assessments conducted in employment settings, such as unstructured job interviews for which no claim of predictive validity is made, are nonstandardized in nature, and it is generally not feasible to apply standards to such assessments. The focus of this chapter, however, is on the use of testing specifically in staffing decisions and credentialing. Many additional issues relevant to uses of testing in organizational settings are discussed in other chapters: technical matters in chapters 1, 2, 4, and 5; documentation in chapter 7; and individualized psychological and personality assessment of job candidates in chapter 10.

As described in chapter 3, the ideal of fairness in testing is achieved if a given test score has the same meaning for all individuals and is not substantially influenced by construct-irrelevant barriers to individuals' performance. For example, a visually impaired person may have difficulty reading questions on a personality inventory or other vocational assessment provided in small print. Young people just entering the workforce may be less sophisticated in test-taking strategies than more experienced job applicants, and their scores may suffer. A person unfamiliar with computer technology may have difficulty with the user interface for a computer simulation assessment. In each of these cases, performance is hindered by a source of variance that is unrelated to the construct of interest. Sound testing practice involves careful monitoring of all aspects of the assessment process and appropriate action when needed to prevent undue disadvantages or advantages for some candidates caused by factors unrelated to the construct being assessed.

Employment Testing

The Influence of Context on Test Use

Employment testing involves using test information to aid in personnel decision making. Both the content and the context of employment testing vary widely. Content may cover various domains of knowledge, skills, abilities, traits, dispositions, values, and other individual characteristics. Some contextual features represent choices made by the employing organization; others represent constraints that must be accommodated by the employing organization. Decisions about the design, evaluation, and implementation of a testing system are specific to the context in which the system is to be used. Important contextual features include the following:

Internal versus external candidate pool. In some instances, such as promotional settings, the candidates to be tested are already employed by the organization. In others, applications are sought from individuals outside the organization. In yet other cases, a mix of internal and external candidates is sought.

Trained versus untrained candidates. In some instances, individuals with little training in a specialized knowledge or skill are sought, either because the job does not require the specialized knowledge or skill or because the organization plans to offer training after the point of hire. In other instances, trained or experienced workers are sought with the expectation that they can immediately perform a specialized job. Thus, a particular job may require very different selection systems, depending on whether trained or untrained individuals will be hired or promoted.

Short-term versus long-term focus. In some instances, the goal of the selection system is to predict performance immediately upon or shortly after hire. In other instances, the concern is with longer-term performance, as in the case of predictions as to whether candidates will successfully complete a multiyear overseas job assignment. Concerns about changing job tasks and job requirements also can lead to a focus on knowledge,

skills, abilities, and other characteristics projected to be necessary for performance on the target job in the future, even if they are not part of the job as currently constituted.

Screening in versus screening out. In some instances, the goal of the selection system is to screen in individuals who are likely to be very high performers on one set of behavioral or outcome criteria of interest to the organization. In others, the goal is to screen out individuals who are likely to be very poor performers. For example, an organization may wish to screen out a small proportion of individuals for whom the risk of pathological, deviant, counterproductive, or criminal behavior on the job is deemed too high. The same organization may want to screen in applicants who have a high probability of superior performance.

Mechanical versus judgmental decision making. In some instances, test information is used in a mechanical, automated fashion. This is the case when scores on a test battery are combined by formula and candidates are selected in strict top-down rank order, or when only candidates above specific cut scores are eligible to continue to subsequent stages of a selection system. In other instances, information from a test is judgmentally integrated with information from other tests and with nontest information to form an overall assessment of the candidate.

Ongoing versus one-time use of a test. In some instances, a test may be used over an extended period in an organization, permitting the accumulation of data and experience using the test in that context. In other instances, concerns about test security are such that repeated use is infeasible, and a new test is required for each test administration. For example, a work-sample test for lifeguards, requiring retrieval of a mannequin from the bottom of a pool, is not compromised if candidates possess detailed knowledge of the test in advance. In contrast, a written job-knowledge test for police officers may be severely compromised if some candidates have access to the test in advance. The key question is whether advance knowledge of test content affects candidates' performance unfairly and consequently changes the constructs measured by the test and the validity of inferences based on the scores.

Fixed applicant pool versus continuous flow. In some instances, an applicant pool can be assembled prior to beginning the selection process, as when an organization's policy is to consider all candidates who apply before a specific date. In other cases, there is a continuous flow of applicants about whom employment decisions need to be made on an ongoing basis. Ranking of candidates is possible in the case of the fixed pool; in the case of a continuous flow, a decision may need to be made about each candidate independent of information about other candidates.

Small versus large sample size. Sample size affects the degree to which different lines of evidence can be used to examine validity and fairness of interpretations of test scores for proposed uses of tests. For example, relying on the local setting to establish empirical linkages between test and criterion scores is not technically feasible with small sample sizes. In employment testing, sample sizes are often small; at the extreme is a job with only a single incumbent. Large sample sizes are sometimes available when there are many incumbents for the job, when multiple jobs share similar requirements and can be pooled, or when organizations with similar jobs collaborate in developing a selection system.

A new job. A special case of the problem of small sample size exists when a new job is created and there are no job incumbents. As new jobs emerge, employers need selection procedures to staff the new positions. Professional judgment may be used to identify appropriate employment tests and provide a rationale for the selection program even though the array of methods for documenting validity may be restricted. Although validity evidence based on criterion-oriented studies can rarely be assembled prior to the creation of a new job, the methods for generalizing validity evidence

in situations with small sample sizes can be used (see the discussion on page 173 concerning settings with small samples), as well as content-oriented studies using the subject matter experts responsible for designing the job.

Size of applicant pool relative to the number of job openings. The size of an applicant pool can constrain the type of testing system that is feasible. For desirable jobs, very large numbers of candidates may compete, and short screening tests may be used to reduce the pool to a size for which the administration of more time-consuming and expensive tests is practical. Large applicant pools may also pose test security concerns, limiting the organization to testing methods that permit simultaneous test administration to all candidates.

Thus, test use by employers is conditioned by contextual features. Knowledge of these features plays an important part in the professional judgment that will influence both the types of testing system developed and the strategies used to evaluate critically the validity of interpretations of test scores for proposed uses of the tests.

The Validation Process in Employment Testing

The validation process often begins with a job analysis in which information about job duties and tasks, responsibilities, worker characteristics, and other relevant information is collected. This information provides an empirical basis for articulating what is meant by *job performance* in the job under consideration, for developing measures of job performance, and for hypothesizing characteristics of individuals that may be predictive of performance.

The fundamental inference to be drawn from test scores in most applications of testing in employment settings is one of prediction: The test user wishes to make an inference from test results to some future job behavior or job outcome. Even when the validation strategy used does not involve empirical predictor-criterion linkages, as in the case of validity evidence based on test content, there is an implied criterion. Thus, although different strategies for gathering evidence may be used, the inference to be supported is that scores on the test can be used to predict subsequent job behavior. The validation process in employment settings involves the gathering and evaluation of evidence relevant to sustaining or challenging this inference. As detailed below and in chapter 1 (in the section "Evidence Based on Relations to Other Variables"), a variety of validation strategies can be used to support the inference.

It follows that establishing this predictive inference requires attention to two domains: that of the test (the predictor) and that of the job behavior or outcome of interest (the criterion). Evaluating the use of a test for an employment decision can be viewed as testing the hypothesis of a linkage between these domains. Operationally, there are many ways of linking these domains, as illustrated by the diagram below.

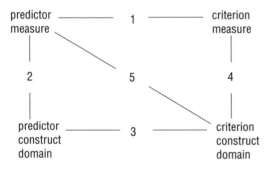

Alternative links between predictor and criterion measures

The diagram differentiates between a predictor construct domain and a predictor measure, and between a criterion construct domain and a criterion measure. A *predictor construct domain* is defined by specifying the set of behaviors, knowledge, skills, abilities, traits, dispositions, and values that will be included under particular construct labels (e.g., verbal reasoning, typing speed, conscientiousness). Similarly, a *criterion construct domain* specifies the set of job behaviors or job outcomes that will be included under particular construct labels (e.g., performance of core job tasks, teamwork, attendance, sales volume, overall job performance). Predictor and criterion measures

are intended to assess an individual's standing on the characteristics assessed in those domains.

The diagram enumerates inferences about a number of linkages that are commonly of interest. The first linkage (labeled 1 in the diagram) is between scores on a predictor measure and scores on a criterion measure. This inference is tested through empirical examination of relationships between the two measures. The second and fourth linkages (labeled 2 and 4) are conceptually similar: Both examine the relationship of an operational measure to the construct domain of interest. Logical analysis, expert judgment, and convergence with or divergence from conceptually similar or different measures are among the forms of evidence that can be examined in testing these linkages. Linkage 3 involves the relationship between the predictor construct domain and the criterion construct domain. This inferred linkage is established on the basis of theoretical and logical analysis. It commonly draws on systematic evaluation of job content and expert judgment as to the individual characteristics linked to successful job performance. Linkage 5 examines a direct relationship of the predictor measure to the criterion construct domain.

Some predictor measures are designed explicitly as samples of the criterion construct domain of interest; thus, isomorphism between the measure and the construct domain constitutes direct evidence for linkage 5. Establishing linkage 5 in this fashion is the hallmark of approaches that rely heavily on what the *Standards* refers to as *validity evidence based on test content.* Tests in which candidates for lifeguard positions perform rescue operations, or in which candidates for word processor positions type and edit text, provide examples of test content that forms the basis for validity.

A prerequisite to the use of a predictor measure for personnel selection is that the inferences concerning the linkage between the predictor measure and the criterion construct domain be established. As the diagram illustrates, there are multiple strategies for establishing this crucial linkage. One strategy is direct, via linkage 5; a second involves pairing linkage 1 and linkage 4; and a third involves pairing linkage 2 and linkage 3.

When the test is designed as a sample of the criterion construct domain, the validity evidence can be established directly via linkage 5. Another strategy for linking a predictor measure and the criterion construct domain focuses on linkages 1 and 4: pairing an empirical link between the predictor and criterion measures with evidence of the adequacy with which the criterion measure represents the criterion construct domain. The empirical link between the predictor measure and the criterion measure is part of what the *Standards* refers to as *validity evidence based on relationships to other variables*. The empirical link of the test and the criterion measure must be supplemented by evidence of the relevance of the criterion measure to the criterion construct domain to complete the linkage between the test and the criterion construct domain. Evidence of the relevance of the criterion measure to the criterion construct domain is commonly based on job analysis, although in some cases the link between the domain and the measure is so direct that relevance is apparent without job analysis (e.g., when the criterion construct of interest is absenteeism or turnover). Note that this strategy does not necessarily rely on a well-developed predictor construct domain. Predictor measures such as empirically keyed biodata measures are constructed on the basis of empirical links between test item responses and the criterion measure of interest. Such measures may, in some instances, be developed without a fully established conception of the predictor construct domain; the basis for their use is the direct empirical link between test responses and a relevant criterion measure. Unless sample sizes are very large, capitalization on chance may be a problem, in which case appropriate steps should be taken (e.g., cross-validation).

Yet another strategy for linking predictor scores and the criterion construct domain focuses on pairing evidence of the adequacy with which the predictor measure represents the predictor construct domain (linkage 2) with evidence of the linkage between the predictor construct domain and the criterion construct domain (linkage 3). As noted above, there is no single direct route to establishing these linkages. They involve lines of evidence subsumed under "construct validity" in prior conceptualizations of the validation process. A combination of lines of evidence (e.g., expert judgment of the characteristics predictive of job success, inferences drawn from an analysis of critical incidents of effective and ineffective job performance, and interview and observation methods) may support inferences about the predictor constructs linked to the criterion construct domain. Measures of these predictor constructs may then be selected or developed, and the linkage between the predictor measure and the predictor construct domain can be established with various lines of evidence for linkage 2, discussed above.

The various strategies for linking predictor scores to the criterion construct domain may differ in their potential applicability to any given employment testing context. While the availability of certain lines of evidence may be constrained, such constraints do not reduce the importance of establishing a validity argument for the predictive inference.

For example, methods for establishing linkages are more limited in settings with only small samples available. In such situations, gathering local evidence of predictor-criterion relationships is not feasible, and approaches to generalizing evidence from other settings may be more useful. A variety of methods exist for generalizing evidence of the validity of the interpretation of the predictive inference from other settings. Validity evidence may be directly transported from another setting in a case where sound evidence (e.g., careful job analysis) indicates that the local job is highly comparable to the job for which the validity data are being imported. These methods may rely on evidence for linkage 1 and linkage 4 that have already been established in other studies, as in the case of the transportability study described previously. Evidence for linkage 1 may also be established using techniques such as meta-analysis to combine results from multiple studies, and a careful job analysis may establish evidence for linkage 4 by showing the focal job to be similar to other jobs included in the meta-analysis. At the extreme, a selection system may be developed for a newly created job with no current incumbents. Here, generalizing evidence from other settings may be especially helpful.

For many testing applications, there is a considerable cumulative body of research that speaks to some, if not all, of the inferences discussed above. A meta-analytic integration of this research can form an integral part of the strategy for linking test information to the construct domain of interest. The value of collecting local validation data varies with the magnitude, relevance, and consistency of research findings using similar predictor measures and similar criterion construct domains for similar jobs. In some cases, a small and inconsistent cumulative research record may lead to a validation strategy that relies heavily on local data; in others, a large, consistent research base may make investing resources in additional local data collection unnecessary.

Thus, multiple sources of data and multiple lines of evidence can be drawn upon to evaluate the linkage between a predictor measure and the criterion construct domain of interest. There is no single preferred method of inquiry for establishing this linkage. Rather, the test user must consider the specifics of the testing situation and apply professional judgment in developing a strategy for testing the hypothesis of a linkage between the predictor measure and the criterion domain.

Bases for Evaluating Employment Test Use

Although a primary goal of employment testing is the accurate prediction of subsequent job behaviors or job outcomes, it is important to recognize that there are limits to the degree to which such criteria can be predicted. Perfect prediction is an unattainable goal. First, behavior in work settings is influenced by a wide variety of organizational and extra-organizational factors, including supervisor and peer coaching, formal and informal training, job design, organizational structures and systems, and family responsibilities, among others. Second, behavior in work settings is also influenced by a wide variety of individual characteristics, including knowledge, skills, abilities, personality, and work attitudes, among others.

Thus, any single characteristic will be only an imperfect predictor, and even complex selection systems only focus on the set of constructs deemed most critical for the job, rather than on all characteristics that can influence job behavior. Third, some measurement error always occurs, even in well-developed test and criterion measures.

Thus, testing systems cannot be judged against a standard of perfect prediction. Rather, they should be judged in terms of comparisons with available alternative selection methods. Professional judgment, informed by knowledge of the research literature about the degree of predictive accuracy relative to available alternatives, influences decisions about test use.

Decisions about test use are often influenced by additional considerations, including utility (i.e., cost-benefit) and return on investment, value judgments about the relative importance of selecting for one criterion domain versus others, concerns about applicant reactions to test content and processes, the availability and appropriateness of alternative selection methods, and statutory or regulatory requirements governing test use, fairness, and policy objectives such as workforce diversity. Organizational values necessarily come into play in decisions about test use; thus, even organizations with comparable evidence supporting an intended inference drawn from test scores may reach different conclusions about whether to use any particular test.

Testing in Professional and Occupational Credentialing

Tests are widely used in the credentialing of persons for many occupations and professions. Licensing requirements are imposed by federal, state, and local governments to ensure that those who are licensed possess knowledge and skills in sufficient degree to perform important occupational activities safely and effectively. Certification plays a similar role in many occupations not regulated by governments and is often a necessary precursor to advancement. Certification has also become widely used to indicate that a person has specific skills (e.g., operation of specialized auto repair equipment) or knowledge (e.g., estate planning), which may be only a part of their occupational duties. Licensure and certification will here generically be called *credentialing*.

Tests used in credentialing are intended to provide the public, including employers and government agencies, with a dependable mechanism for identifying practitioners who have met particular standards. The standards may be strict, but not so stringent as to unduly restrain the right of qualified individuals to offer their services to the public. Credentialing also serves to protect the public by excluding persons who are deemed to be not qualified to do the work of the profession or occupation. Qualifications for credentials typically include educational requirements, some amount of supervised experience, and other specific criteria, as well as attainment of a passing score on one or more examinations. Tests are used in credentialing in a broad spectrum of professions and occupations, including medicine, law, psychology, teaching, architecture, real estate, and cosmetology. In some of these, such as actuarial science, clinical neuropsychology, and medical specialties, tests are also used to certify advanced levels of expertise. Relicensure or periodic recertification is also required in some occupations and professions.

Tests used in credentialing are designed to determine whether the essential knowledge and skills have been mastered by the candidate. The focus is on the standards of competence needed for effective performance (e.g., in licensure this refers to safe and effective performance in practice). Test design generally starts with an adequate definition of the occupation or specialty, so that persons can be clearly identified as engaging in the activity. Then the nature and requirements of the occupation, in its current form, are delineated. To identify the knowledge and skills necessary for competent practice, it is important to complete an analysis of the actual work performed and then document the tasks and responsibilities that are essential to the occupation or profession of interest. A wide variety of empirical approaches may be used, including the critical incident technique, job analysis, training needs assessments, or practice studies and surveys of practicing profes-

sionals. Panels of experts in the field often work in collaboration with measurement experts to define test specifications, including the knowledge and skills needed for safe, effective performance and an appropriate way of assessing them. The *Standards* apply to all forms of testing, including traditional multiple-choice and other selected-response tests, constructed-response tasks, portfolios, situational judgment tasks, and oral examinations. More elaborate performance tasks, sometimes using computer-based simulation, are also used in assessing such practice components as, for example, patient diagnosis or treatment planning. Hands-on performance tasks may also be used (e.g., operating a boom crane or filling a tooth), with observation and evaluation by one or more examiners.

Credentialing tests may cover a number of related but distinct areas of knowledge or skill. Designing the testing program includes deciding what areas are to be covered, whether one or a series of tests is to be used, and how multiple test scores are to be combined to reach an overall decision. In some cases, high scores on some tests are permitted to offset (i.e., compensate for) low scores on other tests, so that an additive combination is appropriate. In other cases, a conjunctive decision model requiring acceptable performance on each test in an examination series is used. The type of pass-fail decision model appropriate for a credentialing program should be carefully considered, and the conceptual and/or empirical basis for the decision model should be articulated.

Validation of credentialing tests depends mainly on content-related evidence, often in the form of judgments that the test adequately represents the content domain associated with the occupation or specialty being considered. Such evidence may be supplemented with other forms of evidence external to the test. For example, information may be provided about the process by which specifications for the content domain were developed and the expertise of the individuals making judgments about the content domain. Criterion-related evidence is of limited applicability because credentialing examinations are not intended to predict individual performance in a specific job but rather to provide evidence that candidates have acquired the knowledge, skills, and judgment required for effective performance, often in a wide variety of jobs or settings (we use the term *judgment* to refer to the applications of knowledge and skill to particular situations). In addition, measures of performance in practice are generally not available for those who are not granted a credential.

Defining the minimum level of knowledge and skill required for licensure or certification is one of the most important and difficult tasks facing those responsible for credentialing. The validity of the interpretation of the test scores depends on whether the standard for passing makes an appropriate distinction between adequate and inadequate performance. Often, panels of experts are used to specify the level of performance that should be required. Standards must be high enough to ensure that the public, employers, and government agencies are well served, but not so high as to be unreasonably limiting. Verifying the appropriateness of the cut score or scores on a test used for licensure or certification is a critical element of the validation process. Chapter 5 provides a general discussion of setting cut scores (see Standards 5.21–5.23 for specific topics concerning cut scores).

Legislative bodies sometimes attempt to legislate a cut score, such as answering 70% of test items correctly. Cut scores established in such an arbitrary fashion can be harmful for two reasons. First, without detailed information about the test, job requirements, and their relationship, sound standard setting is impossible. Second, without detailed information about the format of the test and the difficulty of items, such arbitrary cut scores have little meaning.

Scores from credentialing tests need to be precise in the vicinity of the cut score. They may not need to be as precise for test takers who clearly pass or clearly fail. Computer-based mastery tests may include a provision to end the testing when it becomes clear that a decision about the candidate's performance can be made, resulting in a shorter test for candidates whose performance clearly exceeds or falls below the minimum performance required for a passing score. Because

mastery tests may not be designed to provide accurate results over the full score range, many such tests report results as simply "pass" or "fail." When feedback is given to candidates about how well or how poorly they performed, precision throughout the score range is needed. Conditional standard errors of measurement, discussed in chapter 2, provide information about the precision of specific scores.

Candidates who fail may profit from information about the areas in which their performance was especially weak. This is the reason that subscores are sometimes provided. Subscores are often based on relatively small numbers of items and can be much less reliable than the total score. Moreover, differences in subscores may simply reflect measurement error. For these reasons, the decision to provide subscores to candidates should be made carefully, and information should be provided to facilitate proper interpretation. Chapter 2 and Standard 2.3 speak to the importance of subscore reliability.

Because credentialing tends to involve high stakes and is an ongoing process, with tests given on a regular schedule, it is generally not desirable to use the same test form repeatedly. Thus, new forms, or versions of the test, are generally needed on an ongoing basis. From a technical perspective, all forms of a test should be prepared to the same specifications, assess the same content domains, and use the same weighting of components or topics.

Alternate test forms should have the same score scale so that scores can retain their meaning. Various methods of linking or equating alternate forms can be used to ensure that the standard for passing represents the same level of performance on all forms. Note that release of past test forms may compromise the extent to which different test forms are comparable.

Practice in professions and occupations often changes over time. Evolving legal restrictions, progress in scientific fields, and refinements in techniques can result in a need for changes in test content. Each profession or occupation should periodically reevaluate the knowledge and skills measured in its examination used to meet the requirements of the credential. When change is substantial, it becomes necessary to revise the definition of the profession, and the test content, to reflect changing circumstances. These changes to the test may alter the meaning of the score scale. When major revisions are made in the test or when the score scale changes, the cut score should also be reestablished.

Some credentialing groups consider it necessary, as a practical matter, to adjust their passing score or other criteria periodically to regulate the number of accredited candidates entering the profession. This questionable procedure raises serious problems for the technical quality of the test scores and threatens the validity of the interpretation of a passing score as indicating entry-level competence. Adjusting the cut score periodically also implies that standards are set higher in some years than in others, a practice that is difficult to justify on the grounds of quality of performance. The score scale is sometimes adjusted so that a certain number or proportion of candidates will reach the passing score. This approach, while less obvious to the candidates than changing the cut score, is also technically inappropriate because it changes the meaning of the scores from year to year.

Passing a credentialing examination should signify that the candidate meets the knowledge and skill standards set by the credentialing body to ensure effective practice.

Issues of cheating and test security are of special importance for testing practices in credentialing. Issues of test security are covered in chapters 6 and 9. Issues of cheating by test takers are covered in chapter 8 (see Standards 8.9–8.12, addressing testing irregularities).

Fairness and access, discussed in chapter 3, are important for licensing and certification testing. An evaluation of an accommodation or modification for a credentialing test should take into consideration the critical functions performed in the work targeted by the test. In the case of credentialing tests, the criticality of job functions is informed by the public interest as well as the nature of the work itself. When a condition limits an individual's ability to perform a critical function of a job, an accommodation or modification of the licensing or certification exam may not be appropriate (i.e., some changes may fundamentally alter factors that the examination is designed to measure for protection of the public's health, safety, and welfare).

STANDARDS FOR WORKPLACE TESTING AND CREDENTIALING

The standards in this chapter have been separated into three thematic clusters labeled as follows:

1. Standards Generally Applicable to Both Employment Testing and Credentialing
2. Standards for Employment Testing
3. Standards for Credentialing

Cluster 1. Standards Generally Applicable to Both Employment Testing and Credentialing

Standard 11.1

Prior to development and implementation of an employment or credentialing test, a clear statement of the intended interpretations of test scores for specified uses should be made. The subsequent validation effort should be designed to determine how well this has been achieved for all relevant subgroups.

Comment: The objectives of employment and credentialing tests can vary considerably. Some employment tests aim to screen out those least suited for the job in question, while others are designed to identify those best suited for the job. Employment tests also vary in the aspects of job behavior they are intended to predict, which may include quantity or quality of work output, tenure, counterproductive behavior, and teamwork, among others. Credentialing tests and some employment tests are designed to identify candidates who have met some specified level of proficiency in a target domain of knowledge, skills, or judgment.

Standard 11.2

Evidence of validity based on test content requires a thorough and explicit definition of the content domain of interest.

Comment: In general, the job content domain for an employment test should be described in terms of the tasks that are performed and/or the knowledge, skills, abilities, and other characteristics that are required on the job. They should be clearly defined so that they can be linked to test content. The knowledge, skills, abilities, and other characteristics included in the content domain should be those that qualified applicants already possess when being considered for the job in question. Moreover, the importance of these characteristics for the job under consideration should not be expected to change substantially over a specified period of time.

For credentialing tests, the target content domain generally consists of the knowledge, skills, and judgment required for effective performance. The target content domain should be clearly defined so it can be linked to test content.

Standard 11.3

When test content is a primary source of validity evidence in support of the interpretation for the use of a test for employment decisions or credentialing, a close link between test content and the job or professional/occupational requirements should be demonstrated.

Comment: For example, if the test content samples job tasks with considerable fidelity (e.g., with actual job samples such as machine operation) or, in the judgment of experts, correctly simulates job task content (e.g., with certain assessment center exercises), or if the test samples specific job knowledge (e.g., information necessary to perform certain tasks) or skills required for competent performance, then content-related evidence can be offered as the principal form of evidence of validity. If the link between the test content and the job content is not clear and direct, other lines of validity evidence take on greater importance.

When evidence of validity based on test content is presented for a job or class of jobs, the evidence should include a description of the major job characteristics that a test is meant to sample. It is often valuable to also include information about the relative frequency, importance, or criticality of the elements. For a credentialing examination, the evidence should include a description of the major responsibilities, tasks, and/or activities performed by practitioners that the test is meant to sample, as well as the underlying knowledge and skills required to perform those responsibilities, tasks, and/or activities.

Standard 11.4

When multiple test scores or test scores and nontest information are integrated for the purpose of making a decision, the role played by each should be clearly explicated, and the inference made from each source of information should be supported by validity evidence.

Comment: In credentialing, candidates may be required to score at or above a specified minimum on each of several tests (e.g., a practical, skill-based examination and a multiple-choice knowledge test) or at or above a cut score on a total composite score. Specific educational and/or experience requirements may also be mandated. A rationale and its supporting evidence should be provided for each requirement. For tests and assessments, such evidence includes, but is not necessarily limited to, the reliability/precision of scores and the correlations among the tests and assessments.

In employment testing, a decision maker may integrate test scores with interview data, reference checks, and many other sources of information in making employment decisions. The inferences drawn from test scores should be limited to those for which validity evidence is available. For example, viewing a high test score as indicating overall job suitability, and thus precluding the need for reference checks, would be an inappropriate inference from a test measuring a single narrow, albeit relevant, domain, such as job knowledge. In other circumstances, decision makers integrate scores across multiple tests, or across multiple scales within a given test.

Cluster 2. Standards for Employment Testing

Standard 11.5

When a test is used to predict a criterion, the decision to conduct local empirical studies of predictor-criterion relationships and the interpretation of the results should be grounded in knowledge of relevant research.

Comment: The cumulative literature on the relationship between a particular type of predictor and type of criterion may be sufficiently large and consistent to support the predictor-criterion relationship without additional research. In some settings, the cumulative research literature may be so substantial and so consistent that a dissimilar finding in a local study should be viewed with caution unless the local study is exceptionally sound. Local studies are of greatest value in settings where the cumulative research literature is sparse (e.g., due to the novelty of the predictor and/or criterion used), where the cumulative record is inconsistent, or where the cumulative literature does not include studies similar to the study from the local setting (e.g., a study of a test with a large cumulative literature dealing exclusively with production jobs and a local setting involving managerial jobs).

Standard 11.6

Reliance on local evidence of empirically determined predictor-criterion relationships as a validation strategy is contingent on a determination of technical feasibility.

Comment: Meaningful evidence of predictor-criterion relationships is conditional on a number of features, including (a) the job's being relatively stable rather than in a period of rapid evolution; (b) the availability of a relevant and reliable criterion measure; (c) the availability of a sample reasonably representative of the population of interest; and (d) an adequate sample size for estimating the strength of the predictor-criterion relationship. If any of these conditions is not met, some alternative validation strategy should be used. For example, as noted in the comment to Standard 11.5, the cumulative research literature may provide strong evidence of validity.

Standard 11.7

When empirical evidence of predictor-criterion relationships is part of the pattern of evidence used to support test use, the criterion measure(s) used should reflect the criterion construct domain of interest to the organization. All criteria used should represent important work behaviors or work outputs, either on the job or in job-relevant training, as indicated by an appropriate review of information about the job.

Comment: When criteria are constructed to represent job activities or behaviors (e.g., supervisory ratings of subordinates on important job dimensions), systematic collection of information about the job should inform the development of the criterion measures. However, there is no clear choice among the many available job analysis methods. Note that job analysis is not limited to direct observation of the job or direct sampling of subject matter experts; large-scale job-analytic databases often provide useful information. There is not a clear need for job analysis to support criterion use when measures such as absenteeism, turnover, or accidents are the criteria of interest.

Standard 11.8

Individuals conducting and interpreting empirical studies of predictor-criterion relationships should identify artifacts that may have influenced study findings, such as errors of measurement, range restriction, criterion deficiency, criterion contamination, and missing data. Evidence of the presence or absence of such features, and of actions taken to remove or control their influence, should be documented and made available as needed.

Comment: Errors of measurement in the criterion and restrictions on the variability of predictor or criterion scores systematically reduce estimates of the relationship between predictor measures and the criterion construct domain, but procedures for correction for the effects of these artifacts are available. When these procedures are applied, both corrected and uncorrected values should be presented, along with the rationale for the correction procedures chosen. Statistical significance tests for uncorrected correlations should not be used with corrected correlations. Other features to be considered include issues such as missing data for some variables for some individuals, decisions about the retention or removal of extreme data points, the effects of capitalization on chance in selecting predictors from a larger set on the basis of strength of predictor-criterion relationships, and the possibility of spurious predictor-criterion relationships, as in the case of collecting criterion ratings from supervisors who know selection test scores. Chapter 3, on fairness, describes additional issues that should be considered.

Standard 11.9

Evidence of predictor-criterion relationships in a current local situation should not be inferred from a single previous validation study unless the previous study of the predictor-criterion relationships was done under favorable conditions (i.e., with a large sample size and a relevant criterion) and the current situation corresponds closely to the previous situation.

Comment: Close correspondence means that the criteria (e.g., the job requirements or underlying psychological constructs) are substantially the same (e.g., as is determined by a job analysis), and that the predictor is substantially the same. Judgments about the degree of correspondence should be based on factors that are likely to affect the predictor-criterion relationship. For example, a test of situational judgment found to predict performance of managers in one country may or may not predict managerial performance in another country with a very different culture.

Standard 11.10

If tests are to be used to make job classification decisions (e.g., if the pattern of predictor scores will be used to make differential job assignments), evidence that scores are linked to different levels or likelihoods of success among jobs, job groups, or job levels is needed.

Comment: As noted in chapter 1, it is possible for tests to be highly predictive of performance for different jobs but not provide evidence of differential success among the jobs. For example, the same people may be predicted to be successful for each of the jobs.

Standard 11.11

If evidence based on test content is a primary source of validity evidence supporting the use of a test for selection into a particular job, a similar inference should be made about the test in a new situation only if the job and situation are substantially the same as the job and situation where the original validity evidence was collected.

Comment: Appropriate test use in this context requires that the critical job content factors be substantially the same (e.g., as is determined by a job analysis) and that the reading level of the test material not exceed that appropriate for the new job. In addition, the original meaning of the test materials should not be substantially changed in the new situation. For example, "*salt* is to *pepper*" may be the correct answer to the analogy item "*white* is to *black*" in a culture where people ordinarily use black pepper, but the item would have a different meaning in a culture where white pepper is the norm.

Standard 11.12

When the use of a given test for personnel selection relies on relationships between a predictor construct domain that the test represents and a criterion construct domain, two links need to be established. First, there should be evidence that the test scores are reliable and that the test content adequately samples the predictor construct domain; and second, there should be evidence for the relationship between the predictor construct domain and major factors of the criterion construct domain.

Comment: There should be a clear conceptual rationale for these linkages. Both the predictor construct domain and the criterion construct domain to which it is to be linked should be defined carefully. There is no single preferred route to establishing these linkages. Evidence in support of linkages between the two construct domains can include patterns of findings in the research literature and systematic evaluation of job content to identify predictor constructs linked to the criterion domain. The bases for judgments linking the predictor and criterion construct domains should be documented.

For example, a test of cognitive ability might be used to predict performance in a job that is complex and requires sophisticated analysis of many factors. Here, the predictor construct domain would be cognitive ability, and verifying the first link would entail demonstrating that the test is an adequate measure of the cognitive ability domain. The second linkage might be supported by multiple lines of evidence, including a compilation of research findings showing a consistent relationship between cognitive ability and performance on complex tasks, and by judgments from subject matter experts regarding the importance of cognitive ability for performance in the performance domain.

Cluster 3. Standards for Credentialing

Standard 11.13

The content domain to be covered by a credentialing test should be defined clearly and justified in terms of the importance of the content for credential-worthy performance in an occupation or profession. A rationale and evidence should be provided to support the claim that the knowledge or skills being assessed are required for credential-worthy performance in that occupation and are consistent with the purpose for which the credentialing program was instituted.

Comment: Typically, some form of job or practice analysis provides the primary basis for defining the content domain. If the same examination is used in the credentialing of people employed in a variety of settings and specialties, a number of different job settings may need to be analyzed. Although the job analysis techniques may be similar to those used in employment testing, the emphasis for credentialing is limited appropriately to knowledge and skills necessary for effective practice. The knowledge and skills contained in a core curriculum designed to train people for the job or occupation may be relevant, especially if the curriculum has been designed to be consistent with empirical job or practice analyses.

In tests used for licensure, knowledge and skills that may be important to success but are not directly related to the purpose of licensure (e.g., protecting the public) should not be included. For example, in accounting, marketing skills may be important for success, and assessment of those skills might have utility for organizations selecting accountants for employment. However, lack of those skills may not present a threat to the public, and thus the skills would appropriately be excluded from this licensing examination. The fact that successful practitioners possess certain knowledge or skills is relevant but not persuasive. Such information needs to be coupled with an analysis of the purpose of a credentialing program and the reasons that the knowledge or skills are required in an occupation or profession.

Standard 11.14

Estimates of the consistency of test-based credentialing decisions should be provided in addition to other sources of reliability evidence.

Comment: The standards for decision consistency described in chapter 2 are applicable to tests used for licensure and certification. Other types of re-liability estimates and associated standard errors of measurement may also be useful, particularly the conditional standard error at the cut score. However, the consistency of decisions on whether to certify is of primary importance.

Standard 11.15

Rules and procedures that are used to combine scores on different parts of an assessment or scores from multiple assessments to determine the overall outcome of a credentialing test should be reported to test takers, preferably before the test is administered.

Comment: In some credentialing cases, candidates may be required to score at or above a specified minimum on each of several tests. In other cases, the pass-fail decision may be based solely on a total composite score. If tests will be combined into a composite, candidates should be provided information about the relative weighting of the tests. It is not always possible to inform candidates of the exact weights prior to test administration because the weights may depend on empirical properties of the score distributions (e.g., their variances). However, candidates should be informed of the intention of weighting (e.g., test A contributes 25% and test B contributes 75% to the total score).

Standard 11.16

The level of performance required for passing a credentialing test should depend on the knowledge and skills necessary for credential-worthy performance in the occupation or profession and should not be adjusted to control the number or proportion of persons passing the test.

Comment: The cut score should be determined by a careful analysis and judgment of credential-worthy performance (see chap. 5). When there are alternate forms of a test, the cut score should refer to the same level of performance for all forms.

12. EDUCATIONAL TESTING AND ASSESSMENT

BACKGROUND

Educational testing has a long history of use for informing decisions about learning, instruction, and educational policy. Results of tests are used to make judgments about the status, progress, or accomplishments of individual students, as well as entities such as schools, school districts, states, or nations. Tests used in educational settings represent a variety of approaches, ranging from traditional multiple-choice and open-ended item formats to performance assessments, including scorable portfolios. As noted in the introductory chapter, a distinction is sometimes made between the terms *test* and *assessment*, the latter term encompassing broader sources of information than a score on a single instrument. In this chapter we use both terms, sometimes interchangeably, because the standards discussed generally apply to both.

This chapter does not explicitly address issues related to tests developed or selected exclusively to inform learning and instruction at the classroom level. Those tests often have consequences for students, including influencing instructional actions, placing students in educational programs, and affecting grades that may affect admission to colleges. The *Standards* provide desirable criteria of quality that can be applied to such tests. However, as with past editions, practical considerations limit the *Standards'* applicability at the classroom level. Formal validation practices are often not feasible for classroom tests because schools and teachers do not have the resources to document the characteristics of their tests and are not publishing their tests for widespread use. Nevertheless, the core expectations of validity, reliability/precision, and fairness should be considered in the development of such tests.

The *Standards* clearly applies to formal tests whose scores or other results are used for purposes that extend beyond the classroom, such as benchmark or interim tests that schools and districts use to monitor student progress. The *Standards*

also applies to assessments that are adopted for use across classrooms and whose developers make claims for the validity of score interpretations for intended uses. Admittedly, this distinction is not always clear. Increasingly, districts, schools, and teachers are using an array of coordinated instruction and/or assessment systems, many of which are technology based. These systems may include, for example, banks of test items that individual teachers can use in constructing tests for their own purposes, focused assessment exercises that accompany instructional lessons, or simulations and games designed for instruction or assessment purposes. Even though it is not always possible to separate measurement issues from corresponding instructional and learning issues in these systems, assessments that are part of these systems and that serve purposes beyond an individual teacher's instruction fall within the purview of the *Standards*. Developers of these systems bear responsibility for adhering to the *Standards* to support their claims.

Both the introductory discussion and the standards provided in this chapter are organized into three broad clusters: (1) design and development of educational assessments; (2) use and interpretation of educational assessments; and (3) administration, scoring, and reporting of educational assessments. Although the clusters are related to the chapters addressing operational areas of the standards, this discussion draws upon the principles and concepts provided in the foundational chapters on validity, reliability/precision, and fairness and applies them to educational settings. It should also be noted that this chapter does not specifically address the use of test results in mandated accountability systems that may impose performance-based rewards or sanctions on institutions such as schools or school districts or on individuals such as teachers or principals. Accountability applications involving aggregates of scores are addressed in chapter 13 ("Uses of Tests for Program Evaluation, Policy Studies, and Accountability").

Design and Development of Educational Assessments

Educational tests are designed and developed to provide scores that support interpretations for the intended test purposes and uses. Design and development of educational tests, therefore, begins by considering test purpose. Once a test's purposes are established, considerations related to the specifics of test design and development can be addressed.

Major Purposes of Educational Testing

Although educational tests are used in a variety of ways, most address at least one of three major purposes: (a) to make inferences that inform teaching and learning at the individual or curricular level; (b) to make inferences about outcomes for individual students and groups of students; and (c) to inform decisions about students, such as certifying students' acquisition of particular knowledge and skills for promotion, placement in special instructional programs, or graduation.

Informing teaching and learning. Assessments that inform teaching and learning start with clear goals for student learning and may involve a variety of strategies for assessing student status and progress. The goals are typically cognitive in nature, such as student understanding of rational number equivalence, but may also address affective states or psychomotor skills. For example, teaching and learning goals could include increasing student interest in science or teaching students to form letters with a pen or pencil.

Many assessments that inform teaching and learning are used for formative purposes. Teachers use them in day-to-day classroom settings to guide ongoing instruction. For example, teachers may assess students prior to starting a new unit to ascertain whether they have acquired the necessary prerequisite knowledge and skills. Teachers may then gather evidence throughout the unit to see whether students are making anticipated progress

and to identify any gaps and/or misconceptions that need to be addressed.

More formal assessments used for teaching and learning purposes may not only inform classroom instruction but also provide individual and aggregated assessment data that others may use to support learning improvement. For example, teachers in a district may periodically administer commercial or locally constructed assessments that are aligned with the district curriculum or state content standards. These tests may be used to evaluate student learning over one or more units of instruction. Results may be reported immediately to students, teachers, and/or school or district leaders. The results may also be broken down by content standard or subdomain to help teachers and instructional leaders identify strengths and weaknesses in students' learning and/or to identify students, teachers, and/or schools that may need special assistance. For example, special programs may be designed to tutor students in specific areas in which test results indicate they need help. Because the test results may influence decisions about subsequent instruction, it is important to base content domain or subdomain scores on sufficient numbers of items or tasks to reliably support the intended uses.

In some cases, assessments administered during the school year may be used to predict student performance on a year-end summative assessment. If the predicted performance on the year-end assessment is low, additional instructional interventions may be warranted. Statistical techniques, such as linear regression, may be used to establish the predictive relationships. A confounding variable in such predictions may be the extent to which instructional interventions based on interim results improve the performance of initially low-scoring students over the course of the school year; the predictive relationships will decrease to the extent that student learning is improved.

Assessing student outcomes. The assessment of student outcomes typically serves summative functions, that is, to help assess pupils' learning at the completion of a particular instructional sequence (e.g., the end of the school year). Educational testing of student outcomes can be concerned with several types of score interpretations, including standards-based interpretations, growth-based interpretations, and normative interpretations. These outcomes may relate to the individual student or be aggregated over groups of students, for example, classes, subgroups, schools, districts, states, or nations.

Standards-based interpretations of student outcomes typically start with *content standards*, which specify what students are expected to know and be able to do. Such standards are typically established by committees of experts in the area to be tested. Content standards should be clear and specific and give teachers, students, and parents sufficient direction to guide teaching and learning. Academic *achievement standards*, which are sometimes referred to as *performance standards*, connect content standards to information that describes how well students are acquiring the knowledge and skills contained in academic content standards. Performance standards may include labels for levels of performance (e.g., "basic," "proficient," "advanced"), descriptions of what students at different performance levels know and can do, examples of student work that illustrate the range of achievement within each performance level, and cut scores specifying the levels of performance on an assessment that separate adjacent levels of achievement. The process of establishing the cut scores for the academic achievement standards is often referred to as *standard setting*.

Although it follows from a consideration of standards-based testing that assessments should be tightly aligned with content standards, it is usually not possible to comprehensively measure all of the content standards using a single summative test. For example, content standards that focus on student collaboration, oral argumentation, or scientific lab activities do not easily lend themselves to measurement by traditional tests. As a result, certain content standards may be underemphasized in instruction at the expense of standards that can be measured by the end-of-year summative test. Such limitations may be addressed by developing assessment components that focus on various aspects of a set of common content standards.

For example, performance assessments that are more closely connected with instructional units may measure certain content standards that are not easily assessed by a more traditional end-of-year summative assessment.

The evaluation of student outcomes can also involve interpretations related to student progress or growth over time, rather than just performance at a particular time. In standards-based testing, an important consideration is measuring student growth from year to year, both at the level of the individual student and aggregated across students, for example at the teacher, subgroup, or school level. A number of educational assessments are used to monitor the progress or growth of individual students within and/or across school years. Tests used for these purposes are sometimes supported by vertical scales that span a broad range of developmental or educational levels and include (but are not limited to) both conventional multilevel test batteries and computerized adaptive assessments. In constructing vertical scales for educational tests, it is important to align standards and/or learning objectives vertically across grades and to design tests at adjacent levels (or grades) that have substantial overlap in the content measured.

However, a variety of alternative statistical models exist for measuring student growth, not all of which require the use of a vertical scale. In using and evaluating various growth models, it is important to clearly understand which questions each growth model can (and cannot) answer, what assumptions each growth model is based on, and what appropriate inferences can be derived from each growth model's results. Missing data can create challenges for some growth models. Attention should be paid to whether some populations are being excluded from the model due to missing data (for example, students who are mobile or have poor attendance). Other factors to consider in the use of growth models are the relative reliability/precision of scores estimated for groups with different amounts of missing data, and whether the model treats students the same regardless of where they are on the performance continuum.

Student outcomes in educational testing are sometimes evaluated through norm-referenced interpretations. A norm-referenced interpretation compares a student's performance with the performances of other students. Such interpretations may be made when assessing both status and growth. Comparisons may be made to all students, to a particular subgroup (e.g., other test takers who have majored in the test taker's intended field of study), or to subgroups based on many other conditions (e.g., students with similar academic performance, students from similar schools). Norms can be developed for a variety of targeted populations ranging from national or international samples of students to the students in a particular school district (i.e., local norms). Norm-referenced interpretations should consider differences in the target populations at different times of a school year and in different years. When a test is routinely administered to an entire target population, as in the case of a statewide assessment, norm-referenced interpretations are relatively easy to produce and generally apply only to a single point in the school year. However, national norms for a standardized achievement test are often provided at several intervals within the school year. In that case, developers should indicate whether the norms covering a particular time interval were based on data or interpolated from data collected at other times of year. For example, winter norms are often based on an interpolation between empirical norms collected in fall and spring. The basis for calculating interpolated norms should be documented so that users can be made aware of the underlying assumptions about student growth over the school year.

Because of the time and expense associated with developing national norms, many test developers report alternative *user norms* that consist of descriptive statistics based on all those who take their test or a demographically representative subset of those test takers over a given period of time. Although such statistics—based on people who happen to take the test—are often useful, the norms based on them will change as the makeup of the reference group changes. Consequently, user norms should not be confused with norms representative of more systematically sampled groups.

Informing decisions about students. Test results are often used in the process of making decisions about individual students, for example, about high school graduation, placement in certain educational programs, or promotion from one grade to the next. In higher education, test results inform admissions decisions and the placement of admitted students in different courses (e.g., remedial or regular) or instructional programs.

Fairness is a fundamental concern with all tests, but because decisions regarding educational placement, promotion, or graduation can have profound individual effects, fairness is paramount when tests are used to inform such decisions. Fairness in this context can be enhanced through careful consideration of conditions that affect students' opportunities to demonstrate their capabilities. For example, when tests are used for promotion and graduation, the fairness of individual score interpretations can be enhanced by (a) providing students with multiple opportunities to demonstrate their capabilities through repeated testing with alternate forms or other construct-equivalent means; (b) providing students with adequate notice of the skills and content to be tested, along with appropriate test preparation materials; (c) providing students with curriculum and instruction that afford them the opportunity to learn the content and skills to be tested; (d) providing students with equal access to disclosed test content and responses as well as any specific guidance for test taking (e.g., test-taking strategies); (e) providing students with appropriate testing accommodations to address particular access needs; and (f) in appropriate cases, taking into account multiple criteria rather than just a single test score.

Tests informing college admissions decisions are used in conjunction with other information about students' capabilities. Selection criteria may vary within an institution by academic specialization and may include past academic records, transcripts, and grade-point average or rank in class. Scores on tests used to certify students for high school graduation or scores on tests administered at the end of specific high school courses may be used in college admissions decisions. The interpretations inherent in these uses of high school tests should be supported by multiple lines of relevant validity evidence (e.g., both concurrent and predictive evidence). Other measures used by some institutions in making admissions decisions are samples of previous work by students, lists of academic and service accomplishments, letters of recommendation, and student-composed statements evaluated for the appropriateness of the goals and experience of the student and/or for writing proficiency.

Tests used to place students in appropriate college-level or remedial courses play an important role in both community colleges and four-year institutions. Most institutions either use commercial placement tests or develop their own tests for placement purposes. The items on placement tests are typically selected to serve this single purpose in an efficient manner and usually do not comprehensively measure prerequisite content. For example, a placement test in algebra will cover only a subset of algebra content taught in high school. Results of some placement tests are used to exempt students from having to take a course that would normally be required. Other placement tests are used by advisors for placing students in remedial courses or the most appropriate course in an introductory college-level sequence. In some cases, placement decisions are mechanized through the application of locally determined cut scores on the placement exam. Such cut scores should be established through a documented process involving appropriate stakeholders and validated through empirical research.

Results from educational tests may also inform decisions related to placing students in special instructional programs, including those for students with disabilities, English learners, and gifted and talented students. Test scores alone should never be used as the sole basis for including any student in special education programming, or excluding any student from such programming. Test scores should be interpreted in the context of the student's history, functioning, and needs. Nevertheless, test results may provide an important basis for determining whether a student has a disability and what the student's educational needs are.

Development of Educational Tests

As with all tests, once the construct and purposes of an educational test have been delineated, consideration must be given to the intended population of test takers, as well as to practical issues such as available testing time and the resources available to support the development effort. In the development of educational tests, focus is placed on measuring the knowledge, skills, and abilities of all examinees in the intended population without introducing any advantages or disadvantages because of individual characteristics (e.g., age, culture, disability, gender, language, race/ethnicity) that are irrelevant to the construct the test is intended to measure. The principles of universal design—an approach to assessment development that attempts to maximize the accessibility of a test for all of its intended examinees—provide one basis for developing educational assessments in this manner. Paramount in the process is explicit documentation of the steps taken during the development process to provide evidence of fairness, reliability/precision, and validity for the test's intended uses. The higher the stakes associated with the assessment, the more attention needs to be paid to such documentation. More detailed considerations related to the development of educational tests are discussed in the chapters on fairness in testing (chap. 3) and test design and development (chap. 4).

A variety of formats are used in developing educational tests, ranging from traditional item formats such as multiple-choice and open-ended items to performance assessments, including scorable portfolios, simulations, and games. Examples of such performance assessments might include solving problems using manipulable materials, making complex inferences after collecting information, or explaining orally or in writing the rationale for a particular course of government action under given economic conditions. An individual portfolio may be used as another type of performance assessment. Scorable portfolios are systematic collections of educational products typically collected, and possibly revised, over time.

Technology is often used in educational settings to present testing material and to record and score test takers' responses. Examples include enhancements of text by audio instructions to facilitate student understanding, computer-based and adaptive tests, and simulation exercises where attributes of performance assessments are supported by technology. Some test administration formats also may have the capacity to capture aspects of students' processes as they solve test items. They may, for example, monitor time spent on items, solutions tried and rejected, or editing sequences for texts created by test takers. Technologies also make it possible to provide test administration conditions designed to accommodate students with particular needs, such as those with different language backgrounds, attention deficit disorders, or physical disabilities.

Interpretations of scores on technology-based tests are evaluated by the same standards for validity, reliability/precision, and fairness as tests administered through more traditional means. It is especially important that test takers be familiarized with the assessment technologies so that any unfamiliarity with an input device or assessment interface does not lead to inferences based on construct-irrelevant variance. Furthermore, explicit consideration of sources of construct-irrelevant variance should be part of the validation framework as new technologies or interfaces are incorporated into assessment programs. Finally, it is important to describe scoring algorithms used in technology-based tests and the expert models on which they may be based, and to provide technical data supporting their use in the testing system documentation. Such documentation, however, should stop short of jeopardizing the security of the assessment in ways that could adversely affect the validity of score interpretations.

Assessments Serving Multiple Purposes

By evaluating students' knowledge and skills relative to a specific set of academic goals, test results may serve a variety of purposes, including improving instruction to better meet student needs; evaluating curriculum and instruction district-wide; identifying students, schools and/or teachers who need help; and/or predicting each student's likelihood of success on a summative assessment. It is important to validate the interpretations made from test scores on such assessments for each of their intended uses.

There are often tensions associated with using educational assessments for multiple purposes. For example, a test developed to monitor the progress or growth of individual students across school years is unlikely to also effectively provide detailed and actionable diagnostic information about students' strengths and weaknesses. Similarly, an assessment designed to be given several times over the course of the school year to predict student performance on a year-end summative assessment is unlikely to provide useful information about student learning with respect to particular instructional units. Most educational tests will serve one purpose better than others; and the more purposes an educational test is purported to serve, the less likely it is to serve any of those purposes effectively. For this reason, test developers and users should design and/or select educational assessments to achieve the purposes they believe are most important, and they should consider whether additional purposes can be fulfilled and should monitor the appropriateness of any identified additional uses.

Use and Interpretation of Educational Assessments

Stakes and Consequences of Assessment

The importance of the results of testing programs for individuals, institutions, or groups is often referred to as the *stakes* of the testing program. When the stakes for an individual are high, and important decisions depend substantially on test performance, the responsibility for providing evidence supporting a test's intended purposes is greater than might be expected for tests used in low-stakes settings. Although it is never possible to achieve perfect accuracy in describing an individual's performance, efforts need to be made to minimize errors of measurement or errors in classifying individuals into categories such as "pass," "fail," "admit," or "reject." Further, supporting the validity of interpretations for high-stakes purposes, whether individual or institutional, typically entails collecting sound collateral information that can be used to assist in understanding the factors that contributed to test results and to provide corroborating evidence that supports inferences based on the results. For example, test results can be influenced by multiple factors, both institutional and individual, such as the quality of education provided, students' exposure to education (e.g., through regular school attendance), and students' motivation to perform well on the test. Collecting this type of information can contribute to appropriate interpretations of test results.

The high-stakes nature of some testing programs can create special challenges when new test versions are introduced. For example, a state may introduce a series of high school end-of-course tests that are based on new content standards and are partially tied to graduation requirements. The operational use of these new tests must be accompanied by documentation that students have indeed been instructed on content aligned to the new standards. Because of feasibility constraints, this may require a carefully planned phase-in period that includes special surveys or qualitative research studies that provide the needed opportunity-to-learn documentation. Until such documentation is available, the tests should not be used for their intended high-stakes purpose.

Many types of educational tests are viewed as tools of educational policy. Beyond any intended policy goals, it is important to consider potential unintended effects of large-scale testing programs. These possible unintended effects include (a) narrowing of curricula in some schools to focus exclusively on anticipated test content, (b) restriction of the range of instructional approaches to correspond to the testing format, (c) higher dropout rates among students who do not pass the test, and (d) encouragement of instructional or administrative practices that may raise test scores without improving the quality of education. It is essential for those who mandate and use educational tests to be aware of such potential negative consequences (including missed opportunities to improve

teaching and learning), to collect information that bears on these issues, and to make decisions about the uses of assessments that take this information into account.

Assessments for Students With Disabilities and English Language Learners

In the 1999 edition of the *Standards*, the material on educational testing for special populations focused primarily on individualized diagnostic assessment and educational placement for students with special needs. Since then, requirements stemming from federal legislation have significantly increased the participation of special populations in large-scale educational assessment programs. Special populations have also become more diverse and now represent a larger percentage of those test takers who participate in general education programs. More students are being diagnosed with disabilities, and more of these students are included in general education programs and in state standards-based assessments. In addition, the number of students who are English language learners has grown dramatically, and the number included in educational assessments has increased accordingly.

As discussed in chapter 3 ("Fairness in Testing"), assessments for special populations involve a continuum of potential adaptations, ranging from specially developed alternate assessments to modifications and accommodations of regular assessments. The purpose of alternate assessments and adaptations is to increase the accessibility of tests that may not otherwise allow students with some characteristics to display their knowledge and skills. Assessments for special populations may also include assessments developed for English language learners and individually administered assessments that are used for diagnosis and placement.

Alternate assessments. The term *alternate assessments* as used here, in the context of educational testing, refers to assessments developed for students with significant cognitive disabilities. Based on performance standards different from those used for regular assessments, alternate assessments provide these students with the opportunity to demonstrate their standing and progress in learning. An alternate assessment might consist of an observation checklist, a multilevel assessment with performance tasks, or a portfolio that includes responses to selected-response and/or open-ended tasks. The assessment tasks are developed with the special characteristics of this population in mind. For example, a multilevel assessment with performance tasks might include scaffolding procedures in which the examiner eliminates question distracters when students answer incorrectly, in order to reduce question complexity. Or, in a portfolio assessment, the teacher might include work samples and other assessment information tailored specifically to the student. The teacher may assess the same English language arts standard by asking one student to write a story and another to sequence a story using picture cards, depending on which activity provides students with access to demonstrate what they know and can do.

The development and use of alternate assessments in education have been heavily influenced by federal legislation. Federal regulations may require that alternate assessments used in a given state have explicit connections to the content standards measured by the regular state assessment while allowing for content with less depth, breadth, and complexity. Such requirements clearly influence the design and development of alternate assessments in state standards-based programs.

Alternate assessments in education should be held to the same technical requirements that apply to regular large-scale assessments. These include documentation and empirical data that support test development, standard setting, validity, reliability/precision, and technical characteristics of the tests. When the number of students served under alternate assessments is too small to generate stable statistical data, the test developer and users should describe alternate judgmental or other procedures used to document evidence of the validity of score interpretations.

A variety of comparability issues may arise when alternate assessments are used in statewide testing programs, for example, in aggregating the results of alternate and regular assessments or in comparing trend data for subgroups when alternate assessments have been used in some years and regular assessments in other years.

Accommodations and modifications. To enable assessment systems to include all students, accommodations and modifications are provided to those students who need them, including those who participate in alternate assessments because of their significant cognitive disabilities. Adaptations, which include both accommodations and modifications, provide access to educational assessments.

Accommodations are adaptations to test format or administration (such as changes in the way the test is presented, the setting for the test, or the way in which the student responds) that maintain the same construct and produce results that are comparable to those obtained by students who do not use accommodations. Accommodations may be provided to English language learners to address their linguistic needs, as well as to students with disabilities to address specific, individual characteristics that otherwise would interfere with accessibility. For example, a student with extreme dyslexia may be provided with a screen reader to read aloud the scenarios and questions on a test measuring science inquiry skills. The screen reader would be considered an accommodation because reading is not part of the defined construct (science inquiry) and the scores obtained by the student on the test would be assumed to be comparable to those obtained by students testing under regular conditions.

The use of accommodations should be supported by evidence that their application does not change the construct that is being measured by the assessment. Such evidence may be available from studies of similar applications but may also require specially designed research.

Modifications are adaptations to test format or administration that change the construct being measured in order to make it accessible for designated students while retaining as much of the original construct as possible. Modifications result in scores that differ in meaning from those for the regular assessment. For example, a student with extreme dyslexia may be provided with a screen reader to read aloud the passages and questions on a reading comprehension test that includes decoding as part of the construct. In this case, the screen reader would be considered a modification because it changes the construct being measured, and scores obtained by the student on the test would not be assumed to be comparable to those obtained by students testing under regular conditions. In many cases, accommodations can meet student access needs without the use of modifications, but in some cases, modifications are the only option for providing some students with access to an educational assessment. As with alternate assessments, comparability issues arise with the use of modifications in educational testing programs.

Modified tests should be designed and developed with the same considerations of validity, reliability/precision, and fairness as regular assessments. It is not sufficient to assume that the validity evidence associated with a regular assessment generalizes to a modified version.

An extensive discussion of modifications and accommodations for special populations is provided in chapter 3 ("Fairness in Testing").

Assessments for English language proficiency. An increasing focus on the measurement of English language proficiency (ELP) for English language learners (ELLs) has mirrored the growing presence of these students in U.S. classrooms. Like standards-based content tests, ELP tests are based on ELP standards and are held to the same standards for precision of scores and validity and fairness of score interpretations for intended uses as are other large-scale tests.

ELP tests can serve a variety of purposes. They are used to identify students as English learners and qualify them for special ELL programs and services, to redesignate students as English proficient, and for purposes of diagnosis and instruction. States, districts, and schools also use ELP tests to monitor these students' progress and to hold schools and educators accountable for ELL learning and progress toward English proficiency.

As with any educational test, validity evidence for measures of ELP can be provided by examining the test blueprint, the alignment of content with ELP standards, construct comparability across

students, classification consistency, and other claims in the validity argument. The rationale and evidence supporting the ELP domain definition and the roles/relationships of the language modalities (e.g., reading, writing, speaking, listening) to overall ELP are important considerations in articulating the validity argument for an ELP test and can inform the interpretation of test results. Since no single assessment is equally effective in serving all desired purposes, users should consider which uses of ELP tests are their highest priority and choose or develop instruments accordingly.

Accommodations associated with ELP tests should be carefully considered, as adaptations that are appropriate for regular content assessments may compromise the ELP standards being assessed. In addition, users should establish common guidelines for using ELP results in making decisions about ELL students. The guidelines should include explicit policies and procedures for using results in identifying and redesignating ELL students as English proficient, an important process because of the legal and educational importance of these designations. Local education agencies and schools should be provided with easy access to the guidelines.

Individual assessments. Individually administered tests are used by psychologists and other professionals in schools and other related settings to inform decisions about a variety of services that may be administered to students. Services are provided for students who are gifted as well as for those who encounter academic difficulties (e.g., students requiring remedial reading instruction). Still other services are provided for students who display behavioral, emotional, physical, and/or more severe learning difficulties. Services may be provided for students who are taught in regular classrooms as well as for those receiving more specialized instruction (e.g., special education students).

Aspects of the test that may result in construct-irrelevant variance for students with certain relevant characteristics should be taken into account as appropriate by qualified testing professionals when using test results to aid placement decisions. For example, students' English language proficiency or prior educational experience may interfere with their performance on a test of academic ability and, if not taken into account, could lead to misclassification in special education. Once a student is placed, tests may be administered to monitor the progress of the student toward prescribed learning goals and objectives. Test results may also be used to inform evaluations of instructional effectiveness and determinations of whether the special services need to be continued, modified, or discontinued.

Many types of tests are used in individualized and special needs testing. These include tests of cognitive abilities, academic achievement, learning processes, visual and auditory memory, speech and language, vision and hearing, and behavior and personality. These tests typically are used in conjunction with other assessment methods—such as interviews, behavioral observations, and reviews of records—for purposes of identifying and placing students with disabilities. Regardless of the qualities being assessed and the data collection methods employed, assessment data used in making special education decisions are evaluated in terms of evidence supporting intended interpretations as related to the specific needs of the students. The data must also be judged in terms of their usefulness for designing appropriate educational programs for students who have special needs. For further information, see chapter 10 ("Psychological Testing and Assessment").

Assessment Literacy and Professional Development

Assessment literacy can be broadly defined as knowledge about the basic principles of sound assessment practice, including terminology, the development and use of assessment methodologies and techniques, and familiarity with standards by which the quality of testing practices are judged. The results of educational assessments are used in decision making across a variety of settings in classrooms, schools, districts, and states. Given the range and complexity of test purposes, it is important for test developers and those responsible for educational testing programs to encourage educators to be informed consumers of the tests and to fully understand and appropriately use

results that are reported to them. Similarly, as test users, it is the responsibility of educators to pursue and attain assessment literacy as it pertains to their roles in the education system.

Test sponsors and test developers can promote educator assessment literacy in a variety of ways, including workshops, development of written materials and media, and collaboration with educators in the test development process (e.g., development of content standards, item writing and review, and standard setting). In particular, those responsible for educational testing programs should incorporate assessment literacy into the ongoing professional development of educators. In addition, regular attempts should be made to educate other major stakeholders in the educational process, including parents, students, and policy makers.

Administration, Scoring, and Reporting of Educational Assessments

Administration of Educational Tests

Most educational tests involve standardized procedures for administration. These include directions to test administrators and examinees, specifications for testing conditions, and scoring procedures. Because educational tests typically are administered by school personnel, it is important for the sponsoring agency to provide appropriate oversight to the process and for schools to assign local roles and responsibilities (e.g., testing coordination) for training those who will administer the test. Similarly, test developers have an obligation to support the test administration process and to provide resources to help solve problems when they arise. For example, with high-stakes tests administered by computer, effective technical support to the local administration is critical and should involve personnel who understand the context of the testing program as well as the technical aspects of the delivery system.

Those responsible for educational testing programs should have formal procedures for granting testing accommodations and involve qualified personnel in the associated decision-making process. For students with disabilities, changes in both instruction and assessment are typically specified in an individualized education program (IEP). For English language learners, schools may use guidance from the state or district to match students' language proficiency and instructional experience with appropriate language accommodations. Test accommodations should be chosen by qualified personnel on the basis of the individual student's needs. It is particularly important in large-scale assessment programs to establish clear policies and procedures for assigning and using accommodations. These steps help to maintain the comparability of scores for students testing with accommodations on academic assessments across districts and schools. Once selected, accommodations should be used consistently for both instruction and assessment, and test administrators should be fully familiar with procedures for accommodated testing. Additional information related to test administration accommodations is provided in chapter 3 ("Fairness in Testing").

Weighted and Composite Scoring

Scoring educational tests and assessments requires developing rules for combining scores on items and/or tasks to obtain a total score and, in some cases, for combining multiple scores into an overall composite. Scores from multiple tests are sometimes combined into linear composites using nominal weights, which are assigned to each component score in accordance with a logical judgment of its relative importance. Nominal weights may sometimes be misleading because the variance of the composite is also determined by the variances and covariances of the individual component scores. As a result, the "effective weight" of each component may not reflect the nominal weighting. When composite scores are used, differences between nominal and effective weights should be understood and documented.

For a single test, total scores are often based on a simple sum of the item and task scores. However, differential weighting schemes may be applied to reflect differential emphasis on specific content or constructs. For example, in an English language arts test, more weight may be assigned to an extended essay because of the importance of

the task and because it is not feasible to include more than one extended writing task in the test. In addition, scoring based on item response theory (IRT) models can result in item weights that differ from nominal or desired weights. Such applications of IRT should include consideration and explanation of item weights in scoring. In general, the scoring rules used for educational tests should be documented and include a validity-based rationale.

In addition, test developers should discuss with policy makers the various methods of combining the results from different educational tests used to make decisions about students, and should clearly document and communicate the methods, also known as *decision rules*. For example, as part of graduation requirements, a state may require a student to achieve established levels of performance on multiple tests measuring different content areas using either a noncompensatory or a compensatory decision rule. Under a noncompensatory decision rule, the student has to achieve a determined level of performance on each test; under a compensatory decision rule, the student may only have to achieve a certain total composite score based on a combination of scores across tests. For a high-stakes decision, such as one related to graduation, the rules used to combine scores across tests should be established with a clear understanding of the associated implications. In these situations, important consequences such as passing rates and classification error rates will differ depending on the rules for combining test results. Test developers should document and communicate these implications to policy makers to encourage policy decisions that are fully informed.

Reporting Scores

Score reports for educational assessments should support the interpretations and decisions of their intended audiences, which include students, teachers, parents, principals, policy makers, and other educators. Different reports may be developed and produced for different audiences, and the score report layouts may differ accordingly. For example, reports prepared for individual students and parents may include background information about the purpose of the assessment, definitions of performance categories, and more user-friendly representations of measurement error (e.g., error bands around graphical score displays). Those who develop such reports should strive to provide information that can help students make productive decisions about their own learning. In contrast, reports prepared for principals and district-level personnel may include more detailed summaries but less foundational information because these individuals typically have a much better understanding of assessments.

As discussed in chapter 3, when modifications have been made to a test for some test takers that affect the construct being measured, consideration may be given to reporting that a modification was made because it affects the reliability/precision of test scores or the validity of interpretations drawn from test scores. Conversely, when accommodations are made that do not affect the comparability of test scores, flagging those accommodations is not appropriate.

In general, score reports for educational tests should be designed to provide information that is understandable and useful to stakeholders without leading to unwarranted score interpretations. Test developers can significantly improve the design of score reports by conducting supporting research. For example, surveys of available reports for other educational tests can provide ideas for effectively displaying test results. In addition, usability research with consumers of score reports can provide insights into report design. A number of techniques can be used in this type of research, including focus groups, surveys, and analyses of verbal protocols. For example, the advantages and disadvantages of alternate prototype designs can be compared by gathering data about the interpretations and inferences made by users based on the data presented in each report.

Online reporting capabilities give users flexible access to test results. For example, the user can select options online to break down the results by content or subgroup. The options provided to test users for querying the results should support the test's intended uses and interpretations. For example, online systems may discourage or disallow viewing of results, in some cases as required by law, if the sample sizes of particular subgroups fall below an acceptable number. In addition, care should be taken to allow access only to the appropriate individuals. As with score reports, the validity of interpretations from online supporting systems can be enhanced through usability research involving the intended score users.

Technology also facilitates close alignment of instructional materials with the results of educational tests. For example, results reported for an individual student could include not only strengths and weaknesses but direct links to specific instructional materials that a teacher may use with the student in the future. Rationales and documentation supporting the efficacy of the recommended interventions should be provided, and users should be encouraged to consider such information in conjunction with other evidence and judgments about student instructional needs.

When results are reported for large-scale assessments, the test sponsors or users should prepare accompanying guidance to promote sound use and valid interpretations of the data by the media and other stakeholders in the assessment process. Such communications should address likely testing consequences (both positive and negative), as well as anticipated misuses of the results.

STANDARDS FOR EDUCATIONAL TESTING AND ASSESSMENT

The standards in this chapter have been separated into three thematic clusters labeled as follows:

1. Design and Development of Educational Assessments
2. Use and Interpretation of Educational Assessments
3. Administration, Scoring, and Reporting of Educational Assessments

Users of educational tests for evaluation, policy, or accountability should also refer to the standards in chapter 13 ("Uses of Tests for Program Evaluation, Policy Studies, and Accountability").

Cluster 1. Design and Development of Educational Assessments

Standard 12.1

When educational testing programs are mandated by school, district, state, or other authorities, the ways in which test results are intended to be used should be clearly described by those who mandate the tests. It is also the responsibility of those who mandate the use of tests to monitor their impact and to identify and minimize potential negative consequences as feasible. Consequences resulting from the uses of the test, both intended and unintended, should also be examined by the test developer and/or user.

Comment: Mandated testing programs are often justified in terms of their potential benefits for teaching and learning. Concerns have been raised about the potential negative impact of mandated testing programs, particularly when they directly result in important decisions for individuals or institutions. There is concern that some schools are narrowing their curriculum to focus exclusively on the objectives tested, encouraging instructional or administrative practices designed simply to raise test scores rather than improve the quality of education, and losing higher numbers of students because many drop out after failing tests. The need

to monitor the impact of educational testing programs relates directly to fairness in testing, which requires ensuring that scores on a given test reflect the same construct and have essentially the same meaning for all individuals in the intended test-taker population. Consistent with appropriate testing objectives, potential negative consequences should be monitored and, when identified, should be addressed to the extent possible. Depending on the intended use, the person responsible for examining the consequences could be the mandating authority, the test developer, or the user.

Standard 12.2

In educational settings, when a test is designed or used to serve multiple purposes, evidence of validity, reliability/precision, and fairness should be provided for each intended use.

Comment: In educational testing, it has become common practice to use the same test for multiple purposes. For example, interim/benchmark tests may be used for a variety of purposes, including diagnosing student strengths and weaknesses, monitoring individual student growth, providing information to assist in instructional planning for individuals or groups of students, and evaluating schools or districts. No test will serve all purposes equally well. Choices in test design and development that enhance validity for one purpose may diminish validity for other purposes. Different purposes may require different kinds of technical evidence, and appropriate evidence of validity, reliability/precision, and fairness for each purpose should be provided by the test developer. If the test user wishes to use the test for a purpose not supported by the available evidence, it is incumbent on the user to provide the necessary additional evidence. See chapter 1 ("Validity").

Standard 12.3

Those responsible for the development and use of educational assessments should design all relevant steps of the testing process to promote

access to the construct for all individuals and subgroups for whom the assessment is intended.

Comment: It is important in educational contexts to provide for all students—regardless of their individual characteristics—the opportunity to demonstrate their proficiency on the construct being measured. Test specifications should clearly specify all relevant subgroups in the target population, including those for whom the test may not allow demonstration of knowledge and skills. Items and tasks should be designed to maximize access to the test content for all individuals in the intended test-taker population. Tools and strategies should be implemented to familiarize all test takers with the technology and testing format used, and the administration and scoring approach should avoid introducing any construct-irrelevant variance into the testing process. In situations where individual characteristics such as English language proficiency, cultural or linguistic background, disability, or age are believed to interfere with access to the construct(s) that the test is intended to measure, appropriate adaptations should be provided to allow access to the content, context, and response formats of the test items. These may include both accommodations (changes that are assumed to preserve the construct being measured) and modifications (changes that are assumed to make an altered version of the construct accessible). Additional considerations related to fairness and accessibility in educational tests and assessments are provided in chapter 3 ("Fairness in Testing").

Standard 12.4

When a test is used as an indicator of achievement in an instructional domain or with respect to specified content standards, evidence of the extent to which the test samples the range of knowledge and elicits the processes reflected in the target domain should be provided. Both the tested and the target domains should be described in sufficient detail for their relationship to be evaluated. The analyses should make explicit those aspects of the target domain that the test represents, as well as those aspects that the test fails to represent.

Comment: Tests are commonly developed to monitor the status or progress of individuals and groups with respect to local, state, national, or professional content standards. Rarely can a single test cover the full range of performances reflected in the content standards. In developing a new test or selecting an existing test, appropriate interpretation of test scores as indicators of performance on these standards requires documenting and evaluating both the relevance of the test to the standards and the extent to which the test is aligned to the standards. Such alignment studies should address multiple criteria, including not only alignment of the test with the content areas covered by the standards but also alignment with the standards in terms of the range and complexity of knowledge and skills that students are expected to demonstrate. Further, conducting studies of the cognitive strategies and skills employed by test takers, or studies of the relationships between test scores and other performance indicators relevant to the broader target domain, enables evaluation of the extent to which generalizations to that domain are supported. This information should be made available to all who use the test or interpret the test scores.

Standard 12.5

Local norms should be developed when appropriate to support test users' intended interpretations.

Comment: Comparison of examinees' scores to local as well as more broadly representative norm groups can be informative. Thus, sample size permitting, local norms are often useful in conjunction with published norms, especially if the local population differs markedly from the population on which published norms are based. In some cases, local norms may be used exclusively.

Standard 12.6

Documentation of design, models, and scoring algorithms should be provided for tests administered and scored using multimedia or computers.

Comment: Computer and multimedia tests need to be held to the same requirements of technical quality as other tests. For example, the use of technology-enhanced item formats should be supported with evidence that the formats are a feasible way to collect information about the construct, that they do not introduce construct-irrelevant variance, and that steps have been taken to promote accessibility for all students.

Cluster 2. Use and Interpretation of Educational Assessments

Standard 12.7

In educational settings, test users should take steps to prevent test preparation activities and distribution of materials to students that may adversely affect the validity of test score inferences.

Comment: In most educational testing contexts, the goal is to use a sample of test items to make inferences to a broader domain. When inappropriate test preparation activities occur, such as excessive teaching of items that are equivalent to those on the test, the validity of test score inferences is adversely affected. The appropriateness of test preparation activities and materials can be evaluated, for example, by determining the extent to which they reflect the specific test items and by considering the extent to which test scores may be artificially raised as a result, without increasing students' level of genuine achievement.

Standard 12.8

When test results contribute substantially to decisions about student promotion or graduation, evidence should be provided that students have had an opportunity to learn the content and skills measured by the test.

Comment: Students, parents, and educational staff should be informed of the domains on which the students will be tested, the nature of the item types, and the criteria for determining mastery. Reasonable efforts should be made to document the provision of instruction on the tested content and skills, even though it may not be possible or feasible to determine the specific content of instruction for every student. In addition and as appropriate, evidence should also be provided that students have had the opportunity to become familiar with the mode of administration and item formats used in testing.

Standard 12.9

Students who must demonstrate mastery of certain skills or knowledge before being promoted or granted a diploma should have a reasonable number of opportunities to succeed on alternate forms of the test or be provided with technically sound alternatives to demonstrate mastery of the same skills or knowledge. In most circumstances, when students are provided with multiple opportunities to demonstrate mastery, the time interval between the opportunities should allow students to obtain the relevant instructional experiences.

Comment: The number of testing opportunities and the time between opportunities will vary with the specific circumstances of the setting. Further, policy may dictate that some students should be given opportunities to demonstrate their achievement using a different approach. For example, some states that administer high school graduation tests permit students who have participated in the regular curriculum but are unable to demonstrate the required performance level on one or more of the tests to show, through a structured portfolio of their coursework and other indicators (e.g., participation in approved assistance programs, satisfaction of other graduation requirements), that they have the knowledge and skills necessary to obtain a high school diploma. If another assessment approach is used, it should be held to the same standards of technical quality as the primary assessment. In particular, evidence should be provided that the alternative approach measures the same skills and has the same passing expectations as the primary assessment.

Standard 12.10

In educational settings, a decision or characterization that will have major impact on a student should take into consideration not just scores from a single test but other relevant information.

Comment: In general, multiple measures or data sources will often enhance the appropriateness of decisions about students in educational settings and therefore should be considered by test sponsors and test users in establishing decision rules and policy. It is important that in addition to scores on a single test, other relevant information (e.g., school coursework, classroom observation, parental reports, other test scores) be taken into account when warranted. These additional data sources should demonstrate information relevant to the intended construct. For example, it may not be advisable or lawful to automatically accept students into a gifted program if their IQ is measured to be above 130 without considering additional relevant information about their performance. Similarly, some students with measured IQs below 130 may be accepted based on other measures or data sources, such as a test of creativity, a portfolio of student work, or teacher recommendations. In these cases, other evidence of gifted performance serves to compensate for the lower IQ test score.

Standard 12.11

When difference or growth scores are used for individual students, such scores should be clearly defined, and evidence of their validity, reliability/precision, and fairness should be reported.

Comment: The standard error of the difference between scores on the pretest and posttest, the regression of posttest scores on pretest scores, or relevant data from other appropriate methods for examining change should be reported.

In cases where growth scores are predicted for individual students, results based on different versions of tests taken over time may be used. For example, math scores in Grades 3, 4, and 5 may be used to predict the expected math score in Grade 6. In such cases, if complex statistical models are used to predict scores for individual students, the method for constructing the models should be made explicit and should be justified, and supporting technical and interpretive information should be provided to the score users. Chapter 13 ("Uses of Tests for Program Evaluation, Policy Studies, and Accountability") addresses the application of more complex models to groups or systems within accountability settings.

Standard 12.12

When an individual student's scores from different tests are compared, any educational decision based on the comparison should take into account the extent of overlap between the two constructs and the reliability or standard error of the difference score.

Comment: When difference scores between two tests are used to aid in making educational decisions, it is important that the two tests be placed on a common scale, either by standardization or by some other means, and, if appropriate, normed on the same population at about the same time. In addition, the reliability and standard error of the difference scores between the two tests are affected by the relationship between the constructs measured by the tests as well as by the standard errors of measurement of the scores of the two tests. For example, when scores on a nonverbal ability measure are compared with achievement test scores, the overlapping nature of the two constructs may render the reliability of the difference scores lower than test users normally would expect. If the ability and/or achievement tests involve a significant amount of measurement error, this will also reduce the confidence that can be placed in the difference scores. All these factors affect the reliability of difference scores between tests and should be considered when such scores are used as a basis for making important decisions about a student. This standard is also relevant in comparisons of subscores or scores from different components of the same test, such as may be reported for multiple aptitude test batteries, educational tests, and/or selection tests.

Standard 12.13

When test scores are intended to be used as part of the process for making decisions about educational placement, promotion, implementation of individualized educational programs, or provision of services for English language learners, then empirical evidence documenting the relationship among particular test scores, the instructional programs, and desired student outcomes should be provided. When adequate empirical evidence is not available, users should be cautioned to weigh the test results accordingly in light of other relevant information about the students.

Comment: The use of test scores for placement or promotion decisions should be supported by evidence about the relationship between the test scores and the expected benefits of the resulting educational programs. Thus, empirical evidence should be gathered to support the use of a test by a community college to place entering students in different mathematics courses. Similarly, in special education, when test scores are used in the development of specific educational objectives and instructional strategies, evidence is needed to show that the prescribed instruction is (a) directly linked to the test scores, and (b) likely to enhance student learning. When there is limited evidence about the relationship among test results, instructional plans, and student achievement outcomes, test developers and users should stress the tentative nature of the test-based recommendations and encourage teachers and other decision makers to weigh the usefulness of the test scores in light of other relevant information about the students.

Standard 12.14

In educational settings, those who supervise others in test selection, administration, and score interpretation should be familiar with the evidence for the reliability/precision, the validity of the intended interpretations, and the fairness of the scores. They should be able to articulate and effectively train others to articulate a logical explanation of the relationships among the tests used, the purposes served by the tests, and the interpretations of the test scores for the intended uses.

Comment: Appropriate interpretations of scores on educational tests depend on the effective training of individuals who carry out test administration and on the appropriate education of those who make use of test results. Establishing ongoing professional development programs that include a focus on improving the assessment literacy of teachers and stakeholders is one mechanism by which those who are responsible for test use in educational settings can facilitate the validity of test score interpretations. Establishing educational requirements (e.g., an advanced degree, relevant coursework, or attendance at workshops provided by the test developer or test sponsor) are other strategies that might be used to provide documentation of qualifications and expertise.

Standard 12.15

Those responsible for educational testing programs should take appropriate steps to verify that the individuals who interpret the test results to make decisions within the school context are qualified to do so or are assisted by and consult with persons who are so qualified.

Comment: When testing programs are used as a strategy for guiding instruction, the school personnel who are expected to make inferences about instructional planning may need assistance in interpreting test results for this purpose. Such assistance may consist of ongoing professional development, interpretive guides, training, information sessions, and the availability of experts to answer questions that arise as test results are disseminated.

The interpretation of some test scores is sufficiently complex to require that the user have relevant training and experience or be assisted by and consult with persons who have such training and experience. Examples of such tests include individually administered intelligence tests, interest inventories, growth scores on state assessments, projective tests, and neuropsychological tests.

Cluster 3. Administration, Scoring, and Reporting of Educational Assessments

Standard 12.16

Those responsible for educational testing programs should provide appropriate training, documentation, and oversight so that the individuals who administer and score the test(s) are proficient in the appropriate test administration and scoring procedures and understand the importance of adhering to the directions provided by the test developer.

Comment: In addition to being familiar with standardized test administration documentation and procedures (including test security protocols), it is important for test coordinators and test administrators to be familiar with materials and procedures for accommodations and modifications for testing. Test developers should therefore provide appropriate manuals and training materials that specifically address accommodated administrations. Test coordinators and test administrators should also receive information about the characteristics of the student populations included in the testing program.

Standard 12.17

In educational settings, reports of group differences in test scores should be accompanied by relevant contextual information, where possible, to enable meaningful interpretation of the differences. Where appropriate contextual information is not available, users should be cautioned against misinterpretation.

Comment: Differences in test scores between relevant subgroups (e.g., classified by gender, race/ethnicity, school/district, or geographical region) can be influenced, for example, by differences in student characteristics, in course-taking patterns, in curriculum, in teachers' qualifications, or in parental educational levels. Differences in performance of cohorts of students across time may be influenced by changes in the population of students tested or changes in learning opportunities for students. Users should be advised to consider the appropriate contextual information and be cautioned against misinterpretation.

Standard 12.18

In educational settings, score reports should be accompanied by a clear presentation of information on how to interpret the scores, including the degree of measurement error associated with each score or classification level, and by supplementary information related to group summary scores. In addition, dates of test administration and relevant norming studies should be included in score reports.

Comment: Score information should be communicated in a way that is accessible to persons receiving the score report. Empirical research involving score report users can help to improve the clarity of reports. For instance, the degree of uncertainty in the scores might be represented by presenting standard errors of measurement graphically; or the probability of misclassification associated with performance levels might be provided. Similarly, when average or summary scores for groups of students are reported, they should be supplemented with additional information about the sample sizes and the shapes or dispersions of score distributions. Particular care should be taken to portray subscore information in score reports in ways that facilitate proper interpretation. Score reports should include the date of administration so that score users can consider the validity of inferences as time passes. Score reports should also include the dates of relevant norming studies so users can consider the age of the norms in making inferences about student performance.

Standard 12.19

In educational settings, when score reports include recommendations for instructional intervention or are linked to recommended plans or materials for instruction, a rationale for and evidence to support these recommendations should be provided.

Comment: Technology is making it increasingly possible to assign particular instructional interventions to students based on assessment results. Specific digital content (e.g., worksheets or lessons) may be made available to students using a rules-based interpretation of their performance on a standards-based test. In such instances, documentation supporting the appropriateness of instructional assignments should be provided. Similarly, when the pattern of subscores on a test is used to assign students to particular instructional interventions, it is important to provide both a rationale and empirical evidence to support the claim that these assignments are appropriate. In addition, users should be advised to consider such pedagogical recommendations in conjunction with other relevant information about students' strengths and weaknesses.

13. USES OF TESTS FOR PROGRAM EVALUATION, POLICY STUDIES, AND ACCOUNTABILITY

BACKGROUND

Tests are widely used to inform decisions as part of public policy. One example is the use of tests in the context of the design and evaluation of programs or policy initiatives. *Program evaluation* is the set of procedures used to make judgments about a program's design, its implementation, and its outcomes. *Policy studies* are somewhat broader than program evaluations; they contribute to judgments about plans, principles, or procedures enacted to achieve broad public goals. Tests often provide the data that are analyzed to estimate the effect of a policy, program, or initiative on outcomes such as student achievement or motivation. A second broad category of test use in policy settings is in *accountability systems,* which attach consequences (e.g., rewards and sanctions) to the performance of institutions (such as schools or school districts) or individuals (such as teachers or mental health care providers). Program evaluations, policy studies, and accountability systems should not necessarily be viewed as discrete categories. They are frequently adopted in combination with one another, as is the case when accountability systems impose requirements or recommendations to use test results for evaluating programs adopted by schools or districts.

The uses of tests for program evaluations, policy studies, and accountability share several characteristics, including measurement of the performance of a group of people and use of test scores as evidence of the success or shortcomings of an institution or initiative. This chapter examines these uses of tests. The accountability discussion focuses on systems that involve aggregates of scores, such as school-wide or institution-wide averages, percentages of students or patients scoring above a certain level, or growth or value-added

modeling results aggregated at the classroom, school, or institution level. Systems or programs that focus on accountability for individual students, such as through test-based promotion policies or graduation exams, are addressed in chapter 12. (However, many of the issues raised in that chapter are relevant to the use of educational tests for program evaluation or school accountability purposes.) If accountability systems or programs include tests administered to teachers, principals, or other providers for purposes of evaluating their practice or performance (e.g., for teacher pay-for-performance programs that include a test of teacher knowledge or an observation-based measure of their practices), those tests should be evaluated according to the standards related to workplace testing and credentialing in chapter 11.

The contexts in which testing for evaluation and accountability takes place vary in the stakes for test takers and for those who are responsible for promoting specific outcomes (such as teachers or health care providers). Testing programs for institutions can have high stakes when the aggregate performance of a sample or of the entire population of test takers is used to make inferences about the quality of services provided and, as a result, decisions are made about institutional status, rewards, or sanctions. For example, the quality of reading curriculum and instruction may be judged in part on the basis of results of testing for levels of attainment reached by groups of students. Similarly, aggregated scores on psychological tests are sometimes used to evaluate the effectiveness of treatment provided by mental health programs or agencies and may be included in accountability systems. Even when test results are reported in the aggregate and intended for low-stakes purposes, the public release of data may be used to inform judgments about program quality, personnel, or educational programs and may influence policy decisions.

Evaluation of Programs and Policy Initiatives

As noted earlier, program evaluation typically involves making judgments about a single program, whereas policy studies address plans, principles, or procedures enacted to achieve broad public goals. Policy studies may address policies at various levels of government, including local, state, federal, and international, and may be conducted in both public and private organizational or institutional contexts. There is no sharp distinction between policy studies and program evaluations, and in many instances there is substantial overlap between the two types of investigations. Test results are often one important source of evidence for the initiation, continuation, modification, termination, or expansion of various programs and policies.

Tests may be used in program evaluations or policy studies to provide information on the status of clients, students, or other groups before, during, or after an intervention or policy enactment, as well as to provide score information for appropriate comparison groups. Whereas many testing activities are intended to document the performance of individual test takers, program evaluation and policy studies target the performance of groups or the impact of the test results on these groups. A variety of tests can be used for evaluating programs and policies; examples include standardized achievement tests administered by states or districts, published psychological tests that measure outcomes of interest, and measures developed specifically for the purposes of the evaluation. In addition, evaluations of programs and policies sometimes synthesize results from multiple studies or tests.

It is important to evaluate any proposed test in terms of its relevance to the goals of the program or policy and/or to the particular questions its use will address. It is relatively rare for a test to be designed specifically for program evaluation or policy study purposes, and therefore it is often necessary for those who conduct such studies to rely on measures developed for other purposes. In addition, for reasons of cost or convenience, certain tests may be adopted for use in a program evaluation or policy study even though they were developed for a somewhat different population of respondents. Some tests may be selected because they are well known and thought to be especially credible in the view of clients or public consumers, or because useful data already exist from earlier administrations of the tests. Evidence for the validity of test scores for the intended uses should be provided whenever tests are used for program or policy evaluations or for accountability purposes.

Because of administrative realities, such as cost constraints and response burden, methodological refinements may be adopted to increase the efficiency of testing. One strategy is to obtain a sample of participants to be evaluated from the larger set of those exposed to a program or policy. When a sufficient number of clients are affected by the program or policy that will be evaluated, and when there is a desire to limit the time spent on testing, evaluators can create multiple forms of short tests from a larger pool of items. By constructing a number of test forms consisting of relatively few items each and assigning the test forms to different subsamples of test takers (a procedure known as *matrix sampling*), a larger number of items can be included in the study than could reasonably be administered to any single test taker. When it is desirable to represent a domain with a large number of test items, this approach is often used. However, in matrix sample testing, individual scores usually are not created or interpreted. Because procedures for sampling individuals or test items may vary in a number of ways, adequate analysis and interpretation of test results depend on a clear description of how samples were formed and how the tests were designed, scored, and reported. Reports of test results used for evaluation or accountability should describe the sampling strategy and the extent to which the sample is representative of the population that is relevant to the intended inferences.

Evaluations and policy studies sometimes rely on *secondary data analysis:* analysis of data previously collected for other purposes. In some circumstances, it may be difficult to ensure a good match between the existing test and the intervention or policy under examination, or to reconstruct in detail the conditions under which the data were originally collected. Secondary data analysis also requires consideration of the privacy rights of test takers and others affected by the analysis. Sometimes this requires determining whether the informed consent obtained from participants in the original data collection was adequate to allow secondary analysis to proceed without a need for additional consent. It may also require an understanding of the extent to which individually identifiable information has been redacted from the data set consistent with applicable legal standards. In selecting (or developing) a test or deciding whether to use existing data in evaluation and policy studies, careful investigators attempt to balance the purpose of the test, the likelihood that it will be sensitive to the intervention under study, its credibility to interested parties, and the costs of administration. Otherwise, test results may lead to inappropriate conclusions about the progress, impact, and overall value of programs and policies under review.

Interpretation of test scores in program evaluation and policy studies usually entails complex analysis of a number of variables. For example, some programs are mandated for a broad population; others target only certain subgroups. Some are designed to affect attitudes, beliefs, or values; others are intended to have a more direct impact on behavior, knowledge, or skills. It is important that the participants included in any study meet the specified criteria for participating in the program or policy under review, so that appropriate interpretation of test results will be possible. Test results will reflect not only the effects of rules for participant selection and the impact on the participants of taking part in programs or treatments, but also the characteristics of the participants. Relevant background information about clients or students may be obtained to strengthen the inferences derived from the test results. Valid interpretations may depend on additional considerations that have nothing to do with the appropriateness

of the test or its technical quality, including study design, administrative feasibility, and the quality of other available data. This chapter focuses on testing and does not deal with these other considerations in any substantial way. In order to develop defensible conclusions, however, investigators conducting program evaluations and policy studies should supplement test results with data from other sources. These data may include information about program characteristics, delivery, costs, client backgrounds, degree of participation, and evidence of side effects. Because test results lend important weight to evaluation and policy studies, it is critical that any tests used in these investigations be sensitive to the questions of the study and appropriate for the test takers.

Test-Based Accountability Systems

The inclusion of test scores in educational accountability systems has become common in the United States and in other nations. Most test-based educational accountability in the United States takes place at the K–12 level, but many of the issues raised in the K–12 context are relevant to efforts to adopt outcomes-based accountability in postsecondary education. In addition, accountability systems may incorporate information from longitudinal data systems linking students' performance on tests and other indicators, including systems that capture a cohort's performance from preschool through higher education and into the workforce. Test-based accountability sometimes occurs in sectors other than education; one example is the use of psychological tests to create measures of effectiveness for providers of mental health care. These uses of tests raise issues similar to those that arise in educational contexts.

Test-based accountability systems take a variety of approaches to measuring performance and holding individuals or groups accountable for that performance. These systems vary along a number of dimensions, including the unit of accountability (e.g., district, school, teacher), the stakes attached to results, the frequency of measurement, and whether nontest indicators are included in the accountability system. One important measurement concern in accountability stems from the construction of an *accountability index:* a number or label that reflects a set of rules for combining scores and other information to arrive at conclusions and inform decision making. An accountability index could be as simple as an average test score for students in a particular grade in a particular school, but most systems rely on more complex indices. These may involve a set of rules (often called *decision rules*) for synthesizing multiple sources of information, such as test scores, graduation rates, course-taking rates, and teacher qualifications. An accountability index may also be created from applications of complex statistical models such as those used in value-added modeling approaches. As discussed in chapter 12, for high-stakes decisions, such as classification of schools or teachers into performance categories that are linked to rewards or sanctions, the establishment of rules used to create accountability indices should be informed by a consideration of the nature of the information the system is intended to provide and by an understanding of how consequences will be affected by these rules. The implications of the rules should be communicated to decision makers so that they understand the consequences of any policy decisions based on the accountability index.

Test-based accountability systems include interpretations and assumptions that go beyond those for the interpretation of the test scores on which they are based; therefore, they require additional evidence to support their validity. Accountability systems in education typically aggregate scores over the students in a class or school, and may use complex mathematical models to generate a summary statistic, or index, for each teacher or school. These indices are often interpreted as estimates of the effectiveness of the teacher or school. Users of information from accountability systems might assume that the accountability indices provide valid indicators of the intended outcomes of education (e.g., mastery of the skills and knowledge described in the state content standards), that differences among indices can be attributed to differences in the effectiveness of the teacher or school, and that these differences are reasonably

stable over time and across students and items. These assumptions must be supported by evidence. Moreover, those responsible for developing or implementing test-based accountability systems often assert that these systems will lead to specific outcomes, such as increased educator motivation or improved achievement; these assertions should also be supported by evidence. In particular, efforts should be made to investigate any potential positive or negative consequences of the selected accountability system.

Similarly, the choice of specific rules and data that are used to create an accountability index should reflect the goals and values of those who are developing the accountability system, as well as the inferences that the system is designed to support. For example, if a primary goal of an accountability system is to identify teachers who are effective at improving student achievement, the accountability index should be based on assessments that are closely aligned with the content the teacher is expected to cover, and should take into account factors outside the teacher's control. The process typically involves decisions such as whether to measure percentages above a cut score or an average of scale scores, whether to measure status or growth, how to combine information for multiple subjects and grade levels, and whether to measure performance against a fixed target or use a rank-based approach. The development of an accountability index also involves political considerations, such as how to balance technical concerns and transparency.

Issues in Program and Policy Evaluation and Accountability

Test results are sometimes used as one way to motivate program administrators or other service providers as well as to infer institutional effectiveness. This use of tests, including the public reporting of results, is thought to encourage an institution to improve its services for its clients. For example, in some test-based accountability systems, consistently poor results on achievement tests at the school level may result in interventions that affect the school's staffing or operations. The interpretation of test results is especially complex when tests are used both as an institutional policy mechanism and as a measure of effectiveness. For example, a policy or program may be based on the assumption that providing clear goals and general specifications of test content (such as the types of topics, constructs, cognitive domains, and response formats included in the test) may be a reasonable strategy to communicate new expectations to educators. Yet the desire to influence test or evaluation results to show acceptable institutional performance could lead to inappropriate testing practices, such as teaching the test items in advance, modifying test administration procedures, discouraging certain students or clients from participating in the testing sessions, or focusing teaching exclusively on test-taking skills. These responses illustrate that the more an indicator is used for decision making, the more likely it is to become corrupted and distort the process that it was intended to measure. Undesirable practices such as excessive emphasis on test-taking skills might replace practices aimed at helping the test takers learn the broader domains measured by the test. Because results derived from such practices may lead to spuriously high estimates of performance, the diligent investigator should estimate the impact of changes in teaching practices that may result from testing in order to interpret the test results appropriately. Looking at possible inappropriate consequences of tests as well as their benefits will result in more accurate assessment of policy claims that particular types of testing programs lead to improved performance.

Investigators conducting policy studies and program evaluations may give no clear reasons to the test takers for participating in the testing procedure, and they often withhold the results from the test takers. When matrix sampling is used for program evaluation, it may not be feasible to provide such reports. If little effort is made to motivate the test takers to regard the test seriously (e.g., if the purpose of the test is not explained), the test takers may have little reason to maximize their effort on the test. The test results thus may misrepresent the impact of a program, institution, or policy. When there is suspicion that a test has

not been taken seriously, the motivation of test takers may be explored by collecting additional information where feasible, using observation or interview methods. Issues of inappropriate preparation and unmotivated performance raise questions about the validity of interpretations of test results. In every case, it is important to consider the potential impact on the test taker of the testing process itself, including test administration and reporting practices.

Public policy decisions are rarely based solely on the results of empirical studies, even when the studies are of high quality. The more expansive and indirect the policy, the more likely it is that other considerations will come into play, such as the political and economic impact of abandoning, changing, or retaining the policy, or the reactions of various stakeholders when institutions become the targets of rewards or sanctions. Tests used in policy settings may be subjected to intense and detailed scrutiny for political reasons. When the test results contradict a favored position, attempts may be made to discredit the testing procedure, content, or interpretation. Test users should be able to defend the use of the test and the interpretation of results but should also recognize that they cannot control the reactions of stakeholder groups.

It is essential that all tests used in accountability, program evaluation, or policy contexts meet the standards for validity, reliability, and fairness appropriate to the intended test score interpretations and use. Moreover, as described in chapter 6, tests should be administered by personnel who are appropriately trained to implement the test administration procedures. It is also essential that assistance be provided to those responsible for interpreting study results for practitioners, the lay public, and the media. Careful communication about goals, procedures, findings, and limitations increases the likelihood that the interpretations of the results will be accurate and useful.

Additional Considerations

This chapter and its associated standards are directed to users of tests in program evaluations, policy studies, and accountability systems. Users include those who mandate, design, or implement these evaluations, studies, or systems and those who make decisions based on the information they provide. Users include, among others, psychologists who develop, evaluate, or enforce policies, as well as educators, administrators, and policy makers who are engaged in efforts to measure school performance or evaluate the effectiveness of education policies or programs. In addition to the standards below, users should consider other available documents containing relevant standards.

STANDARDS FOR USES OF TESTS FOR PROGRAM EVALUATION, POLICY STUDIES, AND ACCOUNTABILITY

The standards in this chapter have been separated into two thematic clusters labeled as follows:

1. Design and Development of Testing Programs and Indices for Program Evaluation, Policy Studies, and Accountability Systems
2. Interpretations and Uses of Information From Tests Used in Program Evaluation, Policy Studies, and Accountability Systems

Users of educational tests for evaluation, policy, or accountability should also refer to the standards in chapter 12 ("Educational Testing and Assessment") and to the other standards in this volume.

Cluster 1. Design and Development of Testing Programs and Indices for Program Evaluation, Policy Studies, and Accountability Systems

Standard 13.1

Users of tests who conduct program evaluations or policy studies, or monitor outcomes, should clearly describe the population that the program or policy is intended to serve and should document the extent to which the sample of test takers is representative of that population. In addition, when matrix sampling procedures are used, rules for sampling items and test takers should be provided, and error calculations must take the sampling scheme into account. When multiple studies are combined as part of a program evaluation or policy study, information about the samples included in each individual study should be provided.

Comment: It is important to provide information about sampling weights that may need to be applied for accurate inferences about performance. When matrix sampling is used, documentation should address the limitations that stem from this sampling approach, such as the difficulty in creating individual-level scores. Test developers

should also report appropriate sampling error variance estimates if simple random sampling was not used.

Standard 13.2

When change or gain scores are used, the procedures for constructing the scores, as well as their technical qualities and limitations, should be reported. In addition, the time periods between test administrations should be reported, and care should be taken to avoid practice effects.

Comment: The use of change or gain scores presumes that the same test, equivalent forms of the test, or forms of a vertically scaled test are used and that the test (or form or vertical scale) is not materially altered between administrations. The standard error of the difference between scores on pretests and posttests, the error associated with regression of posttest scores on pretest scores, or relevant data from other methods for examining change, such as those based on structural equation modeling, should be reported. In addition to technical or methodological considerations, details related to test administration may also be relevant to interpreting change or gain scores. For example, it is important to consider that the error associated with change scores is higher than the error associated with the original scores on which they are based. If change scores are used, information about the reliability/precision of these scores should be reported. It is also important to report the time period between administrations of tests; and if the same test is used on multiple occasions, the possibility of practice effects (i.e., improved performance due to familiarity with the test items) should be examined.

Standard 13.3

When accountability indices, indicators of effectiveness in program evaluations or policy studies, or other statistical models (such as

value-added models) are used, the method for constructing such indices, indicators, or models should be described and justified, and their technical qualities should be reported.

Comment: An index that is constructed by manipulating and combining test scores should be subjected to the same validity, reliability, and fairness investigations that are expected for the test scores that underlie the index. The methods and rules for constructing such indices should be made available to users, along with documentation of their technical properties. The strengths and limitations of various approaches to combining scores should be evaluated, and information that would allow independent replication of the construction of indices, indicators, or models should be made available for use by appropriate parties.

As with regular test scores, a validity argument should be set forth to justify inferences about indices as measures of a desired outcome. It is important to help users understand the extent to which the models support causal inferences. For example, when value-added estimates are used as measures of teachers' effectiveness in improving student achievement, evidence for the appropriateness of this inference needs to be provided. Similarly, if published ratings of health care providers are based on indices constructed from psychological test scores of their patients, the public information should include information to help users understand what inferences about provider performance are warranted. Developers and users of indices should be aware of ways in which the process of combining individual scores into an index may introduce technical problems that did not affect the original scores. Linking errors, floor or ceiling effects, differences in variability across different measures, and lack of an interval scale are examples of features that may not be problematic for the purpose of interpreting individual test scores but can become problematic when scores are combined into an aggregate measure. Finally, when evaluations or accountability systems rely on measures that combine various sources of information, such as when scores on multiple forms of a test are combined or when

nontest information is included in an accountability index, the rules for combining the information need to be made explicit and must be justified. It is important to recognize that when multiple sources of data are collapsed into a single composite score or rating, the weights and distributional characteristics of the sources will affect the distribution of the composite scores. The effects of the weighting and distributional characteristics on the composite score should be investigated.

When indices combine scores from tests administered under standard conditions with those that involve modifications or other changes to administration conditions, there should be a clear rationale for combining the information into a single index, and the implications for validity and reliability should be examined.

Cluster 2. Interpretations and Uses of Information From Tests Used in Program Evaluation, Policy Studies, and Accountability Systems

Standard 13.4

Evidence of validity, reliability, and fairness for each purpose for which a test is used in a program evaluation, policy study, or accountability system should be collected and made available.

Comment: Evidence should be provided of the suitability of a test for use in program evaluation, policy studies, or accountability systems, including the relevance of the test to the goals of the program, policy, or system under study and the suitability of the test for the populations involved. Those responsible for the release or reporting of test results should provide and explain any supplemental information that will minimize possible misinterpretations or misuse of the data. In particular, if an evaluation or accountability system is designed to support interpretations regarding the effectiveness of a program, institution, or provider, the validity of these interpretations for the intended uses should be investigated and documented. Reports should include cautions against making unwarranted inferences, such as holding health care providers accountable for test-score changes that may not be under their control. If the use involves a classification of persons, institutions, or programs into distinct categories, the consistency, accuracy, and fairness of the classifications should be reported. If the same test is used for multiple purposes (e.g., monitoring achievement of individual students; providing information to assist in instructional planning for individuals or groups of students; evaluating districts, schools, or teachers), evidence related to the validity of interpretations for each of these uses should be gathered and provided to users, and the potential negative effects for certain uses (e.g., improving instruction) that might result from unintended uses (e.g., high-stakes accountability) need to be considered and mitigated. When tests are used to evaluate the performance of personnel, the suitability of the tests for different groups of personnel (e.g., regular teachers, special education teachers, principals) should be examined.

Standard 13.5

Those responsible for the development and use of tests for evaluation or accountability purposes should take steps to promote accurate interpretations and appropriate uses for all groups for which results will be applied.

Comment: Those responsible for measuring outcomes should, to the extent possible, design the testing process to promote access and to maximize the validity of interpretations (e.g., by providing appropriate accommodations) for any relevant subgroups of test takers who participate in program or policy evaluation. Users of secondary data should clearly describe the extent to which the population included in the test-score database includes all relevant subgroups. The users should also document any exclusion rules that were applied and any other changes to the testing process that could affect interpretations of results. Similarly, users of tests for accountability purposes should make every effort to include all relevant subgroups in the testing program; provide docu-

mentation of any exclusion rules, testing modifications, or other changes to the test or administration conditions; and provide evidence regarding the validity of score interpretations for subgroups. When summaries of test scores are reported separately by subgroup (e.g., by racial/ethnic group), test users should conduct analyses to evaluate the reliability/precision of scores for these groups and the validity of score interpretations, and should report this information when publishing the score summaries. Analyses of complex indices used for accountability or for measuring program effectiveness should address the possibility of bias against specific subgroups or against programs or institutions serving those subgroups. If bias is detected (e.g., if scores on the index are shown to be subject to systematic error that is related to examinee characteristics such as race/ethnicity), these indices should not be used unless they are modified in a way that removes the bias. Additional considerations related to fairness and accessibility in educational tests and assessments are provided in chapter 3.

When test results are used to support actions regarding program or policy adoption or change, the professionals who are expected to make interpretations leading to these actions may need assistance in interpreting test results for this purpose. Advances in technology have led to increased availability of data and reports among teachers, administrators, and others who may not have received training in appropriate test use and interpretation or in analysis of test-score data. Those who provide the data or tools have the responsibility to offer support and assistance to users, and users have the responsibility to seek guidance on appropriate analysis and interpretation. Those responsible for the release or reporting of test results should provide and explain any supplemental information that will minimize possible misinterpretations of the data.

Often, the test results for program evaluation or policy analysis are analyzed well after the tests have been given. When this is the case, the user should investigate and describe the context in which the tests were given. Factors such as inclusion/exclusion rules, test purpose, content sampling, instructional alignment, and the attachment of high stakes can affect the aggregated results and should be made known to the audiences for the evaluation or analysis.

Standard 13.6

Reports of group differences in test performance should be accompanied by relevant contextual information, where possible, to enable meaningful interpretation of the differences. If appropriate contextual information is not available, users should be cautioned against misinterpretation.

Comment: Observed differences in average test scores between groups (e.g., classified by gender, race/ethnicity, disability, language proficiency, socioeconomic status, or geographical region) can be influenced by differences in factors such as opportunity to learn, training experience, effort, instructor quality, and level and type of parental support. In education, differences in group performance across time may be influenced by changes in the population of those tested (including changes in sample size) or changes in their experiences. Users should be advised to consider the appropriate contextual information when interpreting these group differences and when designing policies or practices to address those differences. In addition, if evaluations involve comparisons of test scores across national borders, evidence for the comparability of scores should be provided.

Standard 13.7

When tests are selected for use in evaluation or accountability settings, the ways in which the test results are intended to be used, and the consequences they are expected to promote, should be clearly described, along with cautions against inappropriate uses.

Comment: In some contexts, such as evaluation of a specific curriculum program, a test may have a limited purpose and may not be intended to promote specific outcomes other than informing the evaluation. In other settings, particularly with test-based accountability systems, the use of tests

is often justified on the grounds that it will improve the quality of education by providing useful information to decision makers and by creating incentives to promote better performance by educators and students. These kinds of claims should be made explicit when the system is mandated or adopted, and evidence to support their validity should be provided when available. The collection and reporting of evidence for a particular validity claim should be incorporated into the program design. A given claim for the benefits of test use, such as improving students' achievement, may be supported by logical or theoretical argument as well as empirical data. Due weight should be given to findings in the scientific literature that may be inconsistent with the stated claim.

Standard 13.8

Those who mandate the use of tests in policy, evaluation, and accountability contexts and those who use tests in such contexts should monitor their impact and should identify and minimize negative consequences.

Comment: The use of tests in policy, evaluation, and accountability settings may, in some cases, lead to unanticipated consequences. Particularly when high stakes are attached, those who mandate tests, as well as those who use the results, should take steps to identify potential unanticipated consequences. Unintended negative consequences may include teaching test items in advance, modifying test administration procedures, and discouraging or excluding certain test takers from taking the test. These practices can lead to spuriously high scores that do not reflect performance on the underlying construct or domain of interest. In addition, these practices may be prohibited by law. Testing procedures should be designed to minimize the likelihood of such consequences, and users should be given guidance and encouragement to refrain from inappropriate test-preparation practices.

Some consequences can be anticipated on the basis of past research and understanding of how people respond to incentives. For example, research shows that educational accountability tests influence curriculum and instruction by signaling what is important for students to know and be able to do. This influence can be positive if a test encourages a focus on valuable learning outcomes, but it is negative if it narrows the curriculum in unintended ways. These and other common negative consequences, such as possible motivational impact on teachers and students (even when test results are used as intended) and increasing dropout rates, should be studied and the results taken into consideration. The integrity of test results should be maintained by striving to eliminate practices designed to raise test scores without improving performance on the construct or domain measured by the test. In addition, administering an audit measure (i.e., another measure of the tested construct) may detect possible corruption of scores.

Standard 13.9

In evaluation or accountability settings, test results should be used in conjunction with information from other sources when the use of the additional information contributes to the validity of the overall interpretation.

Comment: Performance on indicators other than tests is almost always useful and in many cases essential. Descriptions or analyses of such variables as client selection criteria, services, client characteristics, setting, and resources are often needed to provide a comprehensive picture of the program or policy under review and to aid in the interpretation of test results. In the accountability context, a decision that will have a major impact on an individual such as a teacher or health care provider, or on an organization such as a school or treatment facility, should take into consideration other relevant information in addition to test scores. Examples of other information that may be incorporated into evaluations or accountability systems are measures of educators' or health care providers' practices (e.g., classroom observations, checklists) and nontest measures of student attainment (course taking, college attendance).

In the case of value-added modeling, some researchers have argued for the inclusion of student demographic characteristics (e.g., race/ethnicity and socioeconomic status) as controls, whereas other work suggests that including such variables does not improve the performance of the measures and can promote undesirable consequences such as a perception that lower standards are being set for some students than for others. Decisions regarding what variables to include in such models should be informed by empirical evidence regarding the effects of their inclusion or exclusion.

An additional type of information that is relevant to the interpretation of test results in policy settings is the degree of motivation of the test takers. It is important to determine whether test takers regard the test experience seriously, particularly when individual scores are not reported to test takers or when the scores are not associated with consequences for the test takers. Decision criteria regarding whether to include scores from individuals with questionable motivation should be clearly documented.

GLOSSARY

This glossary provides definitions of terms as used in the text and standards. For many of the terms, multiple definitions can be found in the literature; also, technical usage may differ from common usage.

ability parameter: In item response theory (IRT), a theoretical value indicating the level of a test taker on the ability or trait measured by the test; analogous to the concept of true score in classical test theory.

ability testing: The use of tests to evaluate the current performance of a person in some defined domain of cognitive, psychomotor, or physical functioning.

accessibility: The degree to which the items or tasks on a test enable as many test takers as possible to demonstrate their standing on the target construct without being impeded by characteristics of the item that are irrelevant to the construct being measured. A test that ranks high on this criterion is referred to as *accessible*.

accommodations/test accommodations: Adjustments that do not alter the assessed construct that are applied to test presentation, environment, content, format (including response format), or administration conditions for particular test takers, and that are embedded within assessments or applied after the assessment is designed. Tests or assessments with such accommodations, and their scores, are said to be *accommodated*. Accommodated scores should be sufficiently comparable to unaccommodated scores that they can be aggregated together.

accountability index: A number or label that reflects a set of rules for combining scores and other information to form conclusions and inform decision making in an accountability system.

accountability system: A system that imposes student performance-based rewards or sanctions on institutions such as schools or school systems or on individuals such as teachers or mental health care providers.

acculturation: A process related to the acquisition of cultural knowledge and artifacts that is developmental in nature and dependent upon time of exposure and opportunity for learning.

achievement levels/proficiency levels: Descriptions of test takers' levels of competency in a particular area of knowledge or skill, usually defined in terms of categories ordered on a continuum, for example from "basic" to "advanced," or "novice" to "expert." The categories constitute broad ranges for classifying performance. See *cut score*.

achievement standards: See *performance standards*.

achievement test: A test to measure the extent of knowledge or skill attained by a test taker in a content domain in which the test taker has received instruction.

adaptation/test adaptation: 1. Any change in test content, format (including response format), or administration conditions that is made to increase a test's accessibility for individuals who otherwise would face construct-irrelevant barriers on the original test. An adaptation may or may not change the meaning of the construct being measured or alter score interpretations. An adaptation that changes score meaning is referred to as a *modification;* an adaptation that does not change the score meaning is referred to as an *accommodation* (see definitions in this glossary). 2. Change made to a test that has been translated into the language of a target group and that takes into account the nuances of the language and culture of that group.

adaptive test: A sequential form of individual testing in which successive items, or sets of items, in the test are selected for administration based primarily on their psychometric properties and content, in relation to the test taker's responses to previous items.

adjusted validity or reliability coefficient: A validity or reliability coefficient—most often, a product-moment correlation—that has been adjusted to offset the effects of differences in score variability, criterion variability, or the unreliability of test and/or criterion scores. See *restriction of range or variability*.

aggregate score: A total score formed by combining scores on the same test or across test components. The scores may be raw or standardized. The components of the aggregate score may be weighted or not, depending on the interpretation to be given to the aggregate score.

alignment: The degree to which the content and cognitive demands of test questions match targeted content and cognitive demands described in the test specifications.

alternate assessments/alternate tests: Assessments or tests used to evaluate the performance of students in educational settings who are unable to participate in standardized accountability assessments, even with accommodations. Alternate assessments or tests typically measure achievement relative to alternate content standards.

alternate forms: Two or more versions of a test that are considered interchangeable, in that they measure the same constructs in the same ways, are built to the same content and statistical specifications, and are administered under the same conditions using the same directions. See *equivalent forms, parallel forms.*

alternate or alternative standards: Content and performance standards in educational assessment for students with significant cognitive disabilities.

analytic scoring: A method of scoring constructed responses (such as essays) in which each critical dimension of a particular performance is judged and scored separately, and the resultant values are combined for an overall score. In some instances, scores on the separate dimensions may also be used in interpreting performance. Contrast with *holistic scoring.*

anchor items: Items administered with each of two or more alternate forms of a test for the purpose of equating the scores obtained on these alternate forms.

anchor test: A set of anchor items used for equating.

assessment: Any systematic method of obtaining information, used to draw inferences about characteristics of people, objects, or programs; a systematic process to measure or evaluate the characteristics or performance of individuals, programs, or other entities, for purposes of drawing inferences; sometimes used synonymously with *test.*

assessment literacy: Knowledge about testing that supports valid interpretations of test scores for their intended purposes, such as knowledge about test development practices, test score interpretations, threats to valid score interpretations, score reliability and precision, test administration, and use.

automated scoring: A procedure by which constructed response items are scored by computer using a rules-based approach.

battery: A set of tests usually administered as a unit. The scores on the tests usually are scaled so that they can readily be compared or used in combination for decision making.

behavioral science: A scientific discipline, such as sociology, anthropology, or psychology, in which the actions and reactions of humans and animals are studied through observational and experimental methods.

benchmark assessments: Assessments administered in educational settings at specified times during a curriculum sequence, to evaluate students' knowledge and skills relative to an explicit set of longer-term learning goals. See *interim assessments or tests.*

bias: 1. In test fairness, construct underrepresentation or construct-irrelevant components of test scores that differentially affect the performance of different groups of test takers and consequently the reliability/precision and validity of interpretations and uses of their test scores. 2. In statistics or measurement, systematic error in a test score. See *construct underrepresentation, construct-irrelevant variance, fairness, predictive bias.*

bilingual/multilingual: Having a degree of proficiency in two or more languages.

calibration: 1. In linking test scores, the process of relating scores on one test to scores on another that differ in reliability/precision from those on the first test, so that scores have the same relative meaning for a group of test takers. 2. In item response theory, the process of estimating the parameters of the item response function. 3. In scoring constructed response tasks, procedures used during training and scoring to achieve a desired level of scorer agreement.

certification: A process by which individuals are recognized (or certified) as having demonstrated some level of knowledge and skill in some domain. See *licensing, credentialing.*

classical test theory: A psychometric theory based on the view that an individual's observed score on a test is the sum of a true score component for the test taker and an independent random error component.

classification accuracy: Degree to which the assignment of test takers to specific categories is accurate; the degree to which false positive and false negative classifications are avoided. See *sensitivity, specificity.*

coaching: Planned short-term instructional activities for prospective test takers provided prior to the test administration for the primary purpose of improving their test scores. Activities that approximate the instruction provided by regular school curricula or training programs are not typically referred to as coaching.

coefficient alpha: An internal-consistency reliability coefficient based on the number of parts into which a test is partitioned (e.g., items, subtests, or raters), the interrelationships of the parts, and the total test score variance. Also called *Cronbach's alpha* and, for dichotomous items, *KR-20*. See *internal-consistency coefficient, reliability coefficient.*

cognitive assessment: The process of systematically collecting test scores and related data to make judgments about an individual's ability to perform various mental activities involved in the processing, acquisition, retention, conceptualization, and organization of sensory, perceptual, verbal, spatial, and psychomotor information.

cognitive lab: A method of studying the cognitive processes that test takers use when completing a task such as solving a mathematics problem or interpreting a passage of text, typically involving test takers' thinking aloud while responding to the task and/or responding to interview questions after completing the task.

cognitive science: The interdisciplinary study of learning and information processing.

comparability/score comparability: In test linking, the degree of score comparability resulting from the application of a linking procedure. Score comparability varies along a continuum that depends on the type of linking conducted. See *alternate forms, equating, calibration, linking, moderation, projection, vertical scaling.*

composite score: A score that combines several scores according to a specified formula.

computer-administered test: A test administered by a computer; test takers respond by using a keyboard, mouse, or other response devices.

computer-based mastery test: A test administered by computer that indicates whether the test taker has achieved a specified level of competence in a certain domain, rather than the test takers' degree of achievement in that domain. See *mastery test.*

computer-based test: See *computer-administered test.*

computer-prepared interpretive report: A programmed interpretation of a test taker's test results, based on empirical data and/or expert judgment using various formats such as narratives, tables, and graphs. Sometimes referred to as *automated scoring* or *narrative report.*

computerized adaptive test: An adaptive test administered by computer. See *adaptive test.*

concordance: In linking test scores for tests that measure similar constructs, the process of relating a score on one test to a score on another, so that the scores have the same relative meaning for a group of test takers.

conditional standard error of measurement: The standard deviation of measurement errors that affect the scores of test takers at a specified test score level.

confidence interval: An interval within which the parameter of interest will be included with a specified probability.

consequences: The outcomes, intended and unintended, of using tests in particular ways in certain contexts and with certain populations.

construct: The concept or characteristic that a test is designed to measure.

construct domain: The set of interrelated attributes (e.g., behaviors, attitudes, values) that are included under a construct's label.

construct equivalence: 1. The extent to which a construct measured by one test is essentially the same as the construct measured by another test. 2. The degree to which a construct measured by a test in one cultural or linguistic group is comparable to the construct measured by the same test in a different cultural or linguistic group.

construct-irrelevant variance: Variance in test-taker scores that is attributable to extraneous factors that distort the meaning of the scores and thereby decrease the validity of the proposed interpretation.

construct underrepresentation: The extent to which a test fails to capture important aspects of the construct domain that the test is intended to measure, resulting in test scores that do not fully represent that construct.

constructed-response items, tasks, or exercises: Items, tasks, or exercises for which test takers must create their own responses or products rather than choose a response from a specified set. Short-answer items require a few words or a number as an answer; extended-response items require at least a few sentences and may

GLOSSARY

include diagrams, mathematical proofs, essays, or problem solutions such as network repairs or other work products.

content domain: The set of behaviors, knowledge, skills, abilities, attitudes, or other characteristics to be measured by a test, represented in detailed test specifications and often organized into categories by which items are classified.

content-related validity evidence: Evidence based on test content that supports the intended interpretation of test scores for a given purpose. Such evidence may address issues such as the fidelity of test content to performance in the domain in question and the degree to which test content representatively samples a domain, such as a course curriculum or job.

content standard: In educational assessment, a statement of content and skills that students are expected to learn in a subject matter area, often at a particular grade or at the completion of a particular level of schooling.

convergent evidence: Evidence based on the relationship between test scores and other measures of the same or related construct.

credentialing: Granting to a person, by some authority, a credential, such as a certificate, license, or diploma, that signifies an acceptable level of performance in some domain of knowledge or activity.

criterion domain: The construct domain of a variable that is used as a criterion. See *construct domain.*

criterion-referenced score interpretation: The meaning of a test score for an individual or of an average score for a defined group, indicating the individual's or group's level of performance in relationship to some defined criterion domain. Examples of criterion-referenced interpretations include comparisons to cut scores, interpretations based on expectancy tables, and domain-referenced score interpretations. Contrast with *norm-referenced score interpretation.*

cross-validation: A procedure in which a scoring system for predicting performance, derived from one sample, is applied to a second sample to investigate the stability of prediction of the scoring system.

cut score: A specified point on a score scale, such that scores at or above that point are reported, interpreted, or acted upon differently from scores below that point.

differential item functioning (DIF): For a particular item in a test, a statistical indicator of the extent to which different groups of test takers who are at the same ability level have different frequencies of correct responses or, in some cases, different rates of choosing various item options.

differential test functioning (DTF): Differential performance at the test or dimension level indicating that individuals from different groups who have the same standing on the characteristic assessed by a test do not have the same expected test score.

discriminant evidence: Evidence indicating whether two tests interpreted as measures of different constructs are sufficiently independent (uncorrelated) that they do, in fact, measure two distinct constructs.

documentation: The body of literature (e.g., test manuals, manual supplements, research reports, publications, user's guides) developed by a test's author, developer, user, and/or publisher to support test score interpretations for their intended use.

domain or content sampling: The process of selecting test items, in a systematic way, to represent the total set of items measuring a domain.

effort: The extent to which a test taker appropriately participates in test taking.

empirical evidence: Evidence based on some form of data, as opposed to that based on logic or theory.

English language learner (ELL): An individual who is not yet proficient in English. An ELL may be an individual whose first language is not English, a language minority individual just beginning to learn English, or an individual who has developed considerable proficiency in English. Related terms include *English learner (EL), limited English proficient* (LEP), *English as a second language* (ESL), and *culturally and linguistically diverse.*

equated forms: Alternate forms of a test whose scores have been related through a statistical process known as equating, which allows scale scores on equated forms to be used interchangeably.

equating: A process for relating scores on alternate forms of a test so that they have essentially the same meaning. The equated scores are typically reported on a common score scale.

equivalent forms: See *alternate forms, parallel forms.*

error of measurement: The difference between an observed score and the corresponding true score. See *standard error of measurement, systematic error, random error, true score.*

factor: Any variable, real or hypothetical, that is an aspect of a concept or construct.

factor analysis: Any of several statistical methods of describing the interrelationships of a set of variables by statistically deriving new variables, called *factors,* that are fewer in number than the original set of variables.

fairness: The validity of test score interpretations for intended use(s) for individuals from all relevant subgroups. A test that is fair minimizes the construct-irrelevant variance associated with individual characteristics and testing contexts that otherwise would compromise the validity of scores for some individuals.

fake bad: Exaggerate or falsify responses to test items in an effort to appear impaired.

fake good: Exaggerate or falsify responses to test items in an effort to present oneself in an overly positive way.

false negative: An error of classification, diagnosis, or selection leading to a determination that an individual does not meet the standard based on an assessment for inclusion in a particular group, when, in truth, he or she does meet the standard (or would, absent measurement error). See *sensitivity, specificity.*

false positive: An error of classification, diagnosis, or selection leading to a determination that an individual meets the standard based on an assessment for inclusion in a particular group, when, in truth, he or she does not meet the standard (or would not, absent measurement error). See *sensitivity, specificity.*

field test: A test administration used to check the adequacy of testing procedures and the statistical characteristics of new test items or new test forms. A field test is generally more extensive than a pilot test. See *pilot test.*

flag: An indicator attached to a test score, a test item, or other entity to indicate a special status. A flagged test score generally signifies a score obtained from a modified test resulting in a change in the underlying construct measured by the test. Flagged scores may not be comparable to scores that are not flagged.

formative assessment: An assessment process used by teachers and students during instruction that provides feedback to adjust ongoing teaching and learning with the goal of improving students' achievement of intended instructional outcomes.

gain score: In testing, the difference between two scores obtained by a test taker on the same test or two equated tests taken on different occasions, often before and after some treatment.

generalizability coefficient: An index of reliability/precision based on generalizability theory (G theory). A generalizability coefficient is the ratio of universe score variance to observed score variance, where the observed score variance is equal to the universe score variance plus the total error variance. See *generalizability theory.*

generalizability theory: Methodological framework for evaluating reliability/precision in which various sources of error variance are estimated through the application of the statistical techniques of analysis of variance. The analysis indicates the generalizability of scores beyond the specific sample of items, persons, and observational conditions that were studied. Also called *G theory.*

group testing: Testing for groups of test takers, usually in a group setting, typically with standardized administration procedures and supervised by a proctor or test administrator.

growth models: Statistical models that measure students' progress on achievement tests by comparing the test scores of the same students over time. See *value-added modeling.*

high-stakes test: A test used to provide results that have important, direct consequences for individuals, programs, or institutions involved in the testing. Contrast with *low-stakes test.*

holistic scoring: A method of obtaining a score on a test, or a test item, based on a judgment of overall performance using specified criteria. Contrast with *analytic scoring.*

individualized education program (IEP): A documented plan that delineates special education services for a special-needs student and that includes any adaptations that are required in the regular classroom or for assessments and any additional special programs or services.

informed consent: The agreement of a person, or that person's legal representative, for some procedure to be performed on or by the individual, such as taking a test or completing a questionnaire.

intelligence test: A test designed to measure an individual's level of cognitive functioning in accord with some recognized theory of intelligence. See *cognitive assessment.*

interim assessments or tests: Assessments administered during instruction to evaluate students' knowledge and skills relative to a specific set of academic goals to inform policy-maker or educator decisions at the classroom, school, or district level. See *benchmark assessments.*

internal-consistency coefficient: An index of the reliability of test scores derived from the statistical interrelationships among item responses or scores on separate parts of a test. See *coefficient alpha, split-halves reliability coefficient.*

internal structure: In test analysis, the factorial structure of item responses or subscales of a test.

interpreter: Someone who facilitates cross-cultural communication by converting concepts from one language to another (including sign language).

interrater agreement/consistency: The level of consistency with which two or more judges rate the work or performance of test takers. See *interrater reliability.*

interrater reliability: The level of consistency in rank ordering of ratings across raters. See *interrater agreement.*

intrarater reliability: The level of consistency among repetitions of a single rater in scoring test takers' responses. Inconsistencies in the scoring process resulting from influences that are internal to the rater rather than true differences in test takers' performances result in low intrarater reliability.

inventory: A questionnaire or checklist that elicits information about an individual's personal opinions, interests, attitudes, preferences, personality characteristics, motivations, or typical reactions to situations and problems.

item: A statement, question, exercise, or task on a test for which the test taker is to select or construct a response, or perform a task. See *prompt.*

item characteristic curve (ICC): A mathematical function relating the probability of a certain item response, usually a correct response, to the level of the attribute measured by the item. Also called *item response curve, item response function.*

item context effect: Influence of item position, other items administered, time limits, administration conditions, and so forth, on item difficulty and other statistical item characteristics.

item pool/item bank: The collection or set of items from which a test or test scale's items are selected during test development, or the total set of items from which a particular subset is selected for a test taker during adaptive testing.

item response theory (IRT): A mathematical model of the functional relationship between performance on a test item, the test item's characteristics, and the test taker's standing on the construct being measured.

job analysis: The investigation of positions or job classes to obtain information about job duties and tasks, responsibilities, necessary worker characteristics (e.g. knowledge, skills, and abilities), working conditions, and/or other aspects of the work. See *practice analysis.*

job/job classification: A group of positions that are similar enough in duties, responsibilities, necessary worker characteristics, and other relevant aspects that they may be properly placed under the same job title.

job performance measurement: Measurement of an incumbent's observed performance of a job as evaluated by a job sample test, an assessment of job knowledge, or ratings of the incumbent's actual performance on the job. See *job sample test.*

job sample test: A test of the ability of an individual to perform the tasks comprised by a job. See *job performance measurement.*

licensing: The granting, usually by a government agency, of an authorization or legal permission to practice an occupation or profession. See *certification, credentialing.*

linking/score linking: The process of relating scores on tests. See *alternate forms, equating, calibration, moderation, projection, vertical scaling.*

local evidence: Evidence (usually related to reliability/precision or validity) collected for a specific test and a specific set of test takers in a single institution or at a specific location.

local norms: Norms by which test scores are referred to a specific, limited reference population of particular interest to the test user (e.g., population of a locale, organization, or institution). Local norms are not intended to be representative of populations beyond that limited setting.

low-stakes test: A test used to provide results that have only minor or indirect consequences for individuals, programs, or institutions involved in the testing. Contrast with *high-stakes test.*

mastery test: A test designed to indicate whether a test taker has attained a prescribed level of competence, or mastery, in a domain. See *cut score, computer-based mastery test.*

matrix sampling: A measurement format in which a large set of test items is organized into a number of relatively short item sets, each of which is randomly assigned to a subsample of test takers, thereby avoiding the need to administer all items to all test takers. Equivalence of the short item sets, or subsets, is not assumed.

meta-analysis: A statistical method of research in which the results from independent, comparable studies are combined to determine the size of an overall effect or the degree of relationship between two variables.

moderation: A process of relating scores on different tests so that scores have the same relative meaning.

moderator variable: A variable that affects the direction or strength of the relationship between two other variables.

modification/test modification: A change in test content, format (including response formats), and/or administration conditions that is made to increase accessibility for some individuals but that also affects the construct measured and, consequently, results in scores that differ in meaning from scores from the unmodified assessment.

neuropsychological assessment: A specialized type of psychological assessment of normal or pathological processes affecting the central nervous system and the resulting psychological and behavioral functions or dysfunctions.

norm-referenced score interpretation: A score interpretation based on a comparison of a test taker's performance with the distribution of performance in a specified reference population. Contrast *criterion-referenced score interpretation.*

norms: Statistics or tabular data that summarize the distribution or frequency of test scores for one or more specified groups, such as test takers of various ages or grades, usually designed to represent some larger population, referred to as the *reference population.* See *local norms.*

operational use: The actual use of a test, after initial test development has been completed, to inform an interpretation, decision, or action, based in part or wholly on test scores.

opportunity to learn: The extent to which test takers have been exposed to the tested constructs through their educational program and/or have had exposure to or experience with the language or the majority culture required to understand the test.

parallel forms: In classical test theory, strictly parallel test forms that are assumed to measure the same construct and to have the same means and the same standard deviations in the populations of interest. See *alternate forms.*

percentile: The score on a test below which a given percentage of scores for a specified population occurs.

percentile rank: The rank of a given score based on the percentage of scores in a specified score distribution that are below the score being ranked.

performance assessments: Assessments for which the test taker actually demonstrates the skills the test is intended to measure by doing tasks that require those skills.

performance level: Label or brief statement classifying a test taker's competency in a particular domain, usually defined by a range of scores on a test. For example, labels such as "basic" to "advanced," or "novice" to "expert," constitute broad ranges for classifying proficiency. See *achievement levels, cut score, performance-level descriptor, standard setting.*

performance-level descriptor: Descriptions of what test takers know and can do at specific performance levels.

performance standards: Descriptions of levels of knowledge and skill acquisition contained in content standards, as articulated through performance-level labels (e.g., "basic," "proficient," "advanced"); statements of what test takers at different performance levels know and can do; and cut scores or ranges of scores on the scale of an assessment that differentiate levels of performance.

See *cut score, performance level, performance-level descriptor.*

personality inventory: An inventory that measures one or more characteristics that are regarded generally as psychological attributes or interpersonal tendencies.

pilot test: A test administered to a sample of test takers to try out some aspects of the test or test items, such as instructions, time limits, item response formats, or item response options. See *field test.*

policy study: A study that contributes to judgments about plans, principles, or procedures enacted to achieve broad public goals.

portfolio: In assessment, a systematic collection of educational or work products that have been compiled or accumulated over time, according to a specific set of principles or rules.

position: In employment contexts, the smallest organizational unit, a set of assigned duties and responsibilities that are performed by a person within an organization.

practice analysis: An investigation of a certain occupation or profession to obtain descriptive information about the activities and responsibilities of the occupation or profession and about the knowledge, skills, and abilities needed to engage successfully in the occupation or profession. See *job analysis.*

precision of measurement: The impact of measurement error on the outcome of the measurement. See *standard error of measurement, error of measurement, reliability/precision.*

predictive bias: The systematic under- or over-prediction of criterion performance for people belonging to groups differentiated by characteristics not relevant to the criterion performance.

predictive validity evidence: Evidence indicating how accurately test data collected at one time can predict criterion scores that are obtained at a later time.

proctor: In test administration, a person responsible for monitoring the testing process and implementing the test administration procedures.

program evaluation: The collection and synthesis of evidence about the use, operation, and effects of a program; the set of procedures used to make judgments about a program's design, implementation, and outcomes.

projection: A method of score linking in which scores on one test are used to predict scores on another test for a group of test takers, often using regression methodology.

prompt/item prompt/writing prompt: The question, stimulus, or instruction that elicits a test taker's response.

proprietary algorithms: Procedures, often computer code, used by commercial publishers or test developers that are not revealed to the public for commercial reasons.

psychodiagnosis: Formalization or classification of functional mental health status based on psychological assessment.

psychological assessment: An examination of psychological functioning that involves collecting, evaluating, and integrating test results and collateral information, and reporting information about an individual.

psychological testing: The use of tests or inventories to assess particular psychological characteristics of an individual.

random error: A nonsystematic error; a component of test scores that appears to have no relationship to other variables.

random sample: A selection from a defined population of entities according to a random process with the selection of each entity independent of the selection of other entities. See *sample.*

raw score: A score on a test that is calculated by counting the number of correct answers, or more generally, a sum or other combination of item scores.

reference population: The population of test takers to which individual test takers are compared through the test norms. The reference population may be defined in terms of test taker age, grade, clinical status at the time of testing, or other characteristics. See *norms.*

relevant subgroup: A subgroup of the population for which a test is intended that is identifiable in some way that is relevant to the interpretation of test scores for their intended purposes.

reliability coefficient: A unit-free indicator that reflects the degree to which scores are free of random measurement error. See *generalizability theory.*

reliability/precision: The degree to which test scores for a group of test takers are consistent over repeated applications of a measurement procedure and hence are inferred to be dependable and consistent for an individual test taker; the degree to which scores are free of random errors of measurement for a given group. See *generalizability theory, classical test theory, precision of measurement.*

response bias: A test taker's tendency to respond in a particular way or style to items on a test (e.g., acquiescence, choice of socially desirable options, choice of "true" on a true-false test) that yields systematic, construct-irrelevant error in test scores.

response format: The mechanism that a test taker uses to respond to a test item, such as selecting from a list of options (multiple-choice question) or providing a written response (fill-in or written response to an open-ended or constructed-response question); oral response; or physical performance.

response protocol: A record of the responses given by a test taker to a particular test.

restriction of range or variability: Reduction in the observed score variance of a test-taker sample, compared with the variance of the entire test-taker population, as a consequence of constraints on the process of sampling test takers. See *adjusted validity or reliability coefficient.*

retesting: A repeat administration of a test, using either the same test or an alternate form, sometimes with additional training or education between administrations.

rubric: See *scoring rubric.*

sample: A selection of a specified number of entities, called *sampling units* (test takers, items, etc.), from a larger specified set of possible entities, called the *population*. See *random sample, stratified random sample.*

scale: 1. The system of numbers, and their units, by which a value is reported on some dimension of measurement. 2. In testing, the set of items or subtests used to measure a specific characteristic (e.g., a test of verbal ability or a scale of extroversion-introversion).

scale score: A score obtained by transforming raw scores. Scale scores are typically used to facilitate interpretation.

scaling: The process of creating a scale or a scale score to enhance test score interpretation by placing scores from different tests or test forms on a common scale or

by producing scale scores designed to support score interpretations. See *scale.*

school district: A local education agency administered by a public board of education or other public authority that oversees public elementary or secondary schools in a political subdivision of a state.

score: Any specific number resulting from the assessment of an individual, such as a raw score, a scale score, an estimate of a latent variable, a production count, an absence record, a course grade, or a rating.

scoring rubric: The established criteria, including rules, principles, and illustrations, used in scoring constructed responses to individual tasks and clusters of tasks.

screening test: A test that is used to make broad categorizations of test takers as a first step in selection decisions or diagnostic processes.

selection: The acceptance or rejection of applicants for a particular educational or employment opportunity.

sensitivity: In classification, diagnosis, and selection, the proportion of cases that are assessed as meeting or predicted to meet the criteria and which, in truth, do meet the criteria.

specificity: In classification, diagnosis, and selection, the proportion of cases that are assessed as not meeting or predicted to not meet the criteria and which, in truth, do not meet the criteria.

speededness: The extent to which test takers' scores depend on the rate at which work is performed as well as on the correctness of the responses. The term is not used to describe tests of speed.

split-halves reliability coefficient: An internal-consistency coefficient obtained by using half the items on a test to yield one score and the other half of the items to yield a second, independent score. See *internal-consistency coefficient, coefficient alpha.*

stability: The extent to which scores on a test are essentially invariant over time, assessed by correlating the test scores of a group of individuals with scores on the same test or an equated test taken by the same group at a later time. See *test-retest reliability coefficient.*

standard error of measurement: The standard deviation of an individual's observed scores from repeated administrations of a test (or parallel forms of a test) under identical conditions. Because such data generally cannot be collected, the standard error of measurement is usually estimated from group data. See *error of measurement.*

standard setting: The process, often judgment based, of setting cut scores using a structured procedure that seeks to map test scores into discrete performance levels that are usually specified by performance-level descriptors.

standardization: 1. In test administration, maintaining a consistent testing environment and conducting tests according to detailed rules and specifications, so that testing conditions are the same for all test takers on the same and multiple occasions. 2. In test development, establishing a reporting scale using norms based on the test performance of a representative sample of individuals from the population with which the test is intended to be used.

standards-based assessment: Assessment of an individual's standing with respect to systematically described content and performance standards.

stratified random sample: A set of random samples, each of a specified size, from each of several different sets, which are viewed as strata of a population. See *random sample, sample.*

summative assessment: The assessment of a test taker's knowledge and skills typically carried out at the completion of a program of learning, such as the end of an instructional unit.

systematic error: An error that consistently increases or decreases the scores of all test takers or some subset of test takers, but is not related to the construct that the test is intended to measure. See *bias.*

technical manual: A publication prepared by test developers and/or publishers to provide technical and psychometric information about a test.

test: An evaluative device or procedure in which a systematic sample of a test taker's behavior in a specified domain is obtained and scored using a standardized process.

test design: The process of developing detailed specifications for what a test is to measure and the content, cognitive level, format, and types of test items to be used.

test developer: The person(s) or organization responsible for the design and construction of a test and for the documentation regarding its technical quality for an intended purpose.

test development: The process through which a test is planned, constructed, evaluated, and modified, including consideration of content, format, administration, scoring, item properties, scaling, and technical quality for the test's intended purpose.

test documents: Documents such as test manuals, technical manuals, user's guides, specimen sets, and directions for test administrators and scorers that provide information for evaluating the appropriateness and technical adequacy of a test for its intended purpose.

test form: A set of test items or exercises that meet requirements of the specifications for a testing program. Many testing programs use alternate test forms, each built according to the same specifications but with some or all of the test items unique to each form. See *alternate forms.*

test format/mode: The manner in which test content is presented to the test taker: with paper and pencil, via computer terminal or Internet, or orally by an examiner.

test information function: A mathematical function relating each level of an ability or latent trait, as defined under item response theory (IRT), to the reciprocal of the corresponding conditional measurement error variance.

test manual: A publication prepared by test developers and/or publishers to provide information on test administration, scoring, and interpretation and to provide selected technical data on test characteristics. See *user's guide, technical manual.*

test modification: Changes made in the content, format, and/or administration procedure of a test to increase the accessibility of the test for test takers who are unable to take the original test under standard testing conditions. In contrast to test accommodations, test modifications change the construct being measured by the test to some extent and hence change score interpretations. See *adaptation/test adaptation, modification/test modification.* Contrast with *accommodations/test accommodations.*

test publisher: An entity, individual, organization, or agency that produces and/or distributes a test.

test-retest reliability coefficient: A reliability coefficient obtained by administering the same test a second time to the same group after a time interval and correlating the two sets of scores; typically used as a measure of stability of the test scores. See *stability.*

test security: Protection of the content of a test from unauthorized release or use, to protect the integrity of the test scores so they are valid for their intended use.

test specifications: Documentation of the purpose and intended uses of a test as well as of the test's content, format, length, psychometric characteristics (of the items and test overall), delivery mode, administration, scoring, and score reporting.

test-taking strategies: Strategies that test takers might use while taking a test to improve their performance, such as time management or the elimination of obviously incorrect options on a multiple-choice question before responding to the question.

test user: A person or entity responsible for the choice and administration of a test, for the interpretation of test scores produced in a given context, and for any decisions or actions that are based, in part, on test scores.

timed test: A test administered to test takers who are allotted a prescribed amount of time to respond to the test.

top-down selection: Selection of applicants on the basis of rank-ordered test scores from highest to lowest.

true score: In classical test theory, the average of the scores that would be earned by an individual on an unlimited number of strictly parallel forms of the same test.

unidimensional test: A test that measures only one dimension or only one latent variable.

universal design: An approach to assessment development that attempts to maximize the accessibility of a test for all of its intended test takers.

universe score: In generalizability theory, the expected value over all possible replications of a procedure for the test taker. See *generalizability theory.*

user norms: Descriptive statistics (including percentile ranks) for a group of test takers that does not represent a well-defined reference population, for example, all persons tested during a certain period of time, or a set of self-selected test takers. See *local norms, norms.*

user's guide: A publication prepared by test developers and/or publishers to provide information on a test's

purpose, appropriate uses, proper administration, scoring procedures, normative data, interpretation of results, and case studies. See *test manual.*

validation: The process through which the validity of a proposed interpretation of test scores for their intended uses is investigated.

validity: The degree to which accumulated evidence and theory support a specific interpretation of test scores for a given use of a test. If multiple interpretations of a test score for different uses are intended, validity evidence for each interpretation is needed.

validity argument: An explicit justification of the degree to which accumulated evidence and theory support the proposed interpretation(s) of test scores for their intended uses.

validity generalization: Application of validity evidence obtained in one or more situations to other similar situations on the basis of methods such as meta-analysis.

value-added modeling: Estimating the contribution of individual schools or teachers to student performance by means of complex statistical techniques that use multiple years of student outcome data, which typically are standardized test scores. See *growth models.*

variance components: Variances accruing from the separate constituent sources that are assumed to contribute to the overall variance of observed scores. Such variances, estimated by methods of the analysis of variance, often reflect situation, location, time, test form, rater, and related effects. See *generalizability theory.*

vertical scaling: In test linking, the process of relating scores on tests that measure the same construct but differ in difficulty. Typically used with achievement and ability tests with content or difficulty that spans a variety of grade or age levels.

vocational assessment: A specialized type of psychological assessment designed to generate hypotheses and inferences about interests, work needs and values, career development, vocational maturity, and indecision.

weighted scores/scoring: A method of scoring a test in which a different number of points is awarded for a correct (or diagnostically relevant) response for different items. In some cases, the scoring formula awards differing points for each different response to the same item.

INDEX